THE WORM

For Marie,
my little silkworm

Library and Archives Canada Cataloguing in Publication

Gravel, Elise
[Ver. English]
        The worm / Elise Gravel.

(Disgusting critters)
Translation of: Le ver.
Previously published by Tundra Books, 2014.
ISBN 978-1-101-91841-8 (paperback)

        I. Worms—Juvenile literature. I. Title. II. Title: Ver.
English. III. Series: Gravel, Élise. Disgusting critters.

QL386.6.G7213 2016   j592'.3   C2015-904012-4

Published simultaneously in the United States of America by Tundra Books of Northern New York,
a division of Random House of Canada Limited, a Penguin Random House Company

Library of Congress Control Number: 2013940757

English edition edited by Samantha Swenson
Designed by Elise Gravel and Tundra Books
The artwork in this book was rendered digitally
Printed and bound in China

www.penguinrandomhouse.ca

1 2 3 4 5 6   21 20 19 18 17 16

TUNDRA BOOKS | Penguin Random House

Elise Gravel

THE WORM

Tundra Books

LADIES AND GENTLEMEN,
I present to you

THE WORM.

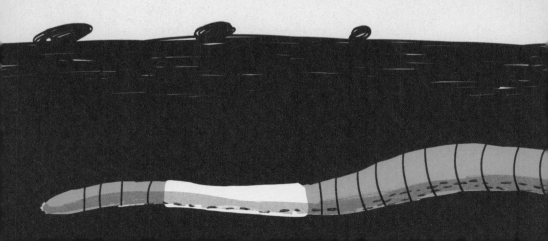

The worm is a long animal that's shaped like a tube. It doesn't have a

SKELETON

or a spine: it's an

INVERTEBRATE.

It also doesn't have any legs.

There are many

DIFFERENT

kinds of worms.

HERE ARE SOME OF THEM:

THE FLATWORM

I'm called a worm, but I have legs!

THE WHITE WORM

Many insect larvae, like

THE MAGGOT

(baby fly)

Some worms are so small that you need a microscope to see them. Others can be 115 feet (35 meters) long, like the ribbon worm that lives in oceans and rivers.

Worms can live in different

HABITATS.

Some live in the water. Others live in rotting plants. Some even live inside human or animal bodies!

These worms
are called
parasites.

The most common worm is the

EARTHWORM.

An earthworm is basically a long

DIGESTIVE TRACT

inside a

MUSCLE TUBE.

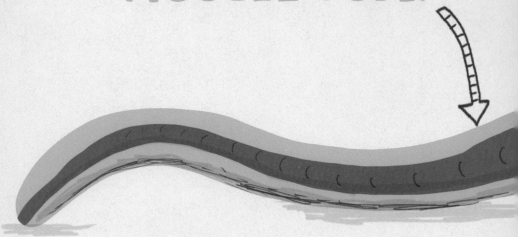

Worms have been on earth for

MiLLiONS
OF
YEARS!

Maybe even billions!

Biologists believe they evolved
with the

DiNOSAURS.

Earthworms have

NO EYES,

but they can sense light with something called

PHOTORECEPTORS:

sensors in the worm's skin that react to light.

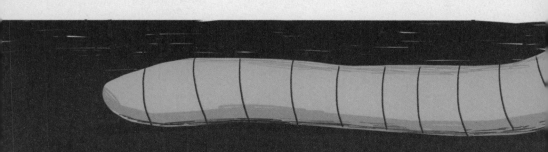

Earthworms move by

SQUEEZING

their

MUSCLES,

causing their bodies to contract and expand.

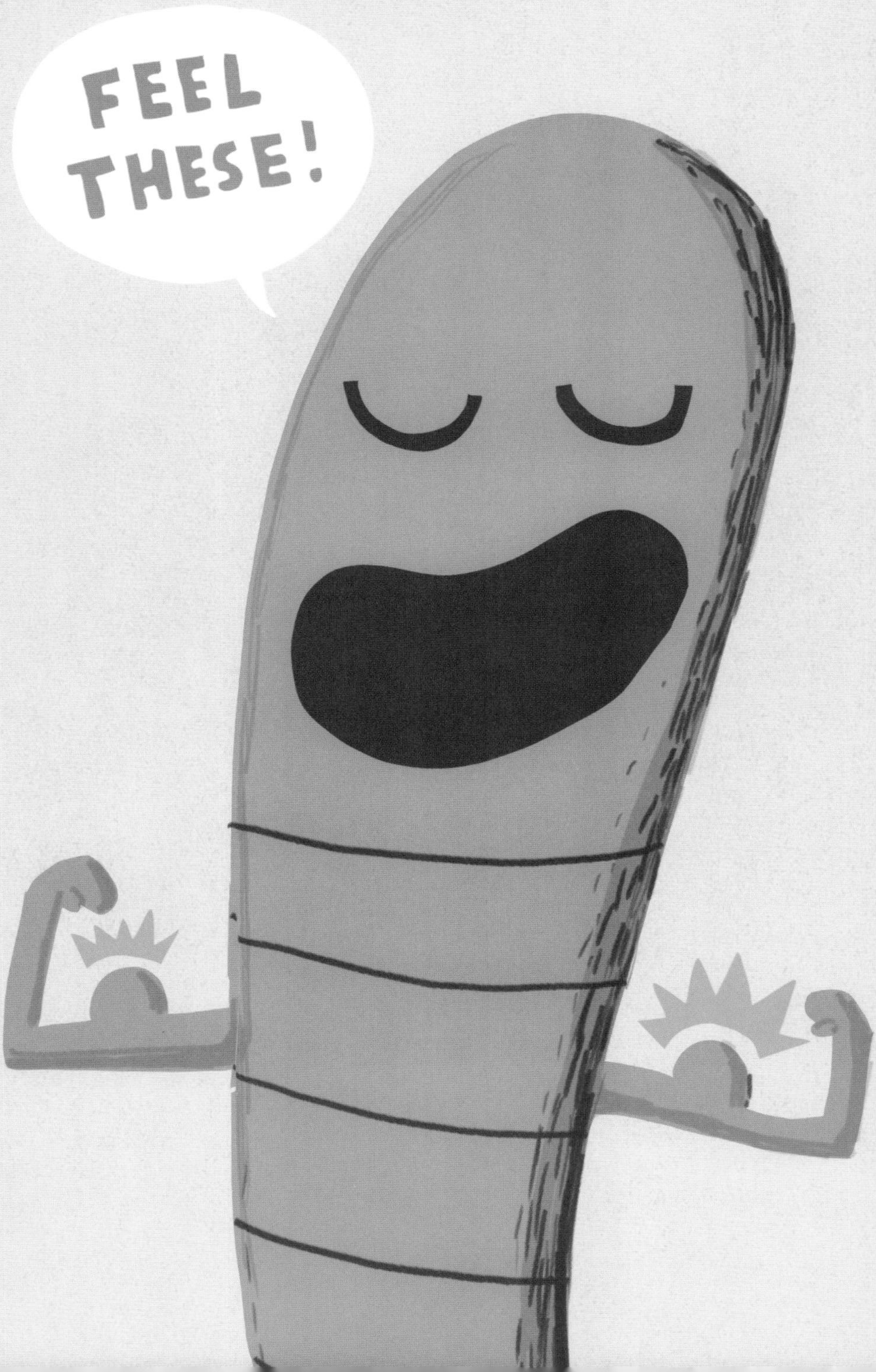
FEEL THESE!

IT'S GOOD for NATURE!

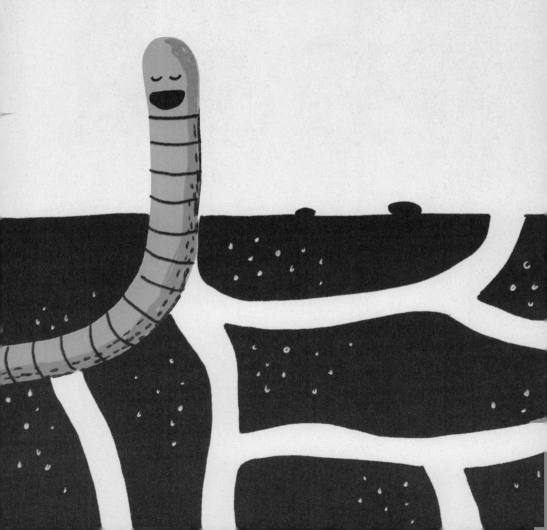

Many kinds of worms are hermaphrodites, which means they have both

MALE

and

FEMALE

reproductive organs.

In other words, an earthworm is a boy and a girl at the same time. They still need a partner to reproduce, though.

Earthworms might seem

PRETTY GROSS,

but they're very useful! They recycle
nature's waste and help turn it into soil.
Farmers and gardeners love earthworms!

Fishermen use earthworms to catch fish, and some people even eat them and find them

DELICIOUS!

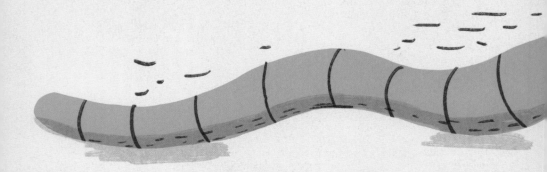

So next time you meet an earthworm,
be polite. Worms are

YOUR FRIENDS!

Hey, want to
play football?

PRAISE FOR DIANE FANNING

"Very few writers have the insight and gift to take a true story and make it one hell of a page-turner. In my opinion, Diane Fanning does just that in *A Poisoned Passion*."
  —Susan Murphy Milano, domestic violence victims' advocate

"Author Diane Fanning tirelessly recounts the young woman's lying ways, theorizes how Anthony might have disposed of her daughter, and concludes that Anthony is 'an individual whose self-absorption and insensitivity to others is a destructive force.'"   —*Orlando Sentinel* on *Mommy's Little Girl*

"I'm sitting on a couch in our newsroom, pouring through the advance copy of your book. Unbelievable stuff!"
  —Mike DeForest, WKMG-TV, on *Mommy's Little Girl*

"I couldn't put it down until I h̶̶̶̶̶̶̶̶̶̶̶ I'm amazed at how much research you ha̶̶̶̶̶̶̶̶̶̶̶ r the parts I actually knew about, th̶̶̶̶̶̶̶̶̶̶̶ I could have expected. I ha̶̶̶̶̶̶̶̶̶̶̶ y read this book, they wil̶̶̶̶̶̶̶̶̶̶̶ ng that I did, just as if they h̶̶̶̶̶̶̶̶̶̶̶ s. I'm a reader and have read many t̶̶̶̶̶̶̶̶̶̶̶ t I'm still surprised at how well you wove̶̶̶̶̶̶̶̶̶̶̶ nto a story that's enjoyable to read and accurate ̶̶̶̶̶̶̶̶̶̶̶."
  —Herb Betz on *Through the Window*

"I was astonished by how good this book was—insightful, well written, and fascinating."
  —Hugh Aynesworth, four-time
  Pulitzer Prize nominee, on *Out There*

"With the publication of Diane Fanning's book, *Written in Blood*, the official record is now complete. Fanning provides a full account of the epic Peterson murder mystery. Her writing is superb. Most importantly, Diane Fanning has written a true crime book focused more on the truth than on the crime, and in that sense, her work honors the spirit of the victim, Kathleen Hunt Atwater."   —Vance Holmes

UNDER COVER OF THE
NIGHT

A True Story of Sex,
Greed, and Murder

DIANE FANNING

BERKLEY BOOKS, NEW YORK

THE BERKLEY PUBLISHING GROUP
Published by the Penguin Group
Penguin Group (USA) LLC
375 Hudson Street, New York, New York 10014

USA • Canada • UK • Ireland • Australia • New Zealand • India • South Africa • China

penguin.com

A Penguin Random House Company

UNDER COVER OF THE NIGHT

A Berkley Book / published by arrangement with the author

For information, address: The Berkley Publishing Group,
a division of Penguin Group (USA) LLC,
375 Hudson Street, New York, New York 10014.

ISBN: 978-0-425-27023-3

PUBLISHING HISTORY
Berkley premium edition / October 2014

PRINTED IN THE UNITED STATES OF AMERICA

10 9 8 7 6 5 4 3 2 1

Cover photos by Shutterstock.
Cover design by Pyrographx.
Interior text design by Kelly Lipovich.

For Jocelyn Branham Earnest, a great friend,
terrific sister, and loving daughter

ACKNOWLEDGMENTS

Writing a true crime book is not a solo effort. I can only get facts with the help of many other people and, at this time, I want to express my appreciation to some of them.

First of all, three people who shared more than information: they shared their hearts and souls. Thank you: Bill Branham, Laura Rogers, and Jennifer Kerns. I wish I'd known your Jocelyn.

Deputy Commonwealth's Attorney Wes Nance and Investigators Gary Babb and Mike Mayhew were of invaluable assistance, as were Joey Sanzone, Sherry Hall, and Cindy Harvey. Thank you for your courtesy and for providing me with work space to review the transcript of the second trial.

I also must express my gratitude to Amherst Circuit Court clerk Roy C. Mayo III; fire chief George Tawes of Smith Mountain Lake Fire/Rescue; Bedford fire chief Brad Creasy; Will Crumpacker, my neighbor and a firefighter and EMT for the Bedford Fire Department; and Pete Fanning.

I owe a special debt to Shannon Jamieson Vazquez for her expert editorial guidance in molding the finished product you now hold in your hands.

As always, I feel deep appreciation to the agent who has made my whole career possible, the incredible Jane Dystel of Dystel & Goderich Literary Management.

Finally, this time Wayne surpassed even himself. Throughout the upheaval of our lives when we moved from Texas to Virginia, he remained my best friend, my foremost cheerleader, and the greatest guy I've ever known. Thank you for giving me the space to stretch and grow.

ONE

Marcy Shepherd often took two weeks off from her job in the human resources department of Genworth Financial around Christmas, to spend time with her children and finish up her holiday preparations, and 2007 was no exception. On Sunday, December 16, 2007, the perky blonde went shopping with her friend and co-worker Jocelyn Earnest, and they made plans to get together again on the evening of Wednesday, December 19. Text messages bounced between the women throughout the day that Wednesday as Marcy ran errands, even briefly stopping at the Genworth offices to deliver popcorn that co-workers had purchased from her son's Cub Scout troop.

At home that evening, Marcy sat down with her eight-year-old son to watch *SpongeBob SquarePants*. Just before seven thirty, she received a text from Jocelyn asking if she was there. Marcy responded, "Y." When she didn't hear back from Jocelyn, Marcy sent another message spelling out her answer more clearly, "Yes, I'm here." Still no reply from Jocelyn, which was unusual since she had answered every other text that day promptly. Marcy knew a momentary pause could have a lot of innocent explanations: another phone call, taking a shower, a temporary separation from her cell phone, whatever. At first, it was not cause for alarm.

When the television show ended, Marcy went upstairs with her son, made sure he brushed his teeth, read a story to him, and tucked him in for the night at eight thirty. She sent an email asking Jocelyn if her text messaging was not working. Jocelyn still remained silent.

Ten minutes later, Marcy left her son with her husband and drove to CVS, still waiting to hear from Jocelyn—still expecting they would meet up that night. She sent another message to Jocelyn while she was in the store, before completing her purchases and leaving at 9:08 P.M.

Marcy was beginning to think that she might not see Jocelyn that evening after all. She had Jocelyn's Christmas present—an enormous box of festive outdoor holiday lights wrapped in gold Santa Claus paper—in her car, however, and not wanting to take the package home for fear its size would stir up her children's heightened state of holiday excitability, Marcy decided to drop it off at the office instead.

She drove fifteen minutes to the downtown Genworth Financial offices and used her key card to gain access to the building after hours. The security system recorded her walking through that door at 9:24 P.M. and taking the elevator to the first floor. She placed Jocelyn's gift on her desk and then returned to her car, checking out at 9:28.

Still not having heard from Jocelyn was making Marcy anxious. She realized that she could be indulging a sense-less agitation, but she could not quiet her escalating fears that something might be wrong. It took a quarter of an hour to drive out to her friend's house, which was situated in a quiet, serene neighborhood in Forest, Virginia, part of scenic Bedford County, nestled up against the Blue Ridge Mountains.

When she arrived, Marcy saw Jocelyn's green Honda parked in the driveway, but while the outside light was lit, only a single low-wattage light burned inside the white-clapboard bungalow with silver metal roof. Had Jocelyn gone out in someone else's vehicle? If so, why hadn't she called or texted about her change of plans? Had she ac-cidentally left her phone behind? Had she fallen asleep? Maybe turned off her cell?

Marcy had planned to just drive by the house without stopping, but instead she turned around in the next drive-way and drove back to her friend's home. She parked and walked up the curved sidewalk to the quiet house and knocked on the front door. There was no response, and no sounds seeped from inside.

Still unsettled, Marcy returned home at a little before ten o'clock. She texted Jocelyn that she was worried and asked her to call. Marcy had difficulty getting to sleep but finally reassured herself that she'd surely get a simple explanation the next morning. Jocelyn would explain what had happened, and they'd laugh about Marcy's unwarranted concern.

The next morning, Marcy rose a little bit after seven and at a quarter past the hour sent Jocelyn another text message. When she still didn't get a response, Marcy set her phone to send her an alert when Jocelyn logged in to the instant messaging system at Genworth. That way, she would know right away that her friend was safely at work.

When by 10 A.M. she had not received any alerts, Marcy called someone who worked for Jocelyn and was told, "We're expecting her but we haven't seen her."

Something was wrong. As long as Marcy had known her, Jocelyn was always one of the first people at her desk. At 11:30, Marcy again made the drive to Jocelyn's home, in escalating anxiety.

Jocelyn's car was still parked in the same spot. Just as the night before, only one weak light glowed beyond the windows. The temperature had risen a bit from the morning's low of twenty-four degrees, but with the light breeze, it was still cool enough to make Marcy shiver on the way up the sidewalk.

Once again, she knocked on the front door. When she got no answer, she balled up her fists and pounded on it as hard as she could, desperate to capture her friend's attention. The possibility of calamity roared in Marcy's ears. Was Jocelyn sick? Injured? An innocent explanation (could Jocelyn have gone to bed early, turned off her phone, and overslept?) seemed less and less likely.

Marcy moved around the exterior of the home; coverings on all the windows prevented her from seeing the interior, but she knocked on each one. Still no sound from inside. She called a mutual friend and co-worker, Maysa Munsey, hoping she had answers. But Maysa did not know where Jocelyn was, either—and she, too, was worried.

Maysa knew the code to the home's alarm system, and Marcy knew where to find the keypad—if only she could get inside. Then Marcy remembered Jocelyn telling her about a spare key she kept in the shed, inside the six-foot fence that surrounded the swimming pool area. Marcy went over to the gate, surprised to find it unlocked when she tugged on the handle.

Still on the phone with Maysa, Marcy located the spare key inside the outbuilding and ran back to the front door. But it didn't work. She tried again and again, thinking that it was just her anxiety making the simple task difficult. Finally, she gave up and dashed around the house to try the back door instead.

Bingo.

When the door, which opened to the kitchen, swung open, it brought with it a blast of heat, enough to fog up Marcy's eyeglasses and momentarily obscure her vision. She called out, "Jocelyn! Jocelyn, where are you?" Then she tilted her head back to peer under her lenses and gasped. She could see Jocelyn lying still on the floor.

"Maysa, call 9-1-1 right now!" Marcy cried. She disconnected from Maysa and punched 9-1-1 into her own cell phone as well.

The 9-1-1 operators asked her to check for a pulse and try CPR.

Marcy felt her hands trembling with panic as she walked across the living room, still on the phone with 9-1-1. As the fog faded, her vision improved, allowing her to see her friend clearly. Her fears morphed into visceral horror. Jocelyn was dressed as if she just walked in the door in a pair of jeans, a sweater, and her winter coat, but she was lying flat on her back on the floor. Her legs stuck straight out. She appeared stiff and unnatural.

Marcy didn't want to believe what she was seeing. *Maybe Jocelyn just bumped her head*, her heart insisted. But logic kicked back into gear when Marcy saw the pool of dark red surrounding Jocelyn's head, mottling the blue carpet with dark, streaky stains trailing across the floor.

The blood puddle was predominately to Jocelyn's right, so Marcy stepped to the left of the body and kneeled down. That was when she saw the firearm. "There's a gun," she said. She moved away from it, kneeling on her friend's other side. She placed her fingers on Jocelyn's throat. It was stiff. It was cold. And nothing beat beneath her skin.

Marcy got a close look at her friend. Her lips were blue. Her fingernails were blue. Blood stains ran in multiple directions on her face, forming a strange hatch pattern. At the operator's request, she reached down and touched Jocelyn's left wrist. Nothing.

The 9-1-1 operator told Marcy to see if Jocelyn was breathing by placing her hand on the stomach area. Marcy slipped her hand in between Jocelyn's sweater and the shirt beneath, desperate to feel the up-and-down movement of respiration, but it wasn't there. Marcy's heart pounded, her mouth dry. She wanted to breathe life back into her friend, but she knew it was far too late. Jocelyn was obviously past the point where CPR would be of any use.

As Marcy stood there, shaking with grief and horror, she thought about all the times that Jocelyn had expressed fear that her life would end violently—the moments she had expressed her paranoid-sounding thoughts about her estranged husband, the many times Marcy observed Jocelyn gripping the armrest in a fear that she'd see Wesley as soon as they'd completed the last turn in the road approaching the house.

Marcy knew Maysa was on her way to the house and that Maysa would have her own children with her. She did not want them to arrive and walk right inside. Marcy opened the front door and stood there watching and waiting, then suddenly wondered about Jocelyn's pets—her black Lab, Rufus, and her two cats. She left the doorway and went down the hall far enough to look into the master bedroom, where she was relieved to see Rufus safely in his kennel. Locating the cats would have to wait.

She hurried back to stand guard at the front door, the phone still connected to 9-1-1. Maysa Munsey, her long, wavy brown hair flying, arrived before any of the first responders. When she pulled up, Marcy shouted out, "Leave the kids in the car."

The operator agreed, saying, "Don't let them in the house. Don't let them in the house."

Marcy blocked the front door as Maysa joined her on the front porch. Wrapping her arms around Marcy, Maysa asked, "Are you certain she's gone?"

Marcy nodded. The two women hugged and sobbed as they waited for the police cars to pull up. Deputy Jason Jones was the first to arrive at the home in the Pine Bluff subdivision. Speaking to Marcy and Maysa, he said, "Please remain here at the house until investigators arrive and talk to you."

The two women left the porch and waited in the driveway. They felt helpless and out of place. Less than a week until Christmas, and instead of making holiday preparations and wishing "Happy Holidays" to friends, family, and co-workers, they stood together in the cold without a single merry thought. The very idea of Christmas spirit felt obscene on that dark winter's day.

TWO

Bedford County deputies Jason Jones and Robbie Nash had been the first officers to arrive at the scene at 1482 Pine Bluff Drive on Thursday, December 20, 2007. The medic unit was right behind them, but Jones told them to wait outside until they cleared the residence. The two lawmen separated and searched the home, sweating from the heat in the house. Finding no one there except for a black dog in a kennel and two cats, Jones allowed the medics inside but warned them not to disturb the body or anything around it any more than necessary. After determining that Jocelyn Earnest had no vital signs, they gathered up their equipment and went back outside. Jones stayed in the room with Jocelyn's body waiting for the arrival of an investigator.

Gary Babb, the sergeant in charge of investigations for the Bedford County Sheriff's Department, had stopped by his home in the small city of Bedford for lunch when he received a call from the dispatcher requesting that he respond to a DOA in Forest, approximately twenty-two miles away. He grabbed the rest of his sandwich and went out the door.

He took Route 221 toward Lynchburg, then traveled down roads that twisted and turned under canopies of tall trees and past pastures of cows and fields lying fallow for winter until he reached the small suburban development where the body had been discovered.

A lot of civilians sat in cars or milled in the street in front of the house in question. As he walked from his car, they stared at him with expressions of naked longing that blended an unsustainable mixture of hope, hopelessness, and denial.

The outside of the house appeared ordinary enough with white vinyl siding and a large bay window, enhanced by a stunning stone chimney and foundation. A tall weathered wood fence surrounded the backyard. Uniformed officer Robbie Nash stood on the porch in front of the open front door, guarding the scene. Jones stepped out onto the porch upon the detective's arrival, and the two deputies explained what they'd found inside of the home and the futile efforts of the rescue squad.

"Did you find a suicide note?" Detective Babb asked.

Both officers shook their heads and said, "No, sir."

Stepping across the threshold, Babb noted that the deceased thirty-eight-year-old woman was five feet six inches tall, of medium build, with hazel eyes and light brown hair with dark blond highlights. She was lying on her back, wearing jeans, brown shoes, and a car coat. One step inside, he noticed that despite the open door and the winter air slipping through it, an uncomfortable heat filled the home. The smell of death and blood had dissipated to some degree, though, leaving only traces of the ominous odor.

Between the front door and the body, Babb spotted a sheet of paper facedown on the floor, appearing to be insignificant household clutter. But it bore four creases, as if it had once been folded into quarters, and that piqued the detective's interest. He pulled on a pair of gloves and flipped the paper over. On the reverse side, he read:

> Mom, I just can't take it anymore. I've tried so hard to be strong but I just can't continue. The ups and downs are too much to deal with. I keep trying to appear as though I am doing fine but the days are so overwhelming and lonely. My new love will never leave the family. Wes has buried us in debt and starting over is too much. I am so sorry mom. I am so sorry everyone.

Babb was immediately suspicious of the note. To begin with, it was typed and did not bear a signature—unusual for the last words of someone about to commit suicide. In addition, the tone of the message was more impersonal than other final messages he'd read in the past, and it raised more questions than it answered. Nevertheless, the note was not sufficiently unsettling to rule out the possibility that Jocelyn *had* taken her own life.

To avoid tracking through the pathway in the immediate vicinity of the victim, Babb walked through the kitchen and came around the other side to get a closer look at her. Leaning forward, he saw bloody streaks running across her face. A revolver lay on top of her coat—an unusual position for a suicide. Usually, the weapon ended up under the body. But again, Babb knew it was way too soon to reach any firm conclusions.

The detective moved down the hall where he found a thermostat. It had been pushed all the way to the highest setting, as far to the right as it could go. He continued on to the bedroom at the end of the hall and saw a cage containing a large black dog who wasn't barking and didn't appear distressed, but who panted heavily from the heat or lack of water or both.

A cabinet by the bed had a drawer that gaped open three or four inches. Beside it, an unopened condom package lay on the floor. On the bathroom floor, Babb found an empty wrapper for another one in the trash can.

Babb had not seen anything in the home that indicated the possibility of a forced entry.

He backed out of the house to obtain a search warrant. Once he'd gotten the paperwork moving, he went out to talk to the people who'd gathered outside.

The two women who'd found the body, Marcy Shepherd and Maysa Munsey, had telephoned other friends and co-workers while they waited. They wanted no one to learn of Jocelyn's death from a reporter calling with questions.

By now, many others who cared about Jocelyn had gathered in the driveway, wanting to deny the reality of her death and comforting one another in their time of loss.

Marcy's eyes were red from crying, Maysa clung to her boyfriend, and both women seemed too upset to communicate well, so Babb first spoke with other friends of Jocelyn's, Jennifer and Bob Kerns, a nurse and a public school administrator.

Jennifer provided the name and the West Virginia phone number for Laura Rogers, Jocelyn's sister, for Babb to make the next-of-kin death notification call. Then she asked, "He finally killed her?"

"Who?" the investigator asked.

"Wesley."

At Babb's prodding, Jennifer explained that she suspected Jocelyn's estranged husband, Wesley Earnest. He and Jocelyn had been married for twelve years but had been separated for the last two to three years, and were embroiled in an acrimonious divorce. Wesley was a PhD, Jennifer said, who lived on the other side of the state in Chesapeake, working as an assistant principal at a high school. Despite the distance, she claimed that he'd made an unexpected late-night visit to Jocelyn in the past.

The detective assured her, "We'll find who did it."

Jocelyn's sister, Laura, was driving on the interstate when the call arrived, en route to pick up two birthday cakes for co-workers, but all thoughts of celebration fled her mind when detectives delivered the news. As soon as she

heard about her sister's death, she, too, immediately suspected Wesley, and warned the investigator, "You will
not break him. He is narcissistic and has a borderline
personality."

Babb made his first attempt to call Wesley, but couldn't
reach him.

Like Detective Babb, Bedford County sheriff's investigator Mike Mayhew had been on his lunch break when
he got the call about a death scene on Pine Bluff Drive
in Forest. He left his SWAT training exercise to report to
the scene, and fellow investigator Ricky Baldwin pulled
up right after him. The medics with the rescue squad were
still there when they arrived, and Mayhew obtained their
statements about what they observed and how they had
gone through the assessment but found no signs of life
in the victim and their resuscitation attempts were wooden
steps in procedure.

When Mayhew walked through the door, he, too, was
rocked by the high temperature. The smell of cat urine
wafting from a litter box masked the odors of decomposi-
tion, blood, and gunpowder that he might otherwise have
noticed. He looked to the right, where Jocelyn's body lay,
and saw what appeared to be an entry wound in her left
temple and the gun on her right side. *Something's not right
here*, he immediately thought.

Mayhew was also concerned about the way she was
dressed, with her keys just lying there. The victim looked
as if she'd just come in, or was about to leave. Although

her body didn't appear posed, neither did he think it looked natural—it seemed to have been straightened, and he could tell her head had been moved at least three feet by the way her strands of hair appeared as if they were dragged through the blood and remained spread out on the carpet.

The investigators asked everyone on the scene if they had moved the body—none had. Mayhew did a walk-through of the house, snapping photos of each room from the perspective of three different corners. He kept his eyes open for evidence as he proceeded, pausing to collect and bag anything that seemed fragile. While doing so, he also sketched and took measurements of every room. Once the initial documentation was complete, Mayhew turned down the thermostat to a normal level and opened all the windows to cool the house down.

Mayhew and Babb went outside to talk to Maysa and Marcy, respectively. Like Jennifer Kerns, both of the women immediately mentioned Jocelyn's estranged hus-band, Wesley Earnest. Both women had made plans with Jocelyn for Wednesday and Thursday nights. Both insisted that Jocelyn had not been seeing anyone. Jocelyn was happy, they said, and caught up in the Christmas spirit. She'd bought presents for everyone. While the detectives talked to the two friends and co-workers, neighbors milled around on the road in front of the home.

The forensic techs went to work inside, searching for anything that looked as if it could have any significance to the death. The house was ranch-style, with a full finished basement. The front door opened into a living room with a beautiful stone fireplace. The open floor plan wrapped around with a doorway to the dining area and then on to the kitchen. In between the kitchen and the living room was a guest bedroom. A deck stretched across the back of the house.

Going the other way from the front door again, they passed a bathroom on the right and a second guest bedroom on the left. Down the hallway from there was the master bedroom. In the basement there was another bedroom and an entertainment area, and there was a swimming pool in the backyard.

In the master bedroom, the techs secured an unopened LifeStyles ultra-sensitive ribbed condom—its presence reinforcing the statement about a "new love" in the note by the victim's side. In the master closet, behind hanging clothes and underneath a fabric bag of softballs, they collected a very large box of assorted ammunition—.40 caliber shotgun shells, 12-, 20-, and 22-gauge shotgun shells and .40 caliber bullets—but none matched the .357 found lying on the body. In fact, they didn't find any ammunition that fit that particular weapon anywhere in the house.

Among the more notable items found were several handwritten, spiral-bound journals authored by the victim. Their presence raised the question, since she'd written all those pages in longhand, why wouldn't she have handwritten her suicide note, too?

In the craft room, investigators were greeted by holiday chaos: piles of wrapping paper, scissors, ribbons, and wrapped Christmas gifts. They recovered a box of condoms from the guest bedroom, and noted stray hairs and a small amount of blood in the basin and on the pedestal of the sink in the guest bathroom. The bathroom was otherwise dusty and a bit disheveled, as if rarely used and seldom cleaned.

Back in the living room, forensic expert Marjorie Harris pointed to Jocelyn's body and told detectives that it appeared the victim's head had landed in three distinct positions—tilted back and to the right, tilted forward and to the right, and ended up turned to the left. "If her head happened to bounce on the carpet, that might account for the changing positions but it doesn't explain a couple of other things," she told them.

"The pattern of the blood stains on her face, the way her hair is stretched and pinned under her head and the streak of blood across the floor all indicate a distinct possibility that someone dragged the victim's body a couple of feet soon after she was shot."

The detectives wanted to know if the deceased could have dragged her own body across that floor before she died, but they would have to wait for the autopsy report for an answer to that question. The investigators turned their attention to locating the fatal bullet, following possible trajectories for a shot traveling front to back, and looking for evidence in the floor, walls, and ceiling behind her.

With the arrival of Dr. Paul Lilly from the medical examiner's office, however, they realized that they had been looking in all the wrong places for bullet fragments. Lilly noted that the shot had entered the back of Jocelyn's head and exited in the front. They would return to search again using this new line of trajectory.

After his examination, Dr. Lilly ordered the removal of the body and its transport to the medical examiner's office. With that accomplished, the techs then removed a section of stained carpet with its pattern of dried blood. Investigators and forensic personnel gathered everything that might be considered relevant in hopes of piecing together an answer to the big question: homicide or suicide? Was the suspicious nature of the scene mere coincidence? Or had a murder been staged to appear like a self-inflicted death? Detectives did not yet know with any certainty, but what they'd already observed made their instincts twitch.

After trying all day long, Investigator Babb finally reached Jocelyn's estranged husband, Wesley Earnest, at 7 P.M. "Your wife has passed away, Mr. Earnest. I'd like to get with you if you could come in and talk to me."

Without the slightest indication of surprise about the news, Wesley said, "I've been traveling and I'm tired. Could I come around nine tomorrow morning?"

Babb objected. "I'd really like to do it tonight."

"I can't do that," Wesley insisted.

They agreed to a meeting in the morning. Wesley never asked how Jocelyn died. He did not have a single question about what happened.

———

Investigators Babb and Mayhew finally left the scene at Jocelyn's home at 1 A.M. on Friday morning. They hoped the medical examiner's postmortem examination of the deceased and the forensic evidence analysis would provide definitive answers to all their questions. They needed to know one way or another. Until those results were available, all they could do was interview and speculate. For now, it was simply a death investigation, and whether or not they would ever have someone to arrest and charge with a crime was unknown.

If it was a homicide, the three prime suspects would be Marcy Shepherd, the woman who found the body; Wesley Earnest, the estranged husband; and the "new love," identity unknown.

THREE

After grabbing a few hours of sleep, Investigator Mike Mayhew went to the autopsy suite in Roanoke, Virginia, where a body bag lay stretched ominously on the stainless steel table. Assistant medical examiner Dr. Amy Tharp unzipped it, and a tech photographed Jocelyn Earnest's body. They propped a block under her head to facilitate x-rays. Viewing the film, Tharp noted the darkness where the bullet's trajectory created a pocket of air in Jocelyn's skull, while the fillings of her teeth and the outline of her necklace glowed white on the image— though brighter still were the bullet fragments scattered in her brain.

Next, Tharp removed the bags that had been placed on Jocelyn's hands and swabbed the palms and fingers for any gun residue. She observed that there was no blood spatter on Jocelyn's hands (as would typically be present had she been holding the gun when it fired) and noted that there was no injury to the nails, no foreign material visible under them and no debris elsewhere on the hands.

Tharp also documented Jocelyn's personal effects and clothing before undressing the victim. As she removed them, she preserved the victim's green and black coat, jeans, belt, sweater, shirt, shoes, socks, panties, bra, watch, necklace, and cloth bracelet. In the process of removing Jocelyn's clothing, they found a fragment of a bullet lying in the bag that transported her body and saved it as evidence. Tharp thoroughly examined the body, seeking out any external damages, scars, birthmarks, or tattoos. Except for the obvious wounds to Jocelyn's head, she found no other fresh injuries.

Tharp shaved and cleaned around the wounds on the deceased woman's head and examined them closely. On the right side, above and slightly behind Jocelyn's ear, Tharp noted a round, crisp hole with scraped edges and stippling, little red marks created from bits of burning (and unburned) gunpowder, smoke, and flame, which marked the point of entry. It was not a contact wound, meaning the weapon had not been in direct contact with the skin. The gun had obviously been two inches to two feet away when it was fired.

Tharp then turned her attention to the left temple at the outer corner of the eye. The skin was pushed slightly outward, without any abrasion to its surface, just as she expected to see from a tumbling bullet that escaped at a slightly sideways angle. A skull fracture had caused blood to pull in the tissues near the wound, giving Jocelyn a classic black eye. Without a doubt it was an exit wound, confirming the possibility posited by Dr. Paul Lilly at the scene.

Next, Tharp conducted a more invasive examination of Jocelyn's head. Making an incision from ear to ear, she moved the scalp away from the skull and documented the hemorrhage between the two as well as the fractures that caused the fused sutures of the bone to pull apart.

Tharp then removed the top of the skull to follow the deadly track of the projectile. It traversed the right back portion of the brain, causing unconsciousness; cut across the brain stem, causing instant death and a total loss of voluntary and involuntary movement; then went through the other half and exited through the left temple. Jocelyn's death was instantaneous—she could not have moved her own body.

Meanwhile that morning, Investigator Gary Babb reported to the sheriff's office to await the scheduled 9 A.M. arrival of the new widower. That hour came and went with no sign of him. Then Babb received a call from defense attorney Joey Sanzone, informing him that his client, Wesley Earnest, would arrive at 5 P.M.

In the meantime, Mayhew and Babb returned to Jocelyn's house for a second search of the crime scene. They quickly located a bullet fragment, smaller than a pencil eraser, lying in a shoe. They found another fragment on the couch, and the remaining lead wedged between a cushion and the arm of a chair. Each shard of lead was removed and preserved. The investigators looked around the room. *Could Jocelyn have held a gun to her own head at such an angle to have caused the bullet to lodge in those locations?*

No matter how hard they searched, investigators could not find any additional fragments. But two rounds had been fired from that gun. They went down to the basement and examined every inch of the ceiling beneath the living room to see if the other one had been shot through the floor. They found nothing—the second fired bullet remained a mystery.

Before five that afternoon, the investigators were back at the county courthouse with Assistant Commonwealth's Attorney Wes Nance, awaiting the arrival of Wesley Earnest and his attorney, Joey Sanzone. It was after six before they saw Wesley pull up in a pickup truck. Mayhew snapped a photo of the truck just in case they needed it in the future.

At six feet four inches with a trim frame, the dark-haired thirty-seven-year-old Wesley was a gangly man with a disarming, slightly goofy smile. He towered over his shorter, rounder attorney. When they were seated, Babb told him again about Jocelyn's death and asked, "Had you heard about that before receiving my call yesterday?"

"Yes. I arrived at Shameka's between six thirty and seven last night," Wesley said, referring to his girlfriend

Shameka Wright, "and Shameka's mom asked, 'Didn't you used to live on Pine Bluff?' I told her 'yes' and she said there was a story on the news about some woman dying there."

Maybe that accounts for his lack of curiosity, Babb thought, *or maybe not*. He explained to Wesley that in a "normal death investigation" they had to establish the whereabouts of the people connected to the victim in the window of time around the time that Jocelyn died.

Wes gave minute details about everything he'd done on Tuesday.

"What did you do on Wednesday?" Babb asked.

"I went to work at the school. There was a fight there that day. I was tired and didn't feel well after that. I went home and went to bed."

"You didn't go anywhere that night?" Babb continued.

"No."

"You didn't talk to anyone?"

"No."

Despite his vague recollection of Wednesday's events, when Babb asked about Thursday and Friday, Wesley was again very thorough in his descriptions of his actions and activities.

Babb moved on to asking about Wesley's estranged wife. "What was Jocelyn like?"

"She was the greatest woman—a great person, a great athlete. I broke her heart. I hurt her," Wesley said.

Everything Wesley was saying seemed to be in accord with the comments of her friends regarding her personality, her collegiate basketball career, and her black belt in karate, but Babb wondered about what Wesley wasn't saying. "What did you think of Jocelyn?"

"She was wonderful."

"If she was so wonderful, why did you go out with others?"

"Jocelyn was okay with that. She told me to sleep with other women."

Babb knew that directly contradicted what he'd heard from Jocelyn's friends who'd cited his infidelity as what ended the marriage. "Really? I thought you were getting a divorce."

"My brother was the catalyst for that. He caused a big confrontation at the house and I left. He's a very controlling guy. You know, when we separated, it broke Jocelyn's heart. She stopped eating and lost forty pounds. I was just doing my thing," Wesley said with a shrug. "She was very depressed but I didn't do anything about it."

Babb made a mental note to find out everything he could about Wesley's brother, Jocelyn's attitude toward infidelity and any possible dark moods she may have experienced. He said, "My only problem is this: she seems like a real strong person to do what she did with basketball and karate and that image clashes with her being depressed," Babb said.

Most disturbing of all to the investigators was Wesley expressing the belief that Jocelyn had committed suicide. Of all the friends and family members interviewed so far, he was the only person who thought it was possible that she had taken her own life.

Wesley switched subjects. He mentioned one of Jocelyn's co-workers, a man he said he suspected she'd had something going with, since they spent so much time together doing projects.

Wesley admitted that he'd purchased a .357 Magnum in the past but added, "It was a present for my wife, for her protection."

A .357 Magnum was the weapon that they'd found at the scene, the one that in all likelihood took Jocelyn's life. Babb now thought it was in all probability also the same weapon Wesley claimed to have purchased for Jocelyn.

Consulting with Sanzone, Wesley agreed to provide a DNA sample and fingerprints. He would not, however, agree to a polygraph test.

"What kind of vehicles do you have? I know you have a truck," Babb said, referring to the one that Wesley just drove to the meeting.

"That's not my truck. I just borrowed that truck," Wesley answered.

The investigators exchanged a glance. They'd both noticed that Wesley appeared a bit rattled when they asked him about the vehicle. There had to be a reason for that, and they were determined to find it.

FOUR

Saturday, December 22, 2007, detectives questioned Marcy Shepherd and Maysa Munsey separately and found consistency in both women's versions of the events of Thursday morning. Both women insisted that they had not moved Jocelyn Earnest's body.

The investigators were troubled, though, about Marcy's admission that she'd been out to the house the night before. "If you were here last night, why did you come back today?"

"Because, Jocelyn was afraid of Wesley. She just installed a security system because she was afraid of him. If she thought Wesley was outside, she would go into the bathroom, lock the door, and stand frozen in the tub. She said he was still coming into her home and that she was afraid he would kill her. And I think he did."

Detectives wondered if Marcy really believed that or if

she was trying to divert attention from herself. Even more red flags were raised in their minds when they asked Marcy if she knew the identity of the "new love" referenced in the note they found near the victim's body.

She looked down at her feet and didn't speak for a moment. When she did, she said, "That was me. I loved Jocelyn Earnest."

When pushed for further details, Marcy explained. "We started working together in August 2005 and developed a friendship. I started feeling something more and I asked her if she felt the same way and she said, 'No.' So, I said, 'Okay. We'll just be friends.'"

"But then it changed?"

"Yes, it became a romantic relationship."

"Were you and Jocelyn intimate?"

"No. We had feelings for one another but we did not have a sexual relationship."

"No physical intimacy?"

"After the company Christmas party the first year we worked together, I went to her home. We kissed on the sofa. But both of us were married at the time so we didn't pursue it any further." Marcy explained that as of April 2006, she and her husband had legally separated, although they continued to live in the same house in order to care for their young children without disruption. Returning to her relationship with Jocelyn, Marcy added, "We did develop a strong emotional attachment."

"Was that the only time you two got physical?"

"There were a couple of times after that that Jocelyn kissed me—nothing more than that."

The detectives exchanged a glance. Unrequited love or unsatisfied lust could be motive for murder, but it was generally a more personal homicide than a single shot to the head.

The relationship between the two women, however, could also be a motive for Jocelyn's estranged spouse to have taken her life.

When Marcy told the investigators about the text messages she'd exchanged with Jocelyn on the last day of her life, the detectives wanted her BlackBerry. Marcy didn't want to part with it. "I am afraid of Wesley Earnest," she told them. "Jocelyn said that if he knew anything or found out anything, he would kill us both. He could be lurking anywhere. I am afraid to be without my phone."

Was it a reasonable explanation? A diversionary move? Or was Marcy simply buying time because she had something to hide?

That same day, the medical examiner confirmed that Jocelyn had died from a gunshot wound to the head. Although it would be weeks before investigators received the final autopsy report, Dr. Amy Tharp did give them her preliminary findings that indicated it was not suicide and the death was instantaneous. Still, Tharp hesitated to officially define Jocelyn's death as a homicide until receiving the toxicology and other test results.

While the detectives waited for evidence reports from the forensic lab to confirm their suspicions of murder, they reviewed the seventeen spiral notebooks filled with

Jocelyn's handwriting—some found in her home, others discovered when they executed a search warrant on her office at Genworth. Page after page, Jocelyn exposed her deepest thoughts, worries, and joys. The investigators tried to maintain a professional distance, but they felt themselves drawn closer to the deceased woman. It felt as if she were talking to them, explaining her life in intimate detail. They kept reading, hoping they'd find the key to unlock the reason for her death.

And then they did. One entry made in August 2005 jumped off the page. Jocelyn wrote of her growing fear of Wesley and urged her family to suspect "my cheating husband" if she were ever found dead. "Know that he killed me, because I would never kill myself. My guess is he shot me and then killed himself." In another entry, she wrote: "If I die, Wesley killed me and he probably shot me." It was a chillingly prophetic pronouncement about the means of death, but would it prove to be as accurate about the person who pulled the trigger?

Another observation became apparent as they read through the journals. The style and wording found in these notebooks was not consistent with what they'd seen in the note found on the living room floor. Did that point to a different author? Or was it simply because she was more depressed and stressed in the moments before she took her life?

Of particular interest to the detectives was another document they discovered, a timeline of the last eleven years of Jocelyn's life, composed on oversized paper. All of the events listed were handwritten and in first person.

Oddly, though, there were two distinct handwriting styles, indicating that the entries were authored by more than one person. Those entries were bracketed in red, and notably, all were statements that reflected positively on Wesley Earnest.

Some comments in this unfamiliar hand offered an excuse for any possible infidelity on his part. For instance, one entry in 1996 read: "Kept telling Wes to sleep with someone else and come home to me." A year later: "Kept telling Wes, I don't want to be with you sexually."

Other entries praised Wesley. In 1998: "It's okay. Wes took care of me as always." Three years later: "Very understanding husband with me spending late hours at work."

Still other notes in the unknown handwriting placed the blame for difficulties in the marriage squarely on Jocelyn's shoulders. In 2005: "Wes kept trying to talk to me, but I just kept shutting him out," followed in the next year by: "Wes wants another chance to make it work out but finds it highly unlikely because my family has too much influence and never fully embraced Wes and Wes's mother has been left out of the loop."

Who wrote those entries? It certainly didn't appear to be Jocelyn. Could it have been Wesley Earnest? If so, when did he alter that document? Long ago, to aid him in contentious divorce proceedings? Or in the aftermath of murder, to diminish suspicion on the estranged spouse? As in many investigations, every new tidbit of uncovered information generated a roar of unanswered questions.

FIVE

Suspicions against Marcy Shepherd were now a distant second to those pointing to Wesley Earnest. However, Investigators Gary Babb and Mike Mayhew guarded against tunnel vision. They needed more before they settled on any firm conclusions of guilt. The Bedford County Sheriff's Office brought in backup to help make that happen. Personnel from the police departments in the city of Bedford, the seat of the county where Jocelyn died; Lynchburg, the city where Jocelyn worked; and the Campbell County Sheriff's Office, the neighboring area where Wesley stayed when visiting his girlfriend, now became part of the team of investigators.

While the detectives sought answers, Jocelyn Earnest's family, friends, and neighbors sought healing. Lisa Jennings, a former neighbor, was stunned by news of Jocelyn's death. She remembered the Earnests as an athletic, outgoing, and smart couple. "They were nice people as far as we knew," she said to a reporter for the *Virginian-Pilot*.

Next-door neighbor Ernest Daye started double-checking the locks on his windows and doors each night. "It's worrisome," he told Lynchburg's *News & Advance*. "We haven't heard anything. She was my neighbor. I used to see her and wave and speak to her. That's all I know—nothing, to tell the truth."

"It's always been a quiet and peaceful neighborhood," Dorothy Slusher said to the *News & Advance* reporter. "It makes you wonder what happened to her. It's so sad. I keep my doors locked day and night. You just don't know. People are crazy."

The first step on the path back to normalcy for those who knew and cared about Jocelyn was the funeral service.

Initially, Wesley's family said that they wanted her body. Wesley even went to the funeral home insisting that since Jocelyn was his wife, it was his decision. He told them, "I want her cremated in a cardboard box and put in a simple urn."

Since Jocelyn's family wanted to lay her to rest in West Virginia, where they lived and Jocelyn grew up, they enlisted Mayhew's help. In a dispute like this one, he was powerless, but he did make sure nothing was done until a legal decision was reached. He contacted Joey Sanzone and told him that he needed to file the proper paperwork. With the attorney involved, the conflict simply went away. Jocelyn's body was transported to her home state of West Virginia to the Brown Funeral Home in Martinsburg. The family received friends there from 7 to 9 P.M. on December 27, 2007. Services began at 10 A.M. on December 28 with Reverend Ed Taylor officiating. It was a low-key event, made even more mournful because no one knew if the deceased had taken her own life or had been the victim of a violent act. Both possibilities were tragic and painful, but the not-knowing haunted the solemn occasion.

Jocelyn's mother, Joyce Young, was visibly shaken by the experience. While Jocelyn's home was still sealed as a crime scene, Joyce had pleaded with investigators to have something that smelled like her daughter. They'd taken pity on her and had allowed the grieving mother inside—in the presence of law enforcement and Wesley's defense attorney Joey Sanzone—to take possession of a pillow from Jocelyn's bed.

"To go to a funeral, to pick out your child's casket, it just tears you apart," Joyce said.

Jocelyn was interred in nearby Rosedale Cemetery. The obituary notice noted: "In addition to or in lieu of flowers, memorial contributions may be made to the Berkeley County Humane Society."

Her father, Bill Branham, took home her beloved Labrador retriever, Rufus. Homes for her cats were found with feline-loving friends.

On January 16, 2008, questions about Jocelyn's death still hung in the air. Marcy Shepherd, Maysa Munsey, and another friend from work, Dora Farrah, arranged a local memorial service at Timberlake United Methodist Church in Lynchburg. Four hundred people, including some from West Virginia, gathered beneath a sky that threatened snow and entered the sanctuary to express their admiration for their deceased friend.

Co-workers described Jocelyn as a leader who could facilitate the input of others and make decisions on large projects. Friends referred to her special ability to recognize when things were wrong and do something about it. "She didn't wait for that phone call for help. She just offered it. She was my best friend, closer than a sister," Maysa said. When Marcy stood before the gathered mourners to speak of Jocelyn, she said, "She was like a fine wine with a complex bouquet. If I asked everyone in the church what their relationship with Jocelyn was, they'd all have different answers. Yet, she was always herself."

They cried, said good-bye, expressed their love, and waited for more information. Many were already convinced that Jocelyn had not taken her own life and were impatient for authorities to make it official.

SIX

Detectives continued to dig for the solid facts they needed to draw a conclusion, even as more circumstantial evidence piled up that Jocelyn Earnest's death was a homicide. For instance, although there were two printers in the home, neither one was operational at the time of her death, and no draft of the suicide note was found on her computer. And their suspicions about Wesley Earnest were reinforced when they learned that the gun that killed her was registered in his name.

They finally had the proof they needed to call Jocelyn's death a murder when blood stain analysis confirmed that her body had been dragged at least two feet after the instantly fatal gunshot.

In the Department of Forensic Science lab in Roanoke, latent print specialist Kenneth Riding sought evidence on several items. He found no fingerprints of value on the shell casing or on the Smith and Wesson .357.

Then he turned to the note found at the crime scene. There were no visible prints on it, but once he processed it with ninhydrin, a chemical that reacts to the amino acids given off by the fingers, he found two latents—both from the same digit, either the tip of a finger or thumb—one on the front and one on the back of the paper. Using the samples he had retrieved from the morgue, Riding confirmed that the prints did not match those of Jocelyn Earnest. He then compared them to those obtained from Maysa Munsey, Marcy Shepherd, and Dora Farrah—none were a match. However, the latent on the back of the note had ten points of similarity and the one on the front of the note bore fifteen points of similarity to one set of known samples—those belonging to Jocelyn's estranged husband, Wesley Earnest. Although there is no established minimum for identification, experts consider that number of matches to be sufficient for identification purposes.

For verification, they would obtain another set of prints from Wesley and send all the evidence and findings to another latent fingerprint analyst to confirm or dispute Riding's conclusions.

On Monday, December 17, 2007, Wesley had swapped his silver Honda Accord for a maroon Chevrolet Silverado truck, belonging to David Hall, a teacher and wrestling coach at Great Bridge High School as well as Wesley's friend and hunting buddy. Wesley told David that he needed the truck to move some furniture, and he returned the truck to Dave's home early Thursday morning.

"Sorry about the floor mats. They're a little messed up," Wesley apologized for a bleached-out stain he'd caused when cleaning the inside of the truck. Dave noted that Wesley's hair was still wet, as if he'd just gotten out of the shower, but otherwise he looked normal, in his usual button-down shirt and tie.

Dave didn't linger to chat, antsy about being late to work at Great Bridge High, but before he left, he joked to his wife, "If I am late it's not going to be a big deal because I'm with an administrator."

Jesse McCoy, one of Wesley's former students, was trying to start a car detailing business with his uncle, a Baptist preacher. Wesley agreed to try his detailing service, saying that he'd like to have it done to his Honda Accord the week before Christmas break, and they arranged for a 7:30 A.M. pickup on Wednesday, December 19. Close to that date, Wesley called and said, "Wednesday isn't a good day because I'm going to be out of town."

They rescheduled for Thursday at the same time. Early that week, Wesley called again. "I need to push the time back a couple of hours because I don't know if I'll be back yet."

Jesse's uncle picked up Wesley's Honda at 9:15 that morning. Wesley handed him the keys and said, "I have a lot of junk in the back. Don't worry about going back there."

The uncle returned the vehicle, which he described as "the dirtiest car I'd ever cleaned," at 4:15 that afternoon. Wesley paid him $120 in cash.

On January 10, 2008, Wesley borrowed Dave's truck again. He said that he needed the Silverado to straighten out his trailer. Dave told Wesley that he needed it back by six o'clock, since he was driving the wrestling team to an overnight competition after practice that afternoon. Wesley assured him that he'd have the truck back in time.

Wesley drove to Kramer Tire on Providence Road in Virginia Beach, bypassing the two closer Kramer stores in Chesapeake. When approached in the showroom by Rick Keuhne, Wesley introduced himself as Tom Dunbar and said, "I need new tires."

"What's the problem?" Rick asked.

"Well, I'm driving from the Roanoke area and the tires gave me a ride disturbance, shook all the way from there, so I want new tires put on my vehicle."

"Okay," Rick said, making a notation on the work order.

"It's a company vehicle and my employer will reimburse me," Wesley said.

Rick rang up the sale, left the showroom, and carried the ticket into the shop. The truck was put up on the rack, and Rick could not see anything wrong with the tires on it. He spun each of them, looking to see if there was a belt separation defect, but none of the tires wobbled. He ran his hand across the treads and found them completely even from one side to the other, with no visible indication of anything that would cause a ride disturbance.

When Rick returned to the showroom, he asked, "Mr. Dunbar, are you sure you want me to change these tires because I don't see anything wrong with them?" Rick explained what he discovered when he inspected them and added, "I really don't think you need new tires."

"No, get those tires off my vehicle. I want to get new ones," Wesley insisted.

Rick went back into the shop and got the work started. An hour later, Wesley paid for his $688 purchase in cash and drove off.

Wesley returned the truck to Dave by 6:15, and Dave headed off to the wrestling competition. Over the next day, as he ferried the kids back and forth from their hotel rooms to the competition site, he complained constantly about his truck's ride.

On Saturday, he finally checked out his truck's tires and realized there were Dunlops on his vehicle, and not the BFGoodrich all-terrain radials he'd put on it fifteen months earlier.

He called Wesley and left a message asking about the tire change. Wesley responded, "I had popped the two front tires by running over a board with nails in it. I know I could have plugged them but I felt guilty about ruining them. So, when I saw this deal where I could buy three tires and get one free, I bought you four new tires."

Dave accepted Wesley's excuse, but still wished he had the same type of tires he'd had on the truck before.

Molly Sullivan, a teacher at Oscar Smith Middle School, where Wesley had worked in administration before his current position as one of two assistant principals at nearby Great Bridge High School, had heard through the grapevine that Wesley's wife had been killed over the holidays. Apparently, she had not been paying close attention to the details or the rumor mill botched up the story because Molly believed that his wife had died in a car accident. She sent him an email the first week in January 2008.

"I'm very sorry for your loss. Please let me know if there's anything I can do for you," she wrote. She knew that Wesley had opened the email soon after she sent it, but she didn't get a response until twenty-four hours later.

Wes wrote, "What are you talking about?"

Molly responded: "I'm very sorry, please let me know if there's anything I can do."

This time, Wesley did not respond at all.

A few weeks later, on January 23, 2008, Molly was driving home from work debating what to do for dinner. She started calling various friends to see who might be available to join her for a meal somewhere. She called Wesley, then changed her mind and hung up before he answered.

Wesley, however, immediately returned her call. "What are you doing?"

"I was going to see if you wanted to grab a bite to eat," Molly said.

"Well, I'm tied up right now. I'm in Williamsburg," a historic town, fifty miles north-northwest of Chesapeake. "I'm waiting for a pretty lady."

"Oh, you've got a hot date?"

"Yes, I do. You missed your opportunity."

"I'll go home and cook. It's no big deal."

They chatted a bit then Molly remembered about his wife and said, "I'm so sorry about your wife."

In a loud, enraged-sounding voice Wesley said, "What the fuck are you talking about? How many times do I have to tell you I'm not married? Why do you keep asking me over and over again?"

"Whoa, whoa, back off," Molly said.

"Why didn't you call me instead of sending me that email?"

"Because my grandfather died over the holidays, too, and I was tired of getting phone calls so I just sent an email. I'm sorry."

Another Oscar Smith Middle School teacher, Sonya Stevens, had very similar conversations with Wesley. When she, too, expressed her sympathies after hearing the rumors, Wesley blew up at her, too. Neither woman could make sense of his reaction at the time.

Despite their suspicions about Wesley as a suspect in Jocelyn's murder, the detectives still had a concern about the feasibility of his involvement. He was living and working on the other side of the state—a three- to four-hour drive from Jocelyn's home. Was it possible for him to make that trip in the middle of the workweek?

The next day, Detectives Gary Babb and Mike Mayhew drove to Oscar Smith Middle School in Chesapeake, Wesley's first place of employment in the area. Principal Linda Scott was initially reluctant to talk about a former member of her staff, but once the investigators explained a homicide was involved, she cooperated fully.

Scott said that she found Wesley to be very arrogant and demanding, particularly in his attitude toward women in the workplace. "If you had something he could use, he was a friend. If you had nothing he needed, he insisted that you call him Dr. Earnest." She added that Wesley had "hit on" her young adult daughter, who described him as "spooky."

Again and again, on that trip, the investigators spoke to teachers who believed that Wesley was independently wealthy and that he'd never been married. Detective W. B. Satterfield, who worked at the school in 2005 as a resource officer, a member of the local police jurisdiction assigned to the school to help prevent crime, said that Wesley referred to himself as "a small-time millionaire" who didn't need to work to make a living. When Satterfield asked why he wasn't married when he had so much to offer financially, Wesley had answered, "I haven't found the one."

Molly Sullivan said Wesley claimed to own a house on Smith Mountain Lake and another property in California. She said he told her, "I'm worth $5 million. I could retire but I continue working because I love education." Even though at the time she'd considered Wesley a friend, the flaunting of his financial worth still made her uncomfortable—especially since Molly knew he was aware that she herself worked two jobs to make ends meet. Many times, she'd heard him deny that he had ever been married or divorced.

The investigators also went to Great Bridge High School, where Wesley was employed as one of two assistant principals.

A month earlier, on the day after Jocelyn's death was discovered, the central office of Great Bridge High School had informed principal Dr. Janet Andrejco, Wesley's supervisor, that the news media was interested in the death of a woman whom Dr. Earnest knew, and that they might be trying to contact him.

It was the middle of the school holidays, but Andrejco had called Wesley to let him know what she'd heard. Wesley thanked her for calling and expressed his appreciation that she reached out to him. A short while later—right before he first went in to speak to the detectives—Wesley had called her back. "I'm waiting in a parking lot to be questioned," he said, mentioning something about a divorce attorney. He added, "My wife's family often makes me look like I'm evil. Her death was a suicide because of a failing relationship."

Andrejco was confused. She'd thought Wesley was

unmarried, yet now he was talking about divorce? It didn't make any sense. It was beginning to seem as if after working with him for a year and a half she didn't know him at all. But Wesley got off the phone before explaining anything more about the deceased woman or his connection to her.

Now, when the detectives arrived at the high school on January 24, 2008, they found Principal Andrejco in the middle of a meeting, which was jettisoned upon the arrival of the two men in dark suits. The principal allowed the detectives to use her office to talk to the staff.

School resource officer Wallace Chadwick told the investigators that he'd heard similar stories about Wesley's wealth and eligible status. Wallace had met Wesley's girlfriend, Shameka Wright, but when he'd asked Wesley about their relationship, Wesley referred to her as nothing more than "a chick I met in the mountains."

When the detectives talked to Wesley's fellow assistant principal, Jim Clevenger, he had a similar impression about Wesley's net worth. He said, "Wesley indicated in his first year that he didn't necessarily have to work, that he was not like most administrators who had to limit how much they could invest. He said that the folks downtown"—referring to the school district administration—"were investigating how to coordinate the paperwork so that he could invest a large portion of his salary."

Jim Clevenger later described how, on the day the investigators visited the high school, Wesley had approached him looking preoccupied and concerned while Jim was in the common area supervising the students at the beginning of the first lunch period. He said, "Jim, what's going on in the main office?"

"Well, I was in the main office and I saw two gentlemen come in in dark suits. In my experience in high school when two guys in dark suits come in the building, they're law enforcement. Jan and I had this meeting and immediately, I got pushed aside because she's going to entertain and have to deal with those two gentlemen."

"Did Dave Hall come into the office to talk to them?" Wesley asked.

"Yes, I did see Dave come into the main office. But that's all I know. If I learn any more, I'll get back with you."

During a later lunch period, Jim recalled approaching Wesley and telling him, "I haven't learned any more. I just know there are folks meeting; I don't know who's been in the meetings. I've looked in the window to see if we can have our calendar meeting but Jan said, 'That's not happening,' and that's all I know." At the end of the school day, Jim saw Wesley in the hall looking nervous and tense, moving his shoulders and crunching up his neck as if his mind were somewhere far away.

When the detectives left the high school building just after four thirty that afternoon, Wesley immediately called Principal Andrejco on his cell phone. He started crying as soon as she answered the phone. He told her he wanted a leave of absence. He expressed his concern that law enforcement would leak news of his interview to the media and thrust the school into a negative spotlight. But he didn't want anyone to think that he'd been asked to leave. "I fear that people would think I'm leaving because of you," he told Andrejco. "Maybe we could get it clear at a staff meeting."

But before considering that, Dr. Andrejco insisted upon learning more details about Wesley's personal background. She knew that he'd worked at Jefferson Forest High School in Forest and Heritage High School in Lynchburg—both schools were close to each other but more than a three-hour drive away from her school, on the western side of the state—but knew nothing of his personal life from that time. Wesley had never spoken about it before their earlier phone call.

For the first time, he told her about his wife. "Four years ago my wife and I split up. Three years ago I came to the beach," Wesley said, fiddling with the actual timeline either out of carelessness or dishonesty.

Wesley asked Andrejco to give him an opportunity to explain about his marriage and separation to the teachers and other administrators at the school. He wanted to correct the mistaken impressions he'd given to many of the staff in the past.

He continued sobbing through the conversation, his sentences disjointed as if he couldn't find the energy to connect them together. "I love working for you. Would there be another place I could work that is not visible?"

Andrejco didn't have an answer for him. She needed time to figure out what she would do.

Wesley continued to plead with her, contradicting himself as he did. "I don't feel like coming to work tomorrow.

I'm sick to my stomach. It is heavy on my heart. People are coming to me. I only talked to police once. Is my career over? That's all I have to live for. I put a lot into my work and my career. I tried to start a new life coming here. That's all I have to live for. I don't have any family except in West Virginia. I don't have a lot of friends. I don't date a lot. I thought I weathered the worst of everything."

The principal was bothered by this phone call. It was obvious that Wesley had intentionally deceived his co-workers. Besides his marital status, what other misperceptions had he propagated about his past? Could he be hiding something even more serious?

She found Wesley's reaction to his conversation with law enforcement over the top. After all, it was only natural that the detectives would want to question the estranged spouse of someone who died under suspicious circumstances. She suspected that his extreme emotional response likely indicated an underlying problem that was only going to get worse, and her first priority was to prepare for—and try to minimize—any possible collateral damage to the school. She decided to suspend Wesley with pay until she knew whether or not he would be charged with any crime.

SEVEN

As February 2008 drew to a close, Jocelyn Earnest's death was officially deemed a homicide by the medical examiner. Investigators Gary Babb and Mike Mayhew drew up an arrest warrant against Wesley Earnest for the first degree murder of his wife and the use of a firearm in the commission of a felony.

The two detectives, accompanied by a Campbell County officer, went to Wesley Earnest's girlfriend's home, a single-wide trailer way off the main road in the middle of the country in Concord, Virginia, a rural town roughly twenty miles east of the crime scene.

A thin, attractive African American woman who identified herself as Wesley's girlfriend, Shameka Wright, answered the door.

"Is Wes here?" Babb asked.

"Yes," she said. "He's taking a shower."

"May we come in?"

"Yes," she answered, flinging the door open wide and returning to the kitchen to tend to something she had cooking on the stove.

Inside, the investigators found a home that was neat but overcrowded with belongings and furniture. Moments later, Wesley came out to the living room wearing a shirt and a pair of shorts. His hair was wet—his demeanor flat.

"You are under arrest for the murder of Jocelyn Earnest."

"May I go back and get my shoes?"

"Tell us where they are and we'll get them for you," Babb said.

After the retrieved shoes were tied onto his feet, the handcuffs were snapped on his wrists. Wesley was loaded into the backseat of an SUV. Babb sat on one side of him, Mayhew on the other.

The detectives couldn't question Wesley without his lawyer present. Instead, they talked basketball as they headed up the highway, traveling more than thirty miles west to the Blue Ridge Regional Jail Authority's Bedford Adult Detention Center.

The investigators now had sufficient probable cause to request search warrants. They applied for and received the authorization they needed to seek out firearms, ammunition, cell phones, computers, copiers and printers, papers, correspondence, handwritten and printed documents, photographs, biological evidence, and clothing or other apparel from Wesley's $1.3 million house on Smith Mountain Lake and at Shameka's more modest Concord home in Campbell County where Wesley often stayed.

At the lake house, officers entered a beautiful home with an open layout, and decorated with antique wooden ship models. The airy interior of the home offered incredible vistas of the sprawling lake and the woods surrounding it. They brought in a locksmith to drill the safe in the garage, where they discovered a box of .38 caliber bullets, not a caliber that could be used in any of the weapons stored there. They also found a manila folder containing ownership papers for the murder weapon (which did use .357 caliber bullets), a $1,000 bill in a plastic case and an assortment of coins. From elsewhere in the house, they took possession of documents containing samples of Wesley's handwriting as well as financial documents relating to his level of debt and the contentiousness of his divorce from Jocelyn.

At Shameka's residence, they discovered the case for the revolver that took Jocelyn's life, as well as the original box that held the gun at the time of purchase. They also took possession of an album labeled "Our Journey Together" that contained photos and mementoes of trips Shameka and Wesley had taken while Wesley and Jocelyn were still living together in 2004 and 2005—to tourist venues in Tennessee, Florida, and North Carolina. Just miles away from the high school, authorities executed yet another search warrant at Wesley's third identified residence, at an address the school had on file. On December 26, 2007, Wesley's mother and stepfather, Pat and Mike

Wimmer, had delivered their twenty-seven-foot Terry camping trailer to the Chesapeake Campground in the Deep Creek section of Chesapeake for Wesley to occupy for up to the next six months. They'd signed a lease in the name of Wesley Earnest Wimmer.

Law enforcement searched for bullets, LifeStyles condoms, like the ones found in Jocelyn's home, and any electronic media—computers, CDs, or hard drives. All that was recovered was one spiral notebook.

The day after his arrest, Principal Andrejco suspended Wesley without pay, pending the outcome of his trial. She sent a letter to parents informing them that "Dr. Wesley Earnest, Assistant Principal of Great Bridge High School, has been charged with a serious crime in the western part of the state. Dr. Earnest has been away from the school for some time and that will continue until this matter is resolved."

EIGHT

The evidence pointing to possible motives for Wesley Earnest continued to build. Investigators Gary Babb and Mike Mayhew pored over the evidence and their notes looking for answers. They spent hours with prosecutor Wes Nance trying to re-create how Jocelyn had fallen and how she'd been moved. They looked into the possibility of suspects other than Wesley but found no compelling alternatives.

Detectives learned that his affair with Shameka began at least two years before Jocelyn learned of it, hired attorney Jennifer Stille, and filed for divorce in 2006. The legal dissolution of their marriage was still not finalized, as the couple wrangled over the division of communal property. In divorce documents recovered from both of their homes, they learned that Jocelyn had accused her estranged husband of having an affair and of entering her home, after she'd changed the locks, to remove his guns and other property.

As the investigators gathered details about Wesley's financial situation from seized documents, red flags flew high. The court had ordered Jocelyn to pay 25 percent of the mortgage on the 7,000 square foot, seven bedroom, six and a half bath Smith Mountain Lake home, but Wesley still had to come up with three-quarters of the nearly $6,000 monthly mortgage payment.

Making things even worse, Wesley had accumulated more than $100,000 in credit card debt since separating from Jocelyn. Calls from bill collectors were frequent, and Shameka often paid them with her own money.

Between the lake house and his other financial obligations, it became clear that Wesley was more than a million dollars in debt. In an attempt to solve his financial crisis, he'd put the lake home on the market in 2007, but his timing was awful. The housing bubble had burst and the only offers he received would've resulted in a loss on his investment.

Other paperwork they confiscated included a note that appeared to be something Wesley wrote to his attorney in preparation for his divorce. It was a series of complaints written in third person.

"Summer 2004, Jocelyn continues to work up to eighty hours a week at GE or Genworth financial."

"Memorial Day weekend, Jocelyn worked thirty-eight hours over the three-day weekend."

"Jocelyn kept spending increasing amounts of time with people from work, most notably a bachelor named

Leon. She worked on special projects just for him while at home—picture framing projects."

"June 2004, Wesley was going to a conference for work. The conference was located at the resort called the Homestead in Hot Springs, Virginia. Wesley pleaded with Jocelyn to go with him, but she refused, claiming that work at Genworth Financial was more important."

"At the June 2005 graduation party, Wesley asked Jocelyn to join him at the lake house for the celebration. This is the last day Jocelyn spent any quality time at the lake house. Jocelyn was distant and nonresponsive."

"In late June 2005, Jocelyn completely shut Wesley out of her life by refusing to speak to him whatsoever. Wesley continued to pay all the bills while seeking a job promotion."

A typed document contained a list of Jocelyn's family members and friends with a description of the testimony they might deliver at a divorce hearing. Another handwritten note was a list of dates and travel times between Chesapeake, Virginia, and Smith Mountain Lake, and a pad imprinted with "Wesley's Organizational Tools" that contained a sentence: "Add Dave's truck borrowed." Who was Dave? And why and when did Wesley borrow his truck?

They also found a copy of the letter that Wesley had written to Jocelyn detailing options for paying off their joint debt. Even more suspicious was another handwritten note that read: "Weather 12/19/07? Gas up over the drive?"

An additional note in Wesley's handwriting that had

obviously been written between December 19, 2007, and February 27, 2008, read: "Questions of attorney. Death Certificate. Coroner's report. When can house be freed up. Her W-2's. Need to file taxes. Status of $52,000 paying in county taxes. Paid for cars—$6,500 not paid. When can I access my account? Want to know if money from 2006 taxes made it into account. W-2's on escrow. Any updates. If arrested, how? 1482 electrical. Heating. Frozen pipes. Any checking or savings account. Want to know beneficiaries. Will. 60 days limitations."

What had Jocelyn's murder been all about? Was it money? Or was Marcy Shepherd right about her suspicions of Wesley? Had the small physical contact between Marcy and Jocelyn ignited a firestorm of rumors? And if so, did those rumors reach across the state to Jocelyn's estranged husband and send him into a rage? Although law enforcement had not uncovered any indication that this story was circulating, it was too early in the investigation for them to discount the hypothesis.

What had happened in the lives of Jocelyn and Wesley Earnest to cause their marriage to culminate in this fatal, tragic end?

NINE

Jocelyn Denise Branham was born in the early afternoon of Monday, October 13, 1969, in Morgantown, West Virginia. Her parents, Bill Branham and Joyce DeHaven, had met in high school and were married in 1968. After a long labor at University Hospital, Jocelyn arrived with dark brown hair, measuring about eight and a half pounds and twenty inches long. She was "a *big* surprise. Bigger than expected," her mother Joyce recalled.

Bill, who was a biology major studying vertebrate embryology at West Virginia University at the time, looked at his daughter and thought the shape of her head wasn't exactly right. The medical staff told him not to worry, that it would straighten out fine. But the first-time father couldn't help fretting about it until time worked its wonders and put his mind at ease.

By the first of the following March, Jocelyn accomplished a one-handed, two-kneed crawl. Three months later, she was walking. She learned to brush her teeth one month after her first birthday. Jocelyn was a bright and exceptional child. She potty-trained early and rarely got into mischief. Needless to say, Mom and Dad were proud.

Once Bill received his master's degree, his Air Force ROTC obligation sent him and his family to Sheppard Air Force Base in Wichita Falls, Texas. He went through basic training and took advantage of every opportunity for a family trip. They even went to Six Flags and spent the day at the kiddie rides watching their daughter's eyes sparkle with each new thrill.

After three months in Texas, the family spent two months at Vandenberg Air Force Base, situated in California between Los Angeles and San Francisco. In between Bill's training to be a Titan Missile Crew Commander, the family visited Disneyland, Universal Studios, and San Francisco. They then traveled back east to Little Rock Air Force Base in Arkansas, where Bill worked as a Missile Launch Technician.

In February 1974, when Jocelyn was four and a half, the family grew by the addition of a second daughter named Laura. Jocelyn was enchanted with the idea of having a baby sister and proud of her role as big sister—a responsibility she took seriously all of her life.

Jocelyn and Laura had an exemplary sibling relationship from the earliest years. They watched *The Smurfs* together and made friendship bracelets; Jocelyn even let her little sister ride on the handlebars of her pink Huffy bike. They razzed and teased each other, but always with love.

The year of 1976 was one of upheaval for the Branham family. Bill left the Air Force and he and Joyce divorced. For a while, the two separate households both remained in Little Rock, but eventually Joyce and her daughters moved back to Martinsburg, West Virginia.

Jocelyn's and Laura's lives were divided into two parts: the school year with mom, and the summers with dad. Bill would drive down and pick them up when school let out for the year, then bring them back to their mother two and a half months later. At Christmastime, Bill traveled to West Virginia for visits at their mother's apartment and at Bill's parents' home.

The summer trips were full of carefree travel with Bill, though the arrangements, while enjoyable for the girls, would be frowned upon today. Bill had a camper on the back of his pickup truck with a mattress on the floor. In between the cab and the camper-topped truck bed was an inflatable, rectangular rubber access point that they used to pass things back and forth from the front to the back—and sometimes the girls crawled through it. The girls had room to play and hardly noticed the passing miles.

They took off in the truck for a lot of tent camping, canoeing, and hiking, often in the company of Bill's friends and their children. The girls and Bill enjoyed nature hikes, looking for bugs, wildflowers, and wildlife. They visited Willow Springs Water Park. The girls loved to play in the water and were crazy about the waterslide with a little cart that planed out over the water at the bottom of the descent. They also traveled to Lake Sylvia Recreation Area, northwest of Little Rock in the Ouachita

National Forest, and Queen Wilhelmina State Park due west of Little Rock.

Woolly Hollow State Park was also a favorite with the girls where they could swim and ride the paddleboats. The Woolly Cabin, the log-constructed home built by the first settlers, added a historic context to the visit. One year, Jocelyn reached down at something sparkling in the grass and pulled out a diamond ring. Before leaving the park, they stopped at the office and left their contact information in case anyone reported it missing. No one ever did, and Jocelyn got to keep her found treasure.

Each summer, Bill would take the girls with him for one day to the scientific lab where he worked. He would introduce them to the new co-workers and greet the ones they'd met in previous years. Each time, he'd have a fun day of science planned. One year they played with soap, dry ice, and water; another they observed the necropsy of a rat—no matter the activity, Jocelyn and Laura loved their days at work with their dad.

One year, Bill and his daughters saw a commercial on television about making ice cream with orange soda and condensed milk. Bill pulled out his father's old manual ice-cream freezer and they got busy. Bill put the rock salt and ice in the hand crank bucket. Jocelyn and Laura took turns working it until it got too stiff for them to manage and then their dad took over. They had so much fun with that, they experimented with different flavors every week including grape soda, root beer, and cola. They all agreed that orange and grape were best.

Once they went to a spaghetti supper fund-raiser at

a friend's rural Catholic church. Gambling games were set up with a wheel like roulette. Bill gave money to each of the girls and let them play. Jocelyn couldn't stop winning—she came home with an armload of stuffed animals including a three-foot-long stuffed carrot, a toy that was a favorite with the girls for years. Bill worried that he'd contributed to a dangerous lesson and was concerned that Jocelyn would think that gambling was an easy way to riches. Still, when they went to Six Flags in St. Louis with Joyce's family, he didn't object to Jocelyn playing a ringtoss game—the lucky girl won a teddy bear bigger than she was.

Another favorite activity was attending the games played by the Arkansas Travelers, an AA baseball team affiliated with the St. Louis Cardinals. The small ballpark was a safe, enclosed area where kids roamed freely, exploring and playing together. Sometimes Jocelyn would go outside of the park with a group of other kids waiting for foul balls to come over the fence, and Bill would sit up in the back where she could see him and give her a competitive edge by pointing in the direction that balls were headed.

Jocelyn was an athletic girl from a young age. She played tennis and volleyball, and was on the all-star softball team as well as the Berkeley County softball league during her high school years. In her freshman year, on the basketball team, she played point guard. She was the team's star shooting guard, averaging twenty-four points per game in her junior year and twenty-nine in her senior year. She was team captain and the first to earn an all-state honorable mention. Laura often tagged along to basketball practice, softball games, and some of her older sister's get-togethers with friends.

In her spare time, she earned a black belt in karate.

Jocelyn graduated from Hedgesville High School in 1988, and with the help of a four-year full athletic scholarship, she went to West Virginia University where she was a member of the Mountaineer women's basketball team from 1989 to 1992. She was one of the university's best three-point shooters ever, despite her average height, and once tried out for a spot on the women's basketball team for the 1992 Olympics before graduating in 1993 with a double major in economics and marketing. Coach Kittie Blakemore told *48 Hours*, "Her smile, her hard work, her motivation to help her teammates will long be remembered."

TEN

Wesley Brian Earnest was born to Roger and Patricia Earnest on May 19, 1970, in a small town outside of Los Angeles. His father was a California Highway Patrol officer.

Wesley was five years old when the family moved to West Virginia, and twelve years old when his parents' marriage disintegrated. Wesley stayed with his mother, and his younger brother, Tyler, lived with their dad. Patricia referred to Wesley as "the little man around the house." He took care of minor upkeep and repairs in their home like changing the locks on doors, and growing up he played nearly every sport there was.

Wesley entered college at West Virginia University in Morgantown in 1988 and started his academic career as a civil engineering major. But in the middle of his junior year, he changed his major to mathematics when he decided that he wanted to teach math and coach basketball. It was outside of calculus class in 1991 where he met Jocelyn Branham.

Something about Jocelyn grabbed his attention right away. He approached her and he introduced himself to her and said, "Let's go play some basketball."

Wesley's mother described them as a "cute" couple. While they were dating, "both of them would be lying in the middle of the floor watching a ball game together . . . whenever you saw one, you saw the other."

Although according to friends and family, Jocelyn was a confident young woman who had been good at anything she tried to do, she always tried to avoid confrontation, and rarely stood up for herself.

Early in her relationship with Wesley, Jocelyn developed some concern about his controlling and manipulative nature, but it was his anger issues that once led her to break up with him while they were still in college. Jocelyn's sister, Laura, remembered seeing Jocelyn crying after getting off the phone with Wes. They were "polar opposites" whom Laura could never imagine living together in harmony. But when Jocelyn called it off, Wesley told her, "Well, I don't know what I'll do without you. Maybe next time I go skydiving, I won't pull the cord."

Jocelyn couldn't handle the guilt Wesley's comment induced, and she backed down. Soon, the couple was back together again.

When they graduated, Wesley moved to Bedford, Virginia, and took a job as a mathematics teacher and basketball coach at Jefferson Forest High School. Jocelyn remained in West Virginia for another three years, but their relationship grew, and before long, they were engaged.

When Wesley decided to propose marriage, he didn't just pop the question. He filled a box with coins, added a note that read: "Marry me" and buried it in the ground. Then he got Jocelyn, guided her to the general area, and handed her a metal detector. She accomplished her mission, digging up the box and agreeing to become his wife.

In 1994, Wesley joined the coed city volleyball team in Lynchburg. One of his teammates was the nearly six-foot-tall Jennifer Landis, a former basketball player at Virginia Commonwealth University. He told her, "I'm engaged and my fiancée played basketball like you. You guys ought to have a lot in common."

Jennifer thought Wes was a bit socially awkward but he could be very funny and quite interesting, and she liked his competitive spirit on the court. Other teammates, however, found him intimidating. Most of the team would talk to one another about stupid plays, self-interested moves, and other faux pas during the game, but they were afraid to address Wesley about those matters. Jennifer played the front row with him and felt she had the right and the obligation to the team to express her concerns. He always got angry at any criticism she delivered. The rest of the group expressed surprise that she talked to him that way.

The team always went to Taco Bell after games. Typically, Jennifer went to the restroom to wash her hands before ordering. One night, by the time she got to the table, there was only one empty seat and it was directly across from Wesley. "Okay if I sit here?" she asked.

"Sure," Wesley said, "but don't get any ideas, I have a fiancée."

Jennifer was puzzled. She didn't know if his remark stemmed from arrogance, stupidity, or if it was supposed to be a joke—but the expression on his face indicated that he was serious. She shifted subjects to that night's game and snapped back, "Don't try to hit through a double block, okay?"

Jennifer started dating Bob Kerns, another member of their volleyball team, in February 1995. Wesley invited Jennifer and Bob to his and Jocelyn's August 19, 1995, wedding, but scheduling conflicts made it impossible for them to go.

Jennifer and Jocelyn finally met at a going-away party for Bob's former roommate. Jocelyn was sitting in the kitchen, near the food, observing people come and go. Jennifer's first impression was that Jocelyn talked a lot, but she certainly was friendly and bubbly, and within fifteen minutes, Jennifer wanted to get to know her better.

Jocelyn soon joined the other three on the coed volleyball team, and the four became close friends. They frequently had dinners at each other's homes, and often played basketball and paintball together, usually teaming up men-versus-women.

Over the next year, the two couples got to know each other better. Jocelyn and Wesley joined Jennifer and Bob at the Kernses' family cabin on Harris Lake, near the Georgian Bay area of Ontario, Canada, in the summer of 1997.

Bob's grandparents had built the cabin by hand in the mid-sixties. Originally, it had no electricity or telephone, but the grandparents installed both when they got elderly. There was no plumbing, requiring visitors to use an outhouse and bring jugs of drinking water for their stay. The quaint and rustic log structure blended naturally into its surroundings: a rocky coastal shore with big boulders, sparse cabins, and lots of pine and birch trees.

The cabin was inaccessible by road, only by water. The closest town, Pointe au Baril, was a boat ride and a forty-minute drive from the cabin. It consisted of a little grocery store, liquor store, bakeshop, post office, and gas station. The Kernses' place was a secluded retreat made for relaxation. Hiking, fishing, camping, swimming, and reading was the usual order of the day, but there were necessary chores, too. Jocelyn was an enthusiastic helpmeet, turning even dull chores into games. Jennifer recalled her and Jocelyn washing the windows together—one outside and one inside—and laughing themselves silly as they mirrored each other's actions. The trip cemented the friendship between the two women. Jennifer said that Jocelyn was "like an M&M—a lot more on the inside than you see on the outside."

Jocelyn also began developing a close relationship with Jennifer's seven-year-old daughter from her previous marriage, Emily. They went out hunting chipmunks, played with them in their hands, and sometimes dropped one into a pocket where the creature's wriggling induced fits of giggles. The wildlife was an endless source of fascination for Jocelyn, and she developed an undying love for moose and loons.

After the excursion, Jocelyn put together her best photographs of the area—interspersed with lines from her heart like: "The challenge is to see the beauty within others," "A touch of nature makes the whole world smile," "The key to happiness is having dreams—the key to success is making them come true," and "Nothing is more powerful than an inspired landscape"—into a large artful album for Jennifer and Bob with an opening message that read: "We would like to thank you for giving us the experience of a lifetime. This gift is so that you, too, can remember the times there." Jocelyn was clearly in her element up in the woods, far from the everyday comforts of her normal suburban life.

ELEVEN

Both Jocelyn and Wesley Earnest started night classes at Lynchburg College to obtain their master's degrees. Jocelyn obtained her master of business administration degree and got a job with First Colony Life, which became a subsidiary of General Electric Capital Corporation less than a year later. Wesley got a master of education degree and started attending night classes at the University of Virginia in pursuit of a doctorate.

Wesley took Jocelyn by surprise when he decided to become a Jehovah's Witness. Neither she nor Wesley had been raised in religious households.

"What is behind that?" Jocelyn asked.

"It helps me have better control with anger management," Wesley told her.

Although Jocelyn had always wanted children, she'd had doubts about bringing any kids into Wesley's household because of his temper and control issues. Now, she was absolutely sure that she didn't want to do so. Wesley would want any children raised in his new faith, and Jocelyn was adamantly opposed to that. From that point forward, she would not engage in sexual relations unless Wesley wore a condom.

Because of this shift in his life, Wesley developed a different group of friends. Although Jocelyn wouldn't go to services, she would accompany Wesley to church functions like picnics.

Their friends Jennifer and Bob Kerns got married in 1998. When they had their first child, Katelin, in 1999, Jennifer asked Jocelyn if she and Wesley would be the child's godparents. Tearfully, Jocelyn said she had to decline, as Jehovah's Witnesses looked down on infant christening as a Catholic conspiracy.

The tenets that Jehovah's Witnesses live by are quite strict, eschewing modern medicine and regarding all holidays as pagan. In fact, the only special day on the Jehovah's Witnesses' calendar is the Memorial of Christ's Death, which happens every year at about the same time as the Christian holiday of Easter.

Wesley took most of the prohibitions against holidays very seriously. But bringing these restrictions into her home life felt personal to Jocelyn. Wesley knew these days were always spectacular festivities in her family, loaded with tradition and fun. She wondered at his motivations.

One year he agreed to go with Jocelyn to her family's home in West Virginia for Thanksgiving. When they got there, though, he sat in the car while she had dinner with her relatives. Instead of staying over as she usually did so she could go shopping with her mother and sister on Black Friday, she climbed back into the vehicle with Wesley and they drove back to Virginia. Every year after that, she went to her family home without him.

Jocelyn also continued to celebrate Christmas in West Virginia, and with friends like Jennifer, helping her put up the tree, decorate the house, and make cookies—all things Jocelyn wished she could do in her own home. She soon expanded her holiday activities with that family to include helping make Halloween costumes and going trick-or-treating with their kids.

Wesley celebrated one annual event, though: their wedding anniversary. On one of the earlier years, he bought Jocelyn a punching bag and hung it up for her from a support beam in the basement. Some couples would consider this a very odd, decidedly unromantic gift, but the athletic Jocelyn was thrilled.

The Earnests continued to accompany the Kernses on yearly trips to Harris Lake. They loved it so much that when an adjacent lot went up for sale, they considered buying it, but they didn't act fast enough. Wesley had also fallen in love with Smith Mountain Lake in Virginia and suggested that they get a piece of property there instead.

In the 2000 school year, Wesley got a teaching position at Heritage High School in the Lynchburg City Schools system. In August, he finished all the course requirements for his doctorate, and was formally awarded a PhD in administration supervision with finance and technology minors the following January.

The couple now concentrated on finding the perfect place to build on Smith Mountain Lake. Driving through the rolling hills of the Virginia countryside with the glorious Blue Ridge Mountains as a backdrop, the trip to the Smith Mountain Lake home was a pleasure in itself. The peaks lack the majestic angles and stark faces of western mountain ranges but possess the more comforting, ancient beauty of timeworn edges and tree-covered tops.

The drive from Lynchburg cuts through stretches of tall evergreen and deciduous trees and idyllic pastures. In many spots the cultivated areas were overrun by the undulating mystery of kudzu-shrouded landscapes, though an occasional tree manages to fight off the aggressor to stand tall and defiant, stretching its limbs to the sky. Once off the highway, the road winds past vineyards, ticky-tacky houses in need of paint and love and prosperous homesteads with miles of well-maintained wood fencing. In 2001, the Earnests bought the land they wanted nestled on the forested shoreline in the Hickory Point section of Clearwater Estates.

They agreed on the choice of property but little else. Jocelyn envisioned a rustic, restful cabin like the one the Kernses had in Canada. Wesley, on the other hand, wanted an elegant, massive testament to his success—a home that surpassed all the others around him. That is just what he designed: seven bedrooms, each one with a sunset view of the lake, six and a half baths, a spacious deck, and a grandiose three-boat dock.

By this point, Wesley had taken total control of all the couple's finances. He put Jocelyn on a rigid shopping budget, which she only really minded at Christmastime. She wasn't a woman of extravagant tastes, naturally habituated to shopping at Goodwill, thrift stores, and yard sales.

In the summer of 2001, Wesley was unable to make the trip to Canada because he was too busy preparing for the new school year in his position as an assistant principal at Heritage. He didn't want Jocelyn to go without him, but she did anyway. Being there without Wesley further deepened the bond between Jocelyn and Jennifer, who began feeling like a big sister with a ferocious desire to protect and stand up for Jocelyn, and not let her be bullied.

Jennifer was beginning to see a side of Wesley she didn't like. He seemed driven by greed and material goods. He was controlling, overbearing, and manipulative with Jocelyn, and he always seemed to be looking for others to validate his superiority. She felt his high self-esteem treaded on the edges of narcissism. Wesley, on the other hand, related to the troubled, misunderstood genius with a lousy childhood, the title character in *Good Will Hunting*. "That's who I am. That's me," he once told her.

In late 2001, Bob and Jennifer took their daughters over to the Earnest home for pizza. After the kids settled down in front of a movie, Wesley started being very touchy-feely with Jocelyn, who all of them knew was not comfortable with public displays of affection.

"You see this?" Wesley flicked at the wedding band on Jocelyn's finger. "This is the access code. This entitles me to access twenty-four-seven—and I'll tell you twenty-four-seven is not enough for me."

Jocelyn tried to blow him off with a flippant comment: "If that's what you want, you better look elsewhere."

Jennifer tried to distract him. "You talk like most men in America but twice a week is about all that is normal in a marriage."

Wesley seemed to ignore her comment and started talking to Bob about sports.

At Heritage High School, Wesley received a promotion into administration and got involved in Habitat for Humanity. The city required that there be a licensed contractor supervising the work. To save the school the cost of hiring one, Wesley and the head of the Building Trade Department at the school both obtained contractor's licenses.

Wesley worked as the general contractor for his Smith Mountain Lake home. He hired more than eighty subcontractors during the course of the work but did a lot of smaller jobs with his own hands and some assistance from Jocelyn. The house was supposed to be something Wesley and Jocelyn created together, but whenever there was a conflict, Wesley always overruled. Jocelyn wasn't even able to assert herself on the color of the tile.

By nature, Jocelyn was a helper, a problem solver, and a peacemaker. All good qualities—but when combined with a man possessing Wesley's need to control, the end result was not desirable. She tried to make it work, going along to keep the peace. As she did so, though, a creeping resentfulness set in.

Jocelyn later revealed that she'd been worried on her wedding day that she was about to make a serious mistake. It was more than last-minute jitters—she'd had lots of signals that life with Wesley wouldn't be the partnership of equals that she'd always wanted to find in a marriage. But her family had made great efforts and gone to the expense in preparation for the event, and relatives and friends had traveled great distances to celebrate the day. She hadn't wanted to disappoint any of them, so she'd said her vows and hoped for the best.

It was starting to look like the best was not going to happen.

In the summer of 2002, Wesley and Jocelyn went west for a long camping and hiking trip in Oregon with Wesley's brother, Tyler, and his wife. Jocelyn didn't care much for Tyler, and by the time they went home, she had developed suspicions that he was physically abusive to his wife.

While trekking through the wilderness, they ran across a yellow Lab who was in very bad shape. He won Jocelyn's heart in record time and she adopted him on the spot. They named him Rowdie and flew him back with them to Virginia, where he lived comfortably for the few remaining years of his life.

Jocelyn eventually adopted another Labrador, this time a black one, whom she named Rufus.

———

In the fall, they visited Wesley's dad, Roger, at his farm out in the country in West Virginia. One day, the three of them set up targets in a field for shooting practice. Wesley went out with a shotgun and Jocelyn brought a Smith and Wesson short-barreled revolver that Wesley had given to her.

Each one of them took turns firing the Smith and Wesson, using up a couple of boxes of ammunition. Then Wesley fired the shotgun and Jocelyn asked to try it. Roger showed her how to use it and she fired off a shot or two.

Much to her father-in-law's surprise, Jocelyn was a pretty good shot. She actually fired better than Wesley had. Roger kidded his son quite a lot about her outshooting him.

TWELVE

In 2003, Wesley and Jocelyn Earnest prepared their wills, each one giving the bulk of their property and possessions (which at that time included two homes, a boat, and three cars) to the other. They told the Kernses that they were mentioned in the will but did not explain how.

That year was also the first year that Jocelyn started to stand up to Wesley instead of just doing whatever he said to keep the peace. Wesley blamed Jennifer's influence. Jennifer thought he was probably right, and she was glad of it.

Then Wesley took it a step further, accusing Jennifer of romantic feelings for Jocelyn. "You love her. You'd like to sleep with her." Wesley had no real reason to suspect that, but like many controlling men, he probably did not want his wife to have strong relationships outside of the marriage and would stop at nothing to undermine those bonds.

The relationship between Wesley and the Kernses was quickly deteriorating. That summer's trip to Canada shattered the peaceful pattern of the past. Jennifer and Bob's son, Joseph, had been born the year before, and a birthday party was planned for that week on the lake. Wesley was not at all pleased with the celebration and made it abundantly clear to everyone.

That wasn't the worst of Wesley's behavior at the lake, however. One day, when Jennifer's teenage daughter Emily and Wesley had both been drinking Diet Dr Pepper on the dock, Emily had left her can outside. Jennifer sent her back to the dock to get it. Emily retrieved the can but left it on the porch, and again, Jennifer ordered her back outside to pick up the can and crush it.

Later that evening, Jennifer looked out a window and spotted something floating in the lake. Bob went outside to check it out and pulled out a crushed Diet Dr Pepper can. Wesley immediately lit into Emily, scolding her for her irresponsibility. Jennifer knew that Emily had brought in her can, and told Wesley to take responsibility for his own negligence.

"No one is going to speak to me like this," Wesley said. "I'm not going to stay here and listen to this." He stalked outside and yelled for Jocelyn to come out. They stood by the water and talked.

Jocelyn then came into the cabin and said, "I'm supposed to tell you that you have to apologize for how you talked to him and what you did."

"For you, I'd do it," Jennifer said. "But do you think that will even work? If I do it, will he ever let this go?"

Jocelyn said that she didn't think it would work, and went back outside. When she told Wesley that an apology would not be forthcoming, fuming and pacing, he said, "Well, that's it. We're leaving," and sent Jocelyn inside to gather up their belongings.

Bob had the thankless task of taking them by boat over to the mainland, where they got into their car and drove the thirteen-hour trip nonstop straight back to Virginia that night.

After that incident, Wesley grew overtly hostile toward Jennifer. He grew jealous of the time his wife spent with her and expressed his anger about it often. He even forbade Jocelyn to visit Jennifer.

Jocelyn ignored his order, and in fact began to be more open in expressing her difficulties with Wesley to Jennifer—and she had a lot of problems with him, between his attitudes about money, his controlling behavior, his sexual demands, and their conflicts over the lake house, holidays, religion, and family. It seemed to be an endless source of conflict.

Wesley was pressuring Jocelyn to move out with him to the partially finished lake house so that they could work all night and all weekend long on the house. Jocelyn didn't want to have to make that hour-long drive to work even if Wesley was content to make his slightly shorter commute. Additionally, she couldn't see working on the house every single evening after a long day at work.

Further complicating things, when a house two lots

down from their home on Pine Bluff went on the market, Wesley borrowed $100,000 from his dad to purchase it as a rental property. He invited his younger brother, Tyler, to live in the rental, but then rented it to someone else, so Tyler moved in with his brother and sister-in-law. Jocelyn, who didn't like her brother-in-law, believed Wesley had manipulated the situation to pressure her into moving to the lake house to get away from Tyler.

In the spring of 2004, despite all the major construction on the lake house being completed, Wesley became more and more scarce at home on Pine Bluff Drive. Not wanting to be alone with Tyler drove Jocelyn to spend a lot of time at the Kernses' house, to the point that she was eventually only going home to shower and sleep. Wesley made up a story for Jocelyn that being around his brother had resurrected repressed memories about bad things Tyler had done to him when they were growing up. He didn't spell it out, but he left her with the impression that Tyler had sexually abused him, and said that he'd been in therapy because of it. Wesley told Jocelyn that he was spending his nights out at the lake house or in his office at Heritage High School.

At first, Jocelyn took Wesley's statements at face value and was supportive and willing to give him any help she could to "get through his issues." Eventually, though, she chalked up the story about Tyler as just another one of Wesley's lies.

When Jocelyn did see him, he was more evasive, surlier, and more obsessed with finances. That summer, with his brother back on the west coast, Wesley changed his mailing address from Pine Bluff Drive to the house at the lake.

But what was happening behind her back, the real reason for Wesley's increased absence, was that he'd met someone new.

Wesley started dating Shameka Wright, a clerk at Big Lots, shortly after he met her when he'd gone into the store for some painting supplies. Shameka, an attractive African American woman, a few years younger than Wesley, was a former officer with the Lynchburg Police Department. Wesley told the detective that she'd lost that job because she could not pass the shooting proficiency test with her handgun, but according to that same investigator, she'd actually been dismissed for going to an airport and instigating a threatening confrontation while in uniform with a woman whom she thought was seeing her previous boyfriend.

By mid-July 2004, the relationship between Wesley and Shameka was serious enough that they took a trip together to the Homestead, a well-known Virginia mountain spa. That fall, they took several trips together: to the New River Gorge in West Virginia; to Virginia Beach; and to Knoxville, to watch a University of Tennessee football game, then drove down to Gatlinburg; and also paid a visit to SeaWorld, among other places.

In early 2005, Wesley and Shameka went to Florida and visited Universal Studios and the Daytona 500. They went to Chapel Hill, North Carolina, for a college basketball game; they traveled to Charleston, South Carolina, and toured Fort Sumter; and they went to Charlotte, North Carolina, to watch the Bobcats take on the Miami Heat at the Charlotte Coliseum. That summer, they went to the Great Smoky Mountains and toured the Biltmore Estate in Asheville, and later attended a Dave Matthews Band concert in Virginia Beach.

Even when they both got new jobs and their relationship turned long-distance, the affair continued. Wesley accepted an assistant principal position at Oscar Smith Middle School in Chesapeake, all the way across the state in the Tidewater area of Virginia, and Shameka started with the human resources department of the Campbell County government and began work on her doctorate. Nevertheless, the couple continued to see each other nearly every weekend, getting together either in Chesapeake, at Shameka's home in Concord, Virginia, or at Wesley's Smith Mountain Lake retreat.

Jocelyn remained oblivious to all of Wesley's getaways with his new love until one visit she made to the lake house, when she noticed unfamiliar hairs in both the bed and in the bathtub. She confronted Wesley and demanded an explanation.

Wesley said, "That's the cleaning lady, Shameka Wright. I met her in a suicide support group. She's very overweight and unattractive but she desperately needed money so I asked her to clean the place."

Jocelyn was skeptical of his answer but still willing to do anything—to forgive anything—to save her marriage. She talked the situation over with Jennifer, who admitted to having been skeptical of Wesley's faithfulness for a while. "He's overly critical of you and everything about you. He's being mean to you for no reason. He's evasive when you ask a question. Like when you ask, 'Where were you?' he answers, 'Where do you think I was?' And look at him, he's changed his appearance and his mannerisms."

Indeed, Wesley seemed to be on the hunt for more conquests, even in front of his wife. The Kernses once even witnessed Wesley engage in a blatant flirting episode with a waitress, in front of Jocelyn, and when the waitress walked away from the table, Wesley turned to Jennifer and said, "I bet I'll have her phone number before dinner is over."

All the while, Wesley was dangling Jocelyn on a string, not acknowledging his new romantic relationship or the last gasps of his dying marriage. He claimed he just needed some time. However, when Jocelyn asked him to go to a marital counselor with her, he said, "I'm not sitting and paying some stupid asshole to tell me what I should and shouldn't do."

After a search on Google revealed the location of Shameka's parents' Lynchburg home, Jennifer and Jocelyn started driving out at nights during the summer and often saw Wesley's car parked there. One night when they spotted his vehicle in a parking lot, Jennifer pulled a slim-cut red leather jacket out of the passenger's seat. Holding it up, she shook it and said, "Does this look fat to you? This girl is not fat."

Still, Jocelyn always wanted to see the good side of everything and she wanted her marriage to work. She didn't want that failure in her life.

Jocelyn also confided some of the problems in her marriage to her little sister, Laura, telling her, "Wesley won't go to counseling."

"Then you should go by yourself. And you should keep a journal of everything that is happening." Laura added, "Wesley is greedy and selfish and manipulative. He thinks whatever happens that is good is because of him and anything bad is your fault."

Jocelyn took the advice about keeping a record of events and began writing down her thoughts and experiences in wire-bound notebooks. Yet she still clung to the dream that the problems in their relationship might be resolved.

Wesley told her: "I just need a little space. I've got to go on a new medication—the old one was causing a problem."

And Jocelyn believed him.

THIRTEEN

In the summer of 2005, a depressed Jocelyn Earnest decided not to make the annual trip to Canada with the Kerns family. Instead, over the Fourth of July weekend, her sister, Laura, came to visit, and together they went for a drive out to the house on Smith Mountain Lake.

They stopped the car on the opposite shore, giving them a good view of the house Wesley had built—and of Wesley and Shameka Wright, carrying candles out onto the deck, then dancing to music only the couple could hear.

Laura could almost hear the crashing sound of her sister's heart breaking. But it still wasn't enough to convince Jocelyn to leave him.

"Laura, I am 70 percent sure that I want a divorce but I'm not ready to give up yet. I could forgive him if he would come back to me and help rebuild a life for the two of us," Jocelyn told her.

Seeking comfort, serenity, and security—and a respite from reality and its ugly truths—Jocelyn changed her plans and raced to join the Kernses deep in the Canadian woods.

When she returned home from the trip, she honed her focus on work and staying fit. She lost a lot of weight and got very thin—one of the typical reactions of a wife who sees all her dreams for the future crumbling before her eyes.

She still heard from Wesley, who sent an occasional email asking her out, flirting with her, and leading her on. Although they were living separate lives in different homes and Wesley had obviously moved on with a new relationship, he did not want Jocelyn to do the same. He wanted her to continue to believe they had a future. And it worked. With each contact, Jocelyn's hope sprouted new wings and took temporary flight only to crash and burn once again.

One such email Wesley wrote said that he was "on the absolute edge of committing suicide." He complained about losing contact with his old friends and expressed a desire for Jocelyn to be set for life financially. He wrote that his feelings for her had returned when he restarted his career in Chesapeake. He said that he often drove past her house but had no intention of doing her any harm. "You are an incredible person—one that I am so very proud of . . . To see the hurt that I caused you is the most painful of all."

Jennifer told her that the reason for Wesley's emails

was simple. "He is just keeping tabs on you and your activities because he is a control freak. He wants to keep the wool over your eyes while he is hiding his assets and establishing his financial future."

Still, Jocelyn resisted the advice of friends and family and her own common sense. She took no steps to end the marriage that was causing her so much pain.

She did start counseling, in the hopes that it would help her adjust and cope with the intense self-anger she felt for allowing herself to be controlled and manipulated for such a long time, and had her first session with Susan Roehrich, on July 13, 2005. In August, Jocelyn wrote in her journal: "If I am ever found dead, my killer is my cheating husband. Know that he killed me, because I would never kill myself. My guess is he shot me and then killed himself."

When he moved to Chesapeake to take the position as assistant principal at Oscar Smith Middle School, Wesley rented a room in a home owned by Neil Phillips and his wife, Linda. He told the landlord that he was taking a new job in Chesapeake and his wife would be joining him as soon as he was sure the job would work out and he found a place for them to live. The Phillipses never met Jocelyn; it was Shameka who helped Wesley move in, and who came to visit every other weekend.

Wesley soon became an unsettling tenant. When he habitually left the front door open, Linda spoke up about it. On one occasion, she followed him upstairs and Wesley went ballistic, cursing and shouting. He threatened to break her hand by slamming it in the door.

Linda later told WVEC TV news that Wesley "didn't like women who had any ability to assert themselves. He liked them very mousy and quiet . . . He was very vindictive. When you crossed him, he would get back at you whatever way he could."

In November 2005, the Phillipses had an argument that was overheard by Wesley. Afterward, Wesley told Neil, "Bitches like my wife and your wife should be dead."

That comment disturbed Neil. He'd had enough. He wrote an eviction letter, asking Wesley to pay his last month's rent and leave. Wesley said, "If you give me any trouble, I will get even with you."

Wesley moved out on December 1 without paying for November, so the Phillipses kept the security deposit instead. In his vacated room, they found dirty dishes, empty beer bottles, a badly soiled mattress, and Wesley's initials carved into the windowsill. And for some reason, he'd also flipped over the plastic floor mat under the chair at the desk so that the pointy side faced up.

In late summer 2005, Jocelyn had led a company-wide challenge for Genworth Financial, where new hire Marcy Shepherd was the training leader. As a result, the two women spent a lot of time together, working long hours. Occasionally, they went out after work for a drink or a bite to eat, and despite the stressful project with its tight timelines, there were moments of unabashed fun.

Jocelyn was also very focused on getting fit at this time, and walking was part of her regimen. Marcy joined her in this exercise—their favorite variation was a three-mile circuit in Wyndhurst, a section of Lynchburg. They talked at length on these walks and often in great depth.

Before long, Marcy had fallen in love with Jocelyn. During a telephone call in late October, Marcy asked, "If I kissed you, would you kiss me back?"

That December, after the Genworth Christmas party, Marcy gave Jocelyn a ride home back home, and Jocelyn invited her inside. As they sat on the couch talking, Marcy leaned over and they shared a kiss. Afterward, they decided it was not a good idea. They were both still married and neither one wanted to violate their vows. The physical side of their relationship never went any further.

Separated from Wesley, Jocelyn grieved the loss of the relationship. At one point, she hired a private investigator who wrote her depressing reports about Wesley's continuing relationship with Shameka Wright. Jocelyn knew there was little hope of resurrecting their connection, but still she hesitated to pull the trigger and file for divorce.

Then, on an evening in March 2006, Jocelyn called Jennifer and asked her to accompany her on a drive out to the Smith Mountain Lake house. When they reached the lake house, they saw cars in the driveway and recognized one of them as Wesley's vehicle. Jennifer parked by the mailbox, then they walked down the driveway to the house. The shades were not pulled down all the way, giving them a clear view of activity inside.

They saw Wesley brushing his teeth and washing his face. Then he turned toward the bathtub and handed a towel to a black woman who rose up from the water. She then brushed her teeth and the light went out in the bathroom.

As the couple moved into the master bedroom, Jocelyn and Jennifer moved around the deck to keep them in view. Jocelyn was cursing under her breath as she watched them climb into bed.

"If that doesn't prove to you what's going on, I don't know what will," Jennifer said.

"I know. I needed to see this and I'm so glad you're here with me."

Jocelyn and Jennifer sat down side by side on some exposed boulders, watching the couple making love—although it took them some time to understand what they were seeing, given the pale illumination. When they did, Jocelyn grew angrier. "This is it. I'm done. I'm over this."

"How badly do you want him to know that you know?" Jennifer asked.

"Real bad," Jocelyn said.

"You want to knock on the door?"

"Fuck the door. I'm going to the window."

"Then, I'm going with you."

Jocelyn stood up and walked over to the house. Jennifer followed her onto the small deck by the bedroom.

Jocelyn raised her hand and rapped hard on the window. She shouted, "I see you Wesley Earnest."

Jocelyn started to walk away, then turned back and banged on the window again. "Hey, how's it going?"

The two people in the bed sat up in surprise. Then the woman rolled over on her side. Wesley swung to the side of the bed and hung his head and shook it from side to side.

The women outside waved and smiled at the pair. "Having fun?" Jocelyn shouted. "Enjoy!" With that parting word, Jocelyn ran back to the car.

When Wesley turned on the light, Jennifer went out to the car. "You need to write this all down, Joce."

"I can't. I have to drive. You write it down."

As they drove away, Jennifer pulled an envelope out of the glove compartment and wrote down the time and the date. She'd never written up anything like this before, but she drew on her training as a nurse, and so described the scene in clinical language: "Observed an undulating motion in a silhouette caused by moonlight coming down through the window."

Jennifer ached for the pain Jocelyn was feeling but thought that this was what her friend needed: a stark confrontation with the truth in order to move on with her life. And it seemed she was right—the change in Jocelyn's attitude was instantaneous. She had been sad and a bit lethargic. After this confrontation, she was proactive and energetic, moving forward with everything she had neglected—including finally filing for divorce.

In the divorce paperwork submitted to the Bedford

Circuit Court that June 2006, Jocelyn cited Wesley's on-going relationship with Shameka, and in addition to adultery, she also alleged cruelty, desertion, and separation in excess of one year. Paragraph five of the complaint stated that "in 2004, the defendant began spending considerable amounts of time away from home. Frequently, your plaintiff did not know where the defendant was. The defendant often told your plaintiff that he was at their lake house in Moneta, Virginia, but plaintiff would call or go to the lake house only to find that the defendant was not there. When he was home at 1482 Pine Bluff Drive in Lynchburg, Virginia, defendant was wooden, distant, and uncommunicative."

Wesley told his attorney, Richard Cunningham, that the complaint shocked him and that the allegations in it were "preposterous." They filed a counterclaim stating that the allegations contained in paragraph five were denied. "The defendant affirmatively states he has a class A contractor's license and undertook the building of the house at Smith Mountain Lake for which the parties received an occupancy permit on August 12th, 2004. In order to obtain the tax benefits, the parties had to declare said home as their principal residence. Defendant commenced residing in said home, but plaintiff refused to do so, claiming she did not want to drive that far to work. Defendant further affirmatively states that it was the plaintiff who was wooden, distant, and uncommunicative. She refused all acts of intimacy and spent an exorbitant amount of time in her place of employment."

In response to Jocelyn's allegation that her husband

was spending a considerable amount of time with Shameka Wright and would not answer when she asked him if he was having an affair with that woman, Wesley stated that the "defendant admits spending time with a friend, Shameka Wright. Plaintiff did ask the defendant whether or not he was having an affair with Shameka Wright, at which time he denied any such affair."

Wesley also denied the statement about Jocelyn not knowing where he was during nonwork hours by saying, "It was the plaintiff who spent less and less time at the marital house, which was now the lake property . . . Defendant did not conceal his whereabouts . . . Any lack of knowledge on the part of the plaintiff was due to her lack of interest in the defendant and her work schedule."

Wesley went on to complain about Jocelyn not attending after-school events with him, and about her solo trip with the Kernses to Canada in 2005. He defended himself on the adultery charges claiming that "plaintiff has continuously encouraged defendant to engage in sexual intercourse with others since she did not want to have an intimate relationship with him." Finally, he accused Jocelyn of "willful and constructive desertion."

He also filed a motion of relief requesting that he be granted exclusive use of the lake house, that Jocelyn provide temporary spousal support, and that $100,000 be deposited in an escrow account to cover the loan made to them by his father.

The interaction between Jocelyn and Wesley had gone wrong some time ago, but now it was about to turn very ugly. Jocelyn would no longer go along to get along. She raised her objection to his solution to financial issues, determined not to let him "get his way for once." She knew he really wanted the lake house, but she wanted the house sold—it was his "love nest with Shameka," and she found it intolerable that he should be allowed to keep it.

She refused to talk with Wesley any longer about anything. She insisted that the lawyers handle all communication. She changed the locks on the house and installed a security system. And she continued seeing her counselor because she enjoyed the empowerment she realized she was getting from her sessions.

FOURTEEN

Laura Rogers visited her sister throughout 2006 whenever she could. Because she knew Jocelyn was not the most diligent housekeeper, she pitched in to get things under control every visit. She'd finish up Jocelyn's laundry, load her dishwasher, and put away dishes in the cabinet. Laura was certain that without the straightening up that she and Jennifer Kerns did when they were there, Jocelyn would have just lived out of a laundry basket or piled her clothes on top of her dresser.

Laura noticed that one thing had changed since her sister separated from her husband, however. Now, Jocelyn was diligent about reminding her to lock the doors.

When the 2006–07 school year began, Wesley Earnest had sought and achieved his goal of a more prestigious position at another facility, Great Bridge High School, also located in Chesapeake. He and Shameka Wright were still together, taking turns driving to each other's homes every weekend when they weren't off vacationing or sky-diving.

Wesley also sent another letter to Jocelyn. "I'm so very sorry for the turmoil in our lives over the last few years." He claimed that his mother called his younger brother, Tyler, "an agent of the devil."

He also resurrected his false claim that Jocelyn had told him to sleep with someone else in order to fix their marriage, but still audaciously claimed that the best thing he'd ever done was marry her. "I want to grow old with you . . . I am a broken man, ready to get my life back, and I need you."

On November 8, 2006, Jocelyn returned home from work to discover that her home had been invaded. The whole house was cold. Not only had the thermostat been turned off, but the pipe to the gas logs in the fireplace and the water pipes to the heater in the pool had been cut.

A lot of property had been removed from the home: a bike, a camera, a shotgun, financial paperwork, a coin barrel with a thousand dollars in change, a safe, a computer, fishing gear—including one rod that belonged to Jennifer's daughter Emily—and some of her clothing.

The greater sense of loss was caused by items of sentimental value, like the pictures, furniture, and gifts that Jocelyn had received from her grandmother; the moose memorabilia decorating the downstairs bathroom—given to her by Jennifer; an inuksuk, a stone figure built by the Inuit of Arctic Canada that Jocelyn had brought home from a trip to the cabin; her diplomas; and three of her personal journals.

Jocelyn immediately suspected that Wesley was behind this violation, and she was most concerned about him having those journals in his possession, because they gave him access to the information the private investigator had provided Jocelyn, and revealed her preparations for the dissolution of the marriage and the personal thoughts she'd shared with her therapist. Jocelyn was convinced that Wesley thought she was too stupid, too dense, or too naïve to take any actions to protect her best interests. Now that he would know otherwise, Jocelyn became extremely frightened of her estranged husband.

Through lawyers, Wesley claimed he had not been there, but said that he *had* hired movers to remove his belongings. It was hard to believe, however, that professional movers would have entered her home, taken items of sentimental value, and committed acts of vandalism.

Jocelyn tried everything to get her possessions back from Wesley. She tried anger, niceness, pleading—but nothing worked.

After this invasion, Jocelyn did a drive-by of her house looking for anything suspicious whenever she returned home at night. On the advice of her therapist she packed "go" bags, each with a change of clothing, copies of any important papers, and money. She kept one in her car, another at the office, one at Jennifer's, and a fourth at her mom's house.

Jocelyn thought only one solution remained: she had to go to the lake house and get her things back from Wesley before the divorce hearing, where she anticipated that the judge would rule that Wesley could not enter her Pine Bluff home, and Jocelyn could not go into his lake house.

On December 4, 2006, the day before the hearing was scheduled, Jocelyn called Jennifer from work. "Would you go with me to the lake to get my belongings? After tomorrow, I won't be able to go in there."

Jennifer agreed. On the drive out, Jocelyn stopped at Penske's. "I want to rent a moving truck," she said.

"When?" the man behind the counter asked.

"Now," Jocelyn said.

"This is the only one I have right now," he said, pointing to a huge truck on the lot.

Jocelyn took it, and the two women drove out to reclaim Jocelyn's property, hoping that Wesley would not be there when they arrived. He wasn't. They searched all over the property, except inside the garage and an outbuilding, both of which were locked and Jocelyn did not want to break inside. Stymied in her quest for her own property, she decided to take some of Wesley's belongings as bargaining chips. They loaded the truck with a large-screen TV, a DVD player, a large wooden trunk, a quilt-like bedcover, a light tan sectional sofa and matching love seat and recliner, a new twin mattress, random tools, a toolbox, a leather tool belt, cleaning supplies, lightbulbs, cans of spray foam insulation, a glass coffee table, two small cutting boards, a small rug, silk plants and ficus trees, documents, and the leftover tile from the installation at the house.

After three hours, just around dusk, they drove away from the lake and unloaded the truck at Jennifer's house for safekeeping. Jocelyn hoped Wesley wouldn't know what she had done until after the court hearing the next day.

FIFTEEN

Jennifer Kerns spent the night with Jocelyn after the lake house expedition, and they went together to the Earnests' divorce hearing. As expected, the judge established exclusive use parameters for the two houses in question. He also ruled against Wesley's request for spousal support, and ordered Jocelyn to pay 25 percent of the mortgage on the lake house (rather than the half Wesley had requested). The two latter decisions were devastating to Wesley's bottom line. His income would be stretched paper-thin.

Throughout the proceedings, Wesley craned his neck around to look straight at Jennifer. He mouthed words that she could not understand. He obviously was trying to tell her something, but she had no idea of what it was.

Afterward, Jocelyn went to work, but Jennifer stayed sentry at the Pine Bluff house. They thought it possible that Wesley would come over there looking for his belongings, but he never showed.

On a weeknight in the latter half of February 2007, Jennifer Kerns was at home with her three children while her husband, Bob, was out at a meeting in Appomattox. The phone rang.

"Ohmigod! Ohmigod! He's here! He's here!" The moment Jennifer heard Jocelyn's quivering, whispery voice, she knew her friend was distressed and terrified.

"What are you talking about?" Jennifer said, pushing down a rising panic.

"I was sitting here watching TV and saw my doorknob turning. He's out there. I've seen him."

"What does he want?"

"I don't know what he wants. I was not expecting him. What is he doing here in the middle of a school week? What could be so important?"

"Are you alright?"

"I'm scared. What should I do?" Jocelyn asked.

"Did he see you? Does he know you're at home?"

"Yes, my car is in the driveway and I turned all the lights off as soon as I saw him."

"Stay down and hide. I will be right there."

"I'm belly crawling around trying to watch where he goes."

"If he gets in or comes after you, get out ASAP and turn your BlackBerry off so the light or noise doesn't give you away. Get into the woods and make your way through them to the bridge. I will look for you there if you're not home when I get there."

"Okay. Be careful but hurry!" Jocelyn pleaded.

"Do not let anyone in even if something happens to me! Just call 9-1-1. Stay on the phone with Emily until I get there! Jocelyn, do not be afraid to call 9-1-1." Jennifer handed the telephone to her high school–aged daughter and said, "Stay on the phone with Jocelyn. If you hear anything suspicious call 9-1-1 and tell them your mom is on the way."

Even though it was a frigid February night, Jennifer didn't pause to change into something warmer than the T-shirt and sweatpants she'd being wearing inside. She slipped on the closest shoes—a pair of flip-flops—got in her car, and drove as fast as she could to Jocelyn's house.

When Jennifer turned onto Pine Bluff Drive, however, she did not see Wesley Earnest anywhere. She looked up and down the street, around the yard and house, around the neighbor's house, and even cracked open her window to listen for any sound that could betray his where- abouts—but saw no sign of him. There were no other vehicles in sight. Not a single person stirred anywhere in the vicinity. The yard was unbroken darkness. The shades were drawn tight on the house. If any lights were on in- side, none of the illumination escaped from the windows.

For a few moments, Jennifer was paralyzed with fear. She knew Wesley hated her, too—maybe even more than he hated Jocelyn. *What would he do if he caught me? What if he ambushed me on the way into the house? What if he was under Jocelyn's car and grabbed my ankle as soon as I stepped out?*

Then, an even more horrifying thought struck her. *What if he was already inside? What if he's hurting Jocelyn right now?* That concern finally propelled her forward. She sucked in a deep breath, opened the car door, and forced herself to step on the ground, her senses on high alert as she peered into the blackness of the cold night and listened intently for any sound that could portend danger. She trembled in fearful anticipation as her panic built. *Was he inside? What if Jocelyn thinks he's gone and opens the door for me and he pushes inside? Where is he? Why can't I see or hear him?*

Jennifer grasped her keys so tightly they formed painful creases in her hands. She stepped up on the deck and headed toward the front door. She laid her hand on the handle of the storm door—and suddenly, there he was.

Wes stepped out of the shadows less than two feet away from her. He was dressed to be nearly invisible in the night, wearing dark shoes, a dark pair of sweatpants, and a dark sweatshirt with the hood up and drawn snugly around his face. As close as he was to Jennifer, it was still difficult to see him.

Jennifer swallowed down a lump of escalating fear and tried to sound chipper. "Oh, there you are," she said. "Joce called me and said you were out here, that's why I'm here."

"It figures she would call you," Wesley said.

"She does not want to see or talk to you and that is why the lawyers are handling everything now."

"That's why I'm here. We are wasting money having

them handle things. We could do this ourselves. I'm here to talk some sense into her. This will end up ruining our finances and credit," Wes said.

"She doesn't want to see you," Jennifer told him. "She wants the lawyers to handle these things."

"I just wanted to talk to her about the financial things and her reasons for wanting the lawyers to handle it. It was going to be financially detrimental for both of us that way. I wanted to get it across to her that she's being unreasonable."

"She doesn't care," Jennifer said. "She just wants it over. She wants it done." Jennifer was shivering from the cold piercing through her inadequate clothing, and her bare toes were totally numb.

Wesley continued arguing his case and complaining about the high financial cost of the attorney process. When he finally realized that Jennifer was not going to encourage Jocelyn to open the door, he asked, "At least tell her a few things for me."

Jennifer ambled toward her car in an effort to draw him farther away from the house. "Okay, Wes, but she's my best friend and I will support any decision she makes that she feels is in her best interest. I will not try to sway her in any way." By this time, she'd led him out to the driveway, but still could see no sign of his vehicle anywhere.

"Okay," Wes said, then started listing the points he wanted her to relay to Jocelyn. He reached up behind his back with his left hand and slipped his right hand around to the small of his back.

At that point, Jennifer realized there was a strap going

over his shoulder and some sort of satchel was hanging behind his back. She cringed. *What was in that bag?* He swung a messenger-type, soft-sided briefcase around to the front and set it down on the hood of Jennifer's car. *Ohmigod, does he have a gun?*

"Maybe you ought to write this stuff down so you remember it all."

Jennifer opened the car door and sat sideways in the driver's seat. She pulled a crayon and a children's book out of the backseat to use as an ersatz desktop. All the while, she kept a close eye on Wesley, still fearful of what might emerge from his bag.

Wes handed her a piece of paper and dictated his thoughts to Jennifer. She wrote with icy, stiffening fingers, wondering if he would ever finish.

Bob Kerns arrived home to find his teenage daughter still on the phone with Jocelyn, his two younger kids in bed, and his wife gone. When Emily updated him on the situation, he called a friend who had a concealed carry permit and the two of them headed out to Pine Bluff Drive. They drove up the road, past the house, and then parked a little way beyond it and sized up the situation between Jennifer and Wesley. When they decided everything appeared to be under control, Bob returned home to his children.

Wesley talked to Jennifer for nearly three hours, as if he were trying to outlast her. While he emphasized certain points, he pulled financial papers, bills, and other documents out of his bag for her to pass on to Jocelyn. Finally, he handed her a letter in an envelope and the deed to the boat. He referred to the latter as a goodwill gesture. Then he turned and walked away, heading out to the road in the direction of a small woods adjacent to the property.

Jennifer waited until he was out of sight. *I'd better go in right away. What if he's been in and out before I got there? What if he already hurt Jocelyn? What if he circles back and catches me going in? I've got to hurry*, she thought as she raced up the sidewalk. She unlocked the door, eased her way into the house, and locked the door behind her.

Then she burst into tears—tears of fear, anger, and relief. Jocelyn was safe. The two women hugged and comforted each other.

In her hand, Jennifer held her notes with all the information, questions, and statements that Wesley wanted her to present to Jocelyn, as well as the other documents including the letter. All the arguments to make her see how the divorce and property settlement could be done in a different way than it was being handled now. She handed everything over to Jocelyn.

Jennifer offered to spend the night, but Jocelyn told her, "I'll be okay. You need to go home to your kids."

"Then, come with me," Jennifer pleaded. "Spend the night with us."

"No, Jen. Bob has to get up for work early tomorrow morning. I'll disrupt his sleep. Just go home. I'll be fine."

Reluctantly, Jennifer left the house, apprehensive about her personal safety until she was inside her locked car. She stared at the house for a moment, still worried about her friend—hoping she wasn't making a huge mistake. Then she backed up and headed home.

After Jennifer had left, Jocelyn looked through all the paperwork and read over the notes Wesley had dictated. She opened the envelope and read the self-serving, manipulative letter from her estranged husband.

Wesley opened by putting the blame for their drawn-out divorce proceedings entirely on Jocelyn. "From day one I have tried to handle this divorce by asking you to communicate with me and to be reasonable rather than this back and forth nonsense and lawyer posturing," he wrote. He claimed that she suspected him of hiding assets because of his willingness to pay the bills and deposit his paycheck in their joint accounts through July 2006. He wrote that he'd told Jocelyn's lawyer, Jennifer Stille, that he "did not want a lawyer and would grant you an uncontested divorce, but she refused to talk to me any longer until I got an attorney," continuing on to give his opinion that if Stille "was truly representing you, her client, she would have just taken advantage of my naïve approach."

He insinuated that it was his lawyer's fault that things had become so contentious, and that he, Wesley, was trying to protect Jocelyn. "Now my attorney wants to prolong all this stuff by taking a recorded deposition from you, trying to catch you in some lies, et cetera. My attorney has indicated the divorce proceedings may drag out another year. I do not want that, I got protective of you when you were on the stand and he was badgering you. I still continue to hold you in high regard and will not say bad things about you or call you names, despite the financial turmoil I have been in the past year without assistance on the bills. My attorney referred to you as a bitch one time, and it made me mad when he talked about you like that. You are an incredible person."

Wesley continued on, despairing about the horrible state of his finances and his fears of losing the house at Smith Mountain Lake because he could not afford the mortgage payments without Jocelyn's income. He told her that his father was likely to sue her for half of the money they owed him, then complained about the poor state of the housing market at that time that made it impossible to sell the lake property without investing thousands more and still running a monumental loss of the investment. Wesley suggested that she allow someone else take over her half of the mortgage in partnership with him. He wrote that in exchange, he would sign over the Pine Bluff house to her with no strings attached.

But Jocelyn knew under the kind words and faux consideration, there lurked a sinister desire to control her and bend her to his will. She was aware that most of his words were lies with a candy coating of truth. She was determined not to let her fear of him make her back down.

SIXTEEN

Wesley Earnest called Bob Kerns the following morning, a Saturday, and invited him to breakfast in Lynchburg. Though obviously both well aware of what had gone down the night before, after ordering their meals the men caught up on everything that had happened since they'd last seen each other several months earlier without touching on the events of the previous night. Then Wesley shared his concerns regarding the financial difficulties he and Jocelyn were experiencing.

Wesley admitted that he had taken things out of Jocelyn's home on Pine Bluff, but explained that it was because, between the mortgage on the lake house and other financial obligations, he was financially strapped and needed to sell those items to be able to make ends meet.

Bob played the role of supportive friend and asked questions in hopes of being able to give him some advice that might defuse the situation. Wesley said that he was very concerned that his credit rating was being trashed. "Would you talk to Jocelyn about the selling of the lake house? If we have to sell it quickly, we stand to lose quite a bit of money. If we're smart about this, and wait until the market improves, we could both come out a lot better off financially."

When Bob asked why he was talking to him instead of Jocelyn, Wesley said, "I'm not really able to speak to her about these matters."

The conversation did not ease the anxiety Bob had had since the events of the night before. He returned home still concerned about the personal safety of both Jocelyn and his wife.

Jocelyn and her sister, Laura Rogers, traveled to Little Rock, Arkansas, to surprise their father for his sixtieth birthday on April 1, 2007. They stayed for a week and had a wonderful time together. They took a day trip down to Crater of Diamonds State Park in Murfreesboro, where they scoured a plowed field hunting for diamonds in all colors of the rainbow. Then they went to Mount Ida, the "Quartz Crystal Capital of the World," and dug for them, too.

In June 2007, Wesley met Realtor Johnny Maddox with Country & Mountain Realty. Wesley wanted land, a big chunk of it that was valued higher than the lake house.

Johnny told him about a 362-acre tract and Wesley was interested. He wanted to trade the lake house for it. The owner, however, was not interested. On June 15, Wesley signed a document granting a six-month authorization to Johnny to sell the lake house for $2,150,000.

In late August, Jocelyn arrived at her therapist Susan Roehrich's office in a state of anger and fear. She pulled out the timeline written on oversized butcher-block paper and pointed out a few entries she was certain had been added to the document by Wesley. She didn't know when he'd entered her home and written on her timeline, but the fact that he'd done so made her very frightened. As she and the therapist went through it, they bracketed the questionable lines.

In 1995: "kept telling Wes, to sleep with someone else and come home to me." Two years later: "kept telling Wes, I don't want to be with you 'sexually.'" In 2001: "very understanding husband with me spending late hours at work." In 2005: "Wes kept trying to talk to me, but I just shut him out." The next year: "Wes wants another opportunity to make a great marriage, but thinks it's highly unlikely because Jocelyn's family has too much influence on her and they never truly embraced Wes." The final entry: "Wes's mother was left out of the loop."

Throughout the fall, Jocelyn played volleyball with Jennifer every Friday night and had dinners at the Kernses' home now and then. She was looking forward to moving on with her life and leaving Wesley behind.

In October 2007, Laura and Jocelyn went to the Virginia Wine and Garlic Festival at Rebec Vineyards and Winery in Amherst. While they were gone, Jocelyn's co-worker Maysa Munsey got busy baking ziti and other goodies for a surprise "In Two Years She'll Be Forty" birthday party. Jocelyn's dad, Bill, had wanted to visit her around her birthday, but his plans had to be scrapped, and he looked forward to seeing both of his daughters at Christmastime.

That November, Jennifer's five-year-old son, Joseph, had a sleepover at Jocelyn's for the first time. They ate popcorn, watched movies, and played video games in the basement rec room.

As usual when Thanksgiving rolled around, Jocelyn traveled to West Virginia for the family feast and Black Friday shopping blowout with her sister and mother. But on Thanksgiving night, November 22, Jocelyn received a phone call from her security company—her alarm had signaled. She called Jennifer Kerns, who went over to Jocelyn's home and walked through the entire house but saw nothing amiss. All was well, but the peace of the holiday had been shattered for both women.

Two weeks later, on December 7, Jennifer rode with Jocelyn to their weekly volleyball game. Jocelyn was jazzed about the terrific gifts she'd found in West Virginia for Jennifer's kids. They made plans to have their Christmas celebration together after Jocelyn returned from her yearly family visit.

The next weekend, Jocelyn and Maysa drove three and a half hours up to West Virginia to deliver Jocelyn's mother Joyce's Christmas gift, a bedroom suite. Joyce said Jocelyn was really excited about giving her the gift. "We were always into the holidays and shopping," Joyce recalled. "She was upbeat and happy. So when I told her about the ice storm coming to West Virginia, she said, 'Well, that's okay, Mom, because I've got a few more things I need to do.'"

Jocelyn and Maysa left midday Saturday, planning to do some more Christmas shopping along the way, keeping an eye on the weather as they did.

That Sunday, Jocelyn went shopping again, this time with Marcy Shepherd. They went to Sam's Club, where Jocelyn picked up Christmas presents for her team at Genworth and more gifts for Jennifer's kids, and made plans to get together again on the following Wednesday.

That Monday, December 17, 2007, Jocelyn called her mother to ask if she really did like her Christmas gift. Jocelyn was bubbly, laughing, and very upbeat. She was looking forward to having time off work to relax. They talked about plans to make cookies, play cards together, and enjoy the time with family. Jocelyn was doing some cooking to bring to the celebration and planned to bring her gifts and everything she needed to wrap them to her mother's house.

After talking to Joyce, Jocelyn called Jennifer to discuss getting together to make cookies before she left for West Virginia.

But it was not to be. Someone was determined that Jocelyn would not see another Christmas.

SEVENTEEN

On Monday, December 17, 2007, Wesley Earnest asked to borrow David Hall's truck in order to move some furniture. He drove off from school in Dave's maroon Chevrolet Silverado, while Dave took Wesley's silver Honda Accord home from school. The next day, Wesley submitted an online application to the University of Alaska for a job as an IT professional.

The team Jocelyn Earnest supervised had a Christmas dinner party Tuesday night at Logan's Roadhouse. Jocelyn worked a little late, but arrived by six, looking happy in a pink sweater. She interrupted the ordering of meals to announce, "Everything is on me."

The next day, Wednesday, December 19, was a busy one for Jocelyn. She went to work at 7:30 A.M. and met

Maysa Munsey. Maysa had been charged with misde-
meanor identity theft after using the social security number of a co-worker (who was dating Maysa's ex-husband)
to have the other woman's utilities turned off when she
was out of town.

Maysa and Jocelyn drove up to the Amherst County
Sheriff's Office to resolve the matter and were back at
Genworth by ten thirty. Jocelyn had several meetings
in the afternoon, but she laughed and giggled with co-
workers and was obviously in a happy mood, looking
forward to seeing her family and still excited about her
new position in the Corporate Frauds Division, and her
increased six-figure salary.

At the end of the day, Jocelyn and colleague Shari
Irving were working on a project that needed to be completed. They gathered documents and worked on other
preparations for the report that was due. When Jocelyn
had to leave for a six o'clock appointment with her counselor, she asked Shari, "Can you stay and finish so we're
ready first thing in the morning to finalize the work?"

Shari said that she would.

"I'm sorry that I have to leave you here working on it
by yourself. If you need anything, let me know. I'll meet
with you as soon as I get in tomorrow morning. Be careful and have a good night."

Just before seven o'clock, Jocelyn got an email from
Shari about approving overtime hours, which she responded to in the affirmative shortly before seven thirty.

Susan Roehrich was pleased with her patient's good
mood and positive attitude—she'd seen such a change in

Jocelyn since she'd accepted that her marriage was over. Afterward, they chatted for a few minutes about their holiday plans. Jocelyn then drove home expecting to see Marcy Shepherd that evening.

Wesley had a busy week, too. On Tuesday night, he stayed at the school late supervising the high school basketball game. On Wednesday, December 19, he roamed the halls monitoring student behavior, managing the crowds, and checking in with the four security guards scattered through the school.

Al Ragas, in charge of technical support at the high school, talked to Wesley around three thirty that afternoon about suspending a student's privileges for violating the usage policies on school computers. When they finished talking, Wesley got into David Hall's truck and drove west.

Law enforcement believed that Jocelyn entered her home around seven thirty, dropped down the duffle bag she used as a briefcase by a chair, turned off the alarm, and let her dog, Rufus, outside.

Forensics indicated that Jocelyn was running away from her killer at the moment the trigger on the .357 was pulled, firing the fatal shot. Her death was virtually instantaneous. Her body crumpled to the floor, landing on the side.

Her killer turned her on her back and dragged her

inert body two feet, then cleaned off the murder weapon and laid it on her body before dropping the prepared "suicide note" on the floor.

Before leaving, her killer crated Rufus and then turned the thermostat up to its highest setting—ninety degrees—presuming that the excessive heat would make it difficult to determine the time of death (and obviously giving little or no thought to the stressful effect that elevated temperature would have on Rufus), then left the house, locking the door.

Jocelyn lay on the floor of her home while friends grew concerned about her lack of response to messages. Marcy Shepherd was worried enough that she drove to Jocelyn's house looking for her.

But no one answered her knock on the door.

EIGHTEEN

Wesley Earnest appeared before Judge Phillip Wallace for his preliminary hearing on April 21, 2008. The prosecution accused Wesley of ambushing his estranged wife, Jocelyn Earnest, when she'd arrived home on the night of December 19, 2007. They introduced evidence that the fingerprints on the note recovered at the scene matched Wesley's, not Jocelyn's, and that although she had two printers in her home, neither one was hooked up to a computer. "That's not a suicide note. It's a homicide note."

Investigator Mike Mayhew read from Jocelyn's journal, citing the line about her "cheating husband" and other passages that indicated her fear of Wesley. Additionally, he presented the box for the snub nose .357 caliber revolver that shot the victim and told the judge that it had been found in the search of Shameka's home.

The medical examiner informed the court that it was not likely a suicide because of the distance that the gun had to be from Jocelyn's head when it was fired. Jocelyn's therapist, Susan Roehrich, testified that on the day of her death, Jocelyn was "very positive," "upbeat," and "not suicidal."

In an effort to end the case right there, the defense argued that Wesley had given the weapon to Jocelyn for her protection and had simply held on to the box. They also contended that since the note mentioned their client, it was illogical to believe he killed her, since a murderer would not name himself in a fabricated suicide message. The defense also said that if they went to trial, they would contest the fingerprint identification because they were only partial prints and, therefore, not definitive.

The judge, however, found probable cause that Wesley Earnest had murdered his wife, and he sent the case to the grand jury. He denied the defense's request for bond, and Wesley was sent back behind bars.

Investigator Gary Babb drove into Lynchburg to interview Shameka Wright's parents. All along the way, he debated whether or not to mention something about Wesley that had been uncovered when he went to jail. He decided that for Shameka's sake, he had to do so.

Babb asked first what the Wrights thought about the possibility that Wesley had killed his wife, and both of Shameka's parents were certain that Wesley was not capable of doing that. Then, he got to the point he'd worried about on the drive. "Did Shameka ever say anything about an STD—sexually transmitted disease?"

Shameka's mother instantly got defensive. "My children are adults and I don't discuss their sex life with them. You are just trying to drive a wedge in our family."

Unperturbed, Babb said, "Wesley has herpes and I think Shameka should know."

When they interviewed Shameka, she asked more questions of the investigators than they asked her. They also wondered about the possibility that Shameka had been involved but decided that although they believed Wesley had been planning the murder since the February incident that Babb called his "Ninja Night," they didn't think his girlfriend had any knowledge before it happened.

She struck the investigators as being a little arrogant. Her experience with the Lynchburg Police Department was evident. She wanted to know about fingerprints, DNA, tire track impressions, and all sorts of forensic evidence. She obviously did not want to give any more information than necessary, answering most questions with nothing more than "yes" or "no." It was easy to tell when she did not want to answer a question because her head immediately swiveled to her attorney.

On May 6, 2008, the grand jury met and delivered a murder indictment against Wesley Earnest. The trial was set to begin on July 29, but no one really expected it would begin then.

At the end of the month, at a bond hearing, Wesley admitted to having replaced all four tires on Dave Hall's truck, but said he did not recall using the name "Tom Dunbar" when he made the purchase. Bedford Circuit Court judge James Updike set Wesley's bond at $200,000 cash or $400,000 in real estate. He prohibited the defendant from leaving the state, contacting the victim's immediate family, co-workers, or friends, or setting foot on any property belonging to the Chesapeake Public Schools system. Wesley walked out of the Bedford County facility on June 5.

The year 2008 passed in a series of ever-pushed-back court dates. As expected, the July 29 hearing date was moved to October 3; then November 25; then moved again to January 13, 2009; and finally set for June 3, 2009.

On October 13, 2008, which would have been Jocelyn's thirty-ninth birthday, her family gathered. They had a birthday balloon and cake. They lit little candles and laughed and cried over their memories.

The first Thanksgiving since Jocelyn's death arrived on November 27, and it was torture for her family. Laura was haunted by memories of Black Friday shopping with her sister, and every time she looked at a sales flyer, she cried. Her mother, Joyce, made a veggie tray just like the ones Jocelyn always brought to the family home on that holiday, and everyone thought of their missing loved one as they munched on the vegetables before dinner.

On December 19, the first anniversary of Jocelyn's death, Laura and Joyce went shopping at Goodwill in memory of Jocelyn. Laura saw a lot of wool sweaters that she knew her sister would love.

On February 12, 2009, the Hedgesville High Eagles girls' basketball team, Jocelyn's high school alma mater, honored their fallen star with a ceremony to retire jersey number 21—the one Jocelyn Branham had worn—and unveiled the framed jersey for the wall of the gymnasium lobby.

Teammates and classmates from the class of 1988 as well as other family and friends were on hand. The short tribute praised Jocelyn as the greatest female basketball player to ever hit the court for Hedgesville.

Coach Denny Fiery said that Jocelyn never took her talent for granted. "She came to play every night. Her highest-scoring games were against the best teams. By the time she was a junior and a senior, we were contending for sectional crowns and regional championships, so we were playing a lot of big games."

He added that Jocelyn went on to be a starting member of the Mountaineers Sweet Sixteen team in 1992. "When she told me they offered her a scholarship—that was one of my happiest days."

NINETEEN

On Friday, March 20, 2009, Wesley Earnest's masterpiece on Smith Mountain Lake caught fire and filled the air with black smoke. Neighbor Dave Wilson stepped outside and smelled a strong kerosene odor before seeing the flames. He called 9-1-1 and reported the blaze at 6:43 P.M.

The fire chief of the Smith Mountain Lake Marine Volunteer Fire/Rescue Department was sitting in his home when he saw the tremendous roll of smoke across the water. It already looked too late to save the house, but he scrambled to pick up the company's third firefighting boat at the Blackwater River. By the time he reached the scene, the other two boats were already there—one shooting water up to the house, the other putting out a grass fire that threatened woods and homes nearby.

Altogether, sixty firefighters from units from the Moneta Volunteer Fire Department, Saunders and Bedford fire companies, and Smith Mountain Lake Marine Volunteer Fire/Rescue Department responded. By the time they arrived, though, the home was already engulfed in flames.

Broken bones had put Investigator Mike Mayhew into a wheelchair temporarily, and at the time the fire erupted, he was sitting at home watching television. He got a call from Bedford investigator Ricky Baldwin. "You're not going to believe what's happening."

When Baldwin told Mayhew about the fire on the lake, Mayhew's wife loaded her husband and his wheelchair into their car and drove him down to the scene. Firemen picked up and carried him and his chair over fallen trees and undergrowth to see the devastation in person. Mayhew immediately called his captain and urged him to send someone to the Earnest home in Forest to make sure that house wasn't burning, too.

Controlling the conflagration and protecting nearby homes was complicated by the lack of fire hydrants in the community and the difficulty that the fireboats had pumping water uphill from the lake. The fire burned for another hour before it was extinguished. The house was a total loss. Another neighbor, Greg Eigenfeld, told the *News & Advance*, "It was just a giant ball of fire. There was very little even that the fire crews could do but put it out. There was certainly nothing to save."

One big concern was the whereabouts of the homeowner, Wesley Earnest. When his defense attorney, Joey Sanzone, reached him by phone the day after the fire, he asked his client where he was. Wesley informed him that he was driving through Loudoun County, Virginia, an area contained in the Washington, D.C., metropolitan area. Sanzone told Wesley to pull over immediately and contact the sheriff's department. The defense attorney knew that Wesley's word would not be good enough— they needed someone official to verify his location.

Investigation to find the cause of the fire began on Saturday afternoon when everything was sufficiently cooled. In a short time, they had a working theory about what had started the blaze: for some inexplicable reason, it appeared that Wesley had been refinishing furniture, not in the garage where someone typically would perform that task, but in the great room of the home. They believed that a slow fuse lit the stain-soaked rags, which lay under a safety light. From that point, it took no time for the flames to run amok in the timber-framed home.

A number of suspicious facts pointed a finger at Wesley. He had received a foreclosure notice on the home, on which he still owed $990,000, and the insurance was scheduled to run out in July. Wesley was the only person who would benefit from the loss.

Nevertheless, despite the suspicious circumstances, the insurance company paid out over $1 million, leaving Wesley with $100,000 after the bank took its share. He presumably paid his attorney with some of that and sent some payments toward Shameka's house.

No one has ever been charged with what appeared to the experts to be a case of arson.

Investigators obtained a search warrant for Shameka Wright's vehicle on March 24, 2009, since Wesley regularly drove it, as well as another warrant for her Concord home on Night Hawk Road. They discovered a handgun in the car and two other firearms in the bedroom of the house.

Armed with that information, prosecutor Wes Nance asked the judge to revoke Wesley Earnest's bond. Another issue was that although Wesley spent most of his nights at his girlfriend's place, he'd never submitted a change of address as required under the terms of release.

Joey Sanzone argued that every time the court had needed to reach his client, he had always been available. The only reason Wesley had changed where he slept was because his primary address had been uninhabitable since the March fire destroyed it. Sanzone also claimed that Wesley was not a flight risk because he'd obtained a building permit to rebuild the lake house.

Judge Updike did not find those grounds sufficient for a revocation, but he did update the address. He also suspended Wesley's concealed carry permit and modified the bond agreement to stipulate that no firearms be in Wesley's possession regardless of whether or not he owned them.

On May 5, all parties were back in the courtroom. Joey Sanzone reported that he was waiting to receive subpoenaed evidence that now appeared unlikely to arrive in time for the scheduled June trial. The date was moved again to December 1, 2009.

Then in October, both the defense and the prosecution asked for a delay until March 23, 2010, because of evidence that the state forensic lab needed more time to analyze. The judge was frustrated. "This case has been pending for a long time and there needs to be a trial. I'm concerned that the public is concerned why this case is not being tried. I've been asked several times, 'Why is this case being continued?'" Nonetheless, Updike granted the joint request.

In March, before the start of the trial, Judge Updike ruled that the prosecution could not use Jocelyn's journals as evidence because it would violate Wesley's constitutional right to confront an accuser. The move virtually silenced the victim, whose voice would not be heard in the trial.

Eighty Bedford County residents were ordered to report to the courthouse on March 22, 2010, for possible inclusion in the jury. By 1:30 P.M. on March 23, seven men and seven women had been selected to serve as the dozen jurors and two alternates.

The lead prosecutor, Wes Nance, with Commonwealth's Attorney Randy Krantz by his side, opened the case. "It's an age-old story of greed and lust and sex and money. Wesley Earnest saw his wife as an obstacle to those things . . .

"He made errors. He made errors before the crime, he made errors during the crime, and he made errors after the crime." Nance told the jury how Wesley drove his friend's borrowed truck after work and returned it before school three mornings later. He argued that evidence would show the only fingerprint found on the suicide note was Wesley's; that the Smith and Wesson revolver belonged to Wesley; that the box for the weapon had been found at his girlfriend's house; and that he was the only one with a motive for killing Jocelyn.

Nance said that Wesley was $125,000 in debt, not including the money he'd owed on his home. Days after Jocelyn's body was found, Nance said, Wesley replaced the tires on Dave Hill's truck. "He was literally and figuratively covering his tracks."

Sanzone & Baker, representing Wesley Earnest, was rooted in a family practice that went back two hundred years. So it was no surprise to courtroom watchers that a father and daughter—Joey and Blair Sanzone—would present this case together, as they had done many others. They, of course, had a different scenario of Jocelyn's death to present the jury.

Joey Sanzone delivered their opening. He spoke about Wesley's life on the day Jocelyn died. "He went home. He took a nap; he got up and then headed out to get something for dinner. He went home, he went to bed. He had to be at work the next morning." Sanzone told the jurors that there was something "fishy" about the suicide note and that they needed to look at Jocelyn's close friends Maysa Munsey and Marcy Shepherd. He accused Marcy of having moved Jocelyn's body after her death.

The stage was set: circumstantial evidence versus third-party guilt. How would the jury decide?

TWENTY

Wes Nance prepared to present the Commonwealth's case against Wesley Earnest with some trepidation. "Once every twenty years, you encounter a case with a complicated nature like this one." He hoped his communication skills were good enough to pull all the pieces together in a way that made sense to the jurors—that was daunting enough. Add to that Nance's knowledge about the opposition. "Joey Sanzone has a lot of natural ability. The courtroom is a natural environment for him. He is quick on his feet. Not going to catch him flat-footed. Facing him is quite a challenge."

The first witness was Marcy Shepherd, Jocelyn's co-worker, who was not only the person who found the body but the one who said she was the "new love" referred to in the suicide note. Over defense objections, Marcy told jurors that Jocelyn had expressed fear of her husband and had said, "If he knew anything or found out anything, he would kill us both." She said that Jocelyn had recently had a security system installed because of her fear.

Marcy sobbed as a large television showed a crime scene photo of Jocelyn lying with her feet to the camera. She told the jury about the events of the night of December 19. Joey Sanzone questioned her aggressively about her text messages and her visit to Jocelyn's home that night and walking through the house on the morning she found the body—he did everything he could to paint her as a likely suspect. Sanzone asked if she went to work that evening in order to type up the suicide note. Marcy denied that allegation and said she'd gone to drop off a Christmas present on Jocelyn's desk.

Bedford County deputy Jason Jones, the first on scene, testified that the thermostat had been set for ninety degrees. He described what he saw in the home and the position of Jocelyn's body. Investigator Gary Babb testified that the revolver was out of place where it was found near her armpit and her hair was stuck in a pool of blood on the carpet. Sheriff's investigator Mike Mayhew testified that two of the cartridges in the gun had been expended, but they did not find any evidence of a second shot at the scene. The murder weapon had been purchased by Wesley Earnest, and there was no indication of a forced entry.

He was later called back to the stand to enter Wesley's will into evidence. The language in that document indicated that Wesley considered himself the owner of the murder weapon.

———

On the next day of the proceedings, Mike Mayhew told the jurors about the journals they'd found at Jocelyn's home and in her office; he read aloud two letters that were sent by Wesley to Jocelyn referring to his suicidal feelings, problems with his brother, Tyler, and his desire to reunite with his wife.

On cross, Mayhew told Joey Sanzone that there were no fingerprints on the thermostat or on the keypad of the security system. He denied Sanzone's allegation that he'd asked Marcy and Maysa to collect files and evidence at Genworth Financial. The defense then asked leading questions about whether the computers of Jocelyn's friends were searched. Mayhew said they were not.

Mayhew was replaced in the witness box by Jocelyn's close friend Jennifer Kerns, who testified that in March 2006, she and Jocelyn had witnessed Wesley having sex with Shameka Wright, whom she referred to as "Wesley's mistress."

A number of Jocelyn's co-workers testified to her positive frame of mind. "She was a friendly person, very upbeat . . . always encouraging, always smiling."

None of the Genworth employees said they'd had any inkling of a romantic relationship between Jocelyn and Marcy Shepherd.

Susan Roehrich, Jocelyn's therapist, told the jury that Jocelyn came to see her in 2005 with "depression issues" caused by the disintegration of her marriage. Her client, however, had gotten over the heartache and was "looking forward to having a life." Roehrich said Jocelyn was "upbeat and happy" the last time they'd met, on the day of her death.

TWENTY-ONE

On the fourth day of the trial, March 26, 2010, Assistant Medical Examiner Amy Tharp, who'd performed the autopsy, testified that Jocelyn Earnest's wounds were inconsistent with suicide. The angle of shot was too awkward. "Individuals who are trying to kill themselves will put the gun tight against their head because they don't want to miss." She also said that the shot would have killed or incapacitated her instantly.

Forensic scientist Marjorie Harris explained how the blood pattern trails on Jocelyn's face indicated her body had been moved after death. "Once she went down, she was pulled and moved." In all, she said, Jocelyn's head was in three different positions after death, and her body was moved about two feet.

Jocelyn's divorce attorney, Jennifer Stille, testified that Wesley claimed $1 million in debts but seemed unwilling to sell the Smith Mountain Lake home before the spring 2007 divorce trial to decide division of property. She also testified that Wesley had accumulated $60,000 in credit card debt in addition to the joint debts. She went into detail about the contentiousness of the divorce.

Bedford County sergeant Brian Neal wrapped up the day, telling the jurors about the evidence seized in the search of Shameka Wright's home. He read the long list of complaints about Jocelyn that Wesley had prepared for his attorney as well as other notes in Wesley's handwriting.

After a two-day break for the weekend, court was back in session on Monday, March 29, 2010. Bank officer Chip Umberger read numerous delinquency warnings sent to the Earnests in 2007, as well as the notice scheduling the foreclosure for January 4, 2008.

Forensic linguist James Fitzgerald, the man who tracked down the Unabomber through writing analysis, told the jury that the lack of emotion, grammatical clumsiness, and limited punctuation of the supposed suicide note was not consistent with Jocelyn's style. "My conclusion is that it's improbable that she wrote the note." He could not issue an opinion on whether or not the note's writing style was consistent with Wesley's.

Defense attorney Joey Sanzone asked, "Did you study the writings of Maysa and Marcy?"

"No," Fitzgerald said.

He was followed by real estate agent Johnny Maddox, whom Wesley contacted in his search for a piece of land

and to sell the lake house for $2 million. After he stepped down, Sergeant Neal got back in the box. He entered documentation about the rental of the lake house into the record as well as the letter that Wesley gave Jocelyn on that frightening night in February 2007.

Two teachers from Oscar Smith Middle School in Chesapeake testified that Wesley claimed to be rich—worth up to $5 million—and that he denied being married. Wesley's onetime landlord Neil Phillips testified about the ugly statements his tenant made about his wife and Wesley's own wife.

Shameka Wright, with her black hair in an updo, was next on the stand. She told the jury that she had been romantically involved with Wesley since 2004, and that they were still together.

Prosecutor Wes Nance asked of that fateful night in 2007, "Did you have any contact with Wesley Earnest on Wednesday, December 19?"

"I spoke with him by phone that morning but I could not reach him that evening. Cell phone reception at his home is spotty and it wasn't unusual for me to have difficulty reaching him."

She said that the drive from her home in Campbell County to visit Wesley in Chesapeake typically took her four hours without stopping.

Forensic scientist Ken Riding testified about Wesley's fingerprints on the suicide note—one on front matching his left thumb and another on the back—and the absence of any prints belonging to Jocelyn. He said the match was "beyond a reasonable doubt," though on cross, the defense worked hard to discredit his testimony.

Much of the testimony over the next two days concerned Wesley borrowing a truck the week his wife died. Dave Hall relayed the sequence of events surrounding the two times in December 2007 and January 2008 that Wesley borrowed his vehicle. He was followed on the stand by tire store manager Rick Keuhne, who told the jurors about selling tires to the defendant. Then Jesse McCoy took the stand and testified about the car detailing he did for Wesley the day after Jocelyn died.

The prosecution rested its case, and as expected, the defense filed a motion to dismiss.

They alleged that twenty-four hours before Jocelyn died, someone deactivated the security system at her home at 7:30 P.M. when she was at a Christmas dinner at Logan's Roadhouse, and that Wesley did not know the code. Although the defense was correct that the initial readout of the system indicated that it was turned off at that time, it was not an accurate reading. When the security company checked the system after Jocelyn's death, they discovered that the internal clock was off. It was possible that the system had not been properly set when it was installed or that a power outage had knocked it off track. However, when the times were recalibrated the inconsistency was resolved. Additionally, Sanzone claimed that the Commonwealth did not introduce any evidence connecting his client to the few unidentified, stray hairs and blood collected by technicians at the scene. Finally, he insisted that there was testimony given to show Wesley did not leave Chesapeake until after 4 P.M. and it would have taken more than four hours for him to reach Jocelyn's home in Forest. The defense insisted on that timeline even though they knew that the prosecution had paperwork that contested the testimony of when Wesley was at the high school, the length of time that it would take to make the drive, and the definitive time that Wesley's legal team wanted to put on Jocelyn's death.

Sanzone added that Marcy Shepherd had opportunity to kill the deceased, and that her actions on the night of Jocelyn's death were questionable. He wrapped up by claiming that Jocelyn was leading a secret life that no one had adequately explained.

The defense motion to dismiss was denied.

The defense began presenting its case at 9 A.M. on Wednesday, March 31, 2010. Since they were under no obligation to prove who had killed Jocelyn—just to establish reasonable doubt about whether it was Wesley—their goal was an obvious attempt to demonstrate that people other than their client had motive and opportunity to kill Jocelyn. Their first witness, Amherst County investigator John Tetterton, talked about the identity theft case and Maysa Munsey's visit to the Amherst County Sheriff's Department accompanied by another woman on the morning of December 19.

Jack Tymchen of Verizon was next on the stand. He told the jury that although they knew that Wesley's phone was in eastern Virginia on December 19 and no calls were received or instigated on it after early morning that day, it did not necessarily mean that Wesley Earnest was in the same location as his cell. It was quite possible that he left his home without his phone.

Campbell County investigator Robert New explained that there were text messages exchanged between Marcy Shepherd and Jocelyn Earnest in the hours before Jocelyn died, but four of those messages were missing from Marcy's phone. Although the defense operated on a premise that these missing texts were intentionally deleted to cover up Marcy's involvement, law enforcement later testified that Marcy showed those messages to them in the immediate aftermath of Jocelyn's death.

One of Wesley's Smith Mountain Lake neighbors told the jury about Jocelyn and Jennifer arriving at Wesley's house with a moving truck in December 2006. This was the trip with a Penske truck that Jennifer described to the investigators but that the defense attempted to portray as a plundering of Wesley's home.

Wesley's father, Roger Earnest, stepped to the stand next and told the jury about loaning Wesley and Jocelyn $100,000 to purchase a rental home right near their house in Forest. He also talked about Jocelyn demonstrating that she had more proficiency with the .357 revolver than Wesley.

Court was then dismissed for lunch. Out in the hallway, Investigator Gary Babb was approached by Roger Earnest, a former California state trooper. They didn't discuss anything about Wesley but just started talking together like old cops often do. Babb wondered what Roger thought about the case against his son but didn't dare ask.

After everyone returned to the courtroom, the prosecution mounted a vigorous challenge to the defense's presentation of the case. Randy Krantz, the Commonwealth's attorney assisting Wes Nance in the prosecution, cited case law stating that if a third party's involvement in the crime were asserted, evidence must be shown that pointed directly to that person's guilt. He said that the defense did not provide that and no one else had been charged or indicted in Jocelyn's death.

Joey Sanzone responded by claiming that it was relevant to the defense of his client because they illustrated events and coincidences that pointed to the possible guilt of others as strongly as the circumstantial case the prosecution made against Wesley. He claimed that the testimony he planned to present would show that some in Jocelyn's circle of friends had the opportunity and motive to have committed this homicide.

Judge Updike said he would take the prosecution's objection under advisement while the testimony continued.

Maysa Munsey, a long-haired brunette, looked stressed even before she stepped into the witness box. In one hand she clutched a piece of paper that appeared to reporter/ blogger Tim Saunders to be a bulletin from Jocelyn's memorial service.

The defense hoped to deflect guilt from their client by resting it on Maysa Munsey, the second person to arrive at the home after Jocelyn's death. She admitted to knowing the code to the security system, to asking Jocelyn to come with her to the Amherst County Sheriff's Department, to staying overnight at Jocelyn's home frequently, and to having spent the night with her the weekend before she died. She had hoped to get together with Jocelyn to wrap gifts on December 19 but then found out that she had dinner plans with Marcy.

Defense attorneys continued to hammer away at third-party guilt, focusing on Maysa Munsey. The defense called a number of Genworth Financial employees to the stand to explain the ability of payroll and human resources—where Maysa worked—to access information like social security numbers and the ease with which others at the company could obtain another employee's email and individual files. They contended that Jocelyn had learned information about Maysa's identity theft that could put her job at risk, giving Maysa motive to kill her friend.

Rodney Wolforth of the state forensic lab in Roanoke testified for the defense that the blood drops found in Jocelyn's guest bathroom came from a male, but not Wesley. Nor did the blood match any of the twenty-five people connected to the case, including first responders and known visitors to the home.

Al Ragas, an IT worker at Great Bridge High, told the jury about the conversation he'd had with Wesley just before 4 P.M. on December 19, 2007, and said that he had worked until after 4 that day. On cross, he admitted that his time card showed that he'd left work at 3:26 P.M., but he explained that that was just his lunch break.

Owen Casey, a forensic computer analyst, testified that

Jocelyn's BlackBerry had been wiped out and he was unable to retrieve any information from it.

Finally, Wesley Earnest brought the courtroom alive with his unexpected decision to take the stand and testify on his own behalf. He said he'd been at his apartment in Chesapeake on December 19, 2007, suffering from seasonal allergies. He told the jury that Jocelyn was "incredible, fun to be around. I admired her a lot . . . [but] she wasn't capable of giving me the affection I wanted. She was a great person, a great friend. We had a great friendship and I didn't want it to drift away." He reiterated his claim that Jocelyn had told him to have sex with other people but to come home to her. "I wanted more out of a marriage." When asked about his nickname for Jocelyn, he replied, "Buddy," with tears in his eyes.

He said he fell in love with Shameka Wright, and that she filled the void in his heart caused by Jocelyn's lack of intimacy. When the job opportunity arose in Chesapeake, he accepted it because of his separation from Jocelyn. "While you don't want to lose a friend, someone you adore, you want to get a fresh start and that's what I was trying to do."

Wesley identified the murder weapon as a firearm he'd purchased for Jocelyn for her self-protection. He insisted that he did not kill Jocelyn or harm her in any way.

TWENTY-TWO

The final day of testimony began when the defense called Susan Cropp, a DNA examiner for the FBI. She discussed her comparison of the six unidentified male hairs found in Jocelyn Earnest's home to samples provided by eight men known to have been in the home. Defense attorney Joey Sanzone asked her if she had tested Marcy Shepherd's DNA, and Cropp said she had not.

When she stepped down, the defense rested its case. The prosecution called three witnesses to rebut the defense claim that Jocelyn had been at Logan's Roadhouse when her security alarm was turned off at 7:30 on the evening of December 18. Restaurant manager Ann Mason said that credit card receipts were preserved for three years, and that she'd been able to locate the one for that Genworth party, which showed that Jocelyn paid the bill at 7:18 P.M. An alarm company official testified that the system was actually deactivated at 7:38. Co-worker Pam Gillespie told the jury that Jocelyn left the restaurant no later than 7:20. These clarifications provided Jocelyn sufficient time to have returned home to shut off the security system herself.

After another motion to strike the case was made by the defense and denied by the judge, the jurors were instructed and the closing arguments began. Prosecutor Wes Nance argued, "To find this man not guilty, you have to believe a liar. Wesley Earnest wanted everyone to believe Jocelyn Earnest committed suicide, but he made mistakes." Itemizing those errors, Nance pointed to when Wesley told the car detailers that he wouldn't be in Chesapeake on December 19; when he dragged Jocelyn two feet through her own blood on carpet; and when he typed a cold and unemotional suicide note for a woman who was a prolific writer who filled seventeen journals by hand.

Sanzone countered, "The real story about this case involves two separate days of two separate people whose lives had split." He pointed to suspicion surrounding Maysa Munsey and Marcy Shepherd, and to the blood drops and hair in the guest bathroom sink that had never been identified. The defense continued on, attempting to make something out of incidental biological evidence left at some time in the past at a location in the home not connected to the crime scene. They wanted the jurors to believe that any number of people could have been there at the time that Jocelyn was killed. "There is great and substantive evidence of other people that did harm to Jocelyn Earnest. If Jocelyn Earnest had two men in her life instead of Marcy Shepherd and Maysa Munsey and she had been keeping the two men apart, kissing one and keeping the other at the house . . . If it was two men, I don't think any of us would have a lot of trouble with that. Could this just be as old as time? I submit to you that just because it's two women, it's not different."

Sanzone talked to the jurors for quite some time, injecting suspicion into any possible circumstance to create reasonable doubt. In fact, Judge Updike later described it as "the longest closing argument I've ever heard in better than thirty-two years."

Nance then delivered the final words on behalf of the prosecution. "I'd like for you to consider murder as a means of solving a problem. Jocelyn Earnest was killed because she is Jocelyn Earnest and who do we know who has a problem with Jocelyn Earnest? [. . .] This mysterious stranger doesn't have to stage a crime scene because nobody knows who they are . . . [The defense] wants you to think about the hair that's right over there but the forensic evidence right at her body? They want you to ignore that . . . Wesley Earnest lied to you. He lied to you about his actions involving the death of Jocelyn Earnest."

After nine days, hundreds of pieces of evidence, and more than fifty witnesses, it was now time for the jury to deliberate. But since it was Friday, they were dismissed for the weekend and charged with returning to make their decision on Monday, April 5, at 9 A.M. Less than six hours after reporting in that morning, at 2:50 that afternoon, the verdict was announced: Wesley Earnest was found guilty of first degree murder and of a felony firearms charge. Wesley showed no reaction to the announcement. Jocelyn's family and friends were visibly relieved that justice had been served. Wesley's mother, Patricia Wimmer, was disbelieving and distraught.

Wesley's father Roger Earnest stood at the door when Detective Gary Babb came out of the courtroom. Roger shook the investigator's hand.

Babb said, "This is nothing personal."

Roger said, "I know." He left the courthouse and did not return for the sentencing phase of the trial.

Eight minutes after the verdict was delivered, that portion began with Joyce Young, Jocelyn's mother, shaking her head as she held a sheet of paper in her hand. The grief of losing her daughter, she said, "felt like a wild animal inside me wanted out . . . Next month is Mother's Day and my birthday falls on Mother's Day this year. I won't get a hug. I won't get a kiss. I won't get an 'I love you, Mom' anymore."

Jocelyn's sister, Laura Rogers, added, "We expected to grow old together, to attend yard sales at eighty years old."

Wesley bowed his head and shook it from side to side as their testament to endless grief filled his ears.

Judge Updike instructed the jury on possible sentences. It took the panel half an hour to return and recommend the maximum: Life in prison, a $100,000 fine, and three more years of prison for the firearms charge.

Wesley's mother, Patricia Wimmer, looked about to collapse to the floor when she heard those words. She told reporters: "I feel that the jury did what they thought that they needed to do, but I think it was done on speculation and distortion of the facts. My son is innocent. I believe that in my heart. I love Jocelyn, but my son did not murder this woman."

Later that afternoon, Jocelyn's mother, father, sister, and two friends came out of the Commonwealth's attorney's office. Holding up two enlarged photos of Jocelyn, the friends read the following statement: "On behalf of Jocelyn's family, friends, and those who cared for her, we are pleased with today's verdict. We realize and appreciate the efforts of all involved—the Commonwealth Attorney's office, law enforcement personnel, the Bedford County court system, and members of the jury. At this time we hope that Jocelyn can be remembered for her character, integrity, and wisdom. As we continue the next leg of our 'new normal' journey, we will always remember her words of encouragement said with a twinkle in her eye and her infectious laugh filling the air."

TWENTY-THREE

After the verdict was rendered, Jocelyn Earnest's family finally had free access to the home where their loved one had lived and died. Her sister and mother, Laura Rogers and Joyce Young, called her friend Jennifer Kerns, who accompanied them to Pine Bluff Drive.

All three hearts clenched and burned when they looked at the cutout chunk in the carpet where Jocelyn fell to the floor and died. Other than what forensics had taken, nothing had been altered since Jocelyn's death more than two years earlier. Jennifer cleaned out the litter box and the refrigerator, now filled with moldy and sour food. The pain of their loss swelled as they went through her belongings.

The prosecution had taken possession of Jocelyn's private journals pretrial, not allowing family, friends, or media to read them at length. They felt a bit freer with the contents after the trial was over. They gave family and select friends copies of one poignant section where, after expressing her fears that Wesley might take her life, Jocelyn said good-bye to the people she loved.

On April 22, 2010, Jocelyn's mother, father, and sister filed a lawsuit against Wesley Earnest, Sanzone & Baker PC, and Shameka Wright over the insurance proceeds from the fire at the lake house. Under the provisions of Virginia's slayer statute, they alleged that Wesley was not entitled to profit from Jocelyn's death in any way. They claimed that Wesley had unlawfully kept the couple's home and properties, including Jocelyn's personal effects and jointly owned vehicles. He then, the documents read, used insurance payments to pay his lawyers and his legal firm knew when they accepted the money that Jocelyn's relatives had a claim on it.

Joey Sanzone wrote on behalf of his client that the family was not entitled to the money. "The insurance proceeds, which the plaintiff alleges to exist . . . were not acquired as a result of the death."

Although officials with the sheriff's office suspected that Wesley burned down the house before the bank could foreclose and before his insurance policy could lapse, no one was ever arrested or charged in the blaze.

A letter from Patricia Wimmer was published in the *Bluefield Daily Telegraph* in West Virginia on May 10. It began, "My son, Wesley Earnest, did not kill his wife, Jocelyn

Earnest. He is innocent and your help is needed to get the verdict set aside."

She went on to itemize the points the defense had raised as issues of reasonable doubt: the length of the drive from his home, the unidentified drop of blood in the bathroom, and the credibility of the fingerprint evidence. She also mentioned things that she either misunderstood or remembered incorrectly from the trial, such as the claim that the prosecution's linguist testified that Wesley could not have written the note found at the scene (he actually said he couldn't make a statement regarding that), or that Jocelyn's body had been moved at least eight hours after her death but before police arrived (no one offered evidence of this claim at trial).

She wrote in summation: "This is a case of justice gone wrong. We must help Wesley; he is innocent. He did not, he would not, he could not have killed Jocelyn." She urged everyone to contact Judge Updike. "Ask him to set aside the jury's misguided and preconceived verdict of guilty."

Although the defense was working on the possibility of entering an appeal in the case and Wesley's mother was desperate to see one, everyone else thought it was all over. And it was—until one day in early July when Laura Rogers was browsing through the website of the Lynchburg *News & Advance* and saw a comment posted back on April 11 from someone self-identifying as "bedford-resident." The anonymous writer claimed to have been a jury member on the Earnest trial and was defending the panel against critics who insisted that they had convicted an innocent man.

The author argued that they had seen lots of evidence—including the journals written by Jocelyn—before finding Wesley guilty. "There was not a doubt in my mind that Wesley Earnest committed murder . . . I personally would have voted for [the] death penalty if it had been a choice we had, but it was not. For anyone to say that we did not give Wesley Earnest a fair trial is absurd."

Laura called Wes Nance and delivered the news that she knew might call the guilty verdict into question. Nance said, "It was a punch in the gut—my heart hurt for the family—it will be devastating for them to have to go through the trial again."

Nance called Investigator Mike Mayhew. "We've got a problem."

"What is it?" Mayhew asked.

"I don't know what to do about it."

"What's going on?"

"Somehow, the journals got into the jury room."

Wes Nance contacted Joey Sanzone and informed him of the latest development. Wesley Earnest had already been scheduled to appear before the judge on Thursday, July 8, for his formal sentencing. Nance and Sanzone delivered the news to the judge, who immediately postponed that day's hearing until September.

The first item on the court's agenda was to discover if

"bedfordresident" was, in fact, an actual member of the jury. Updike ordered the Lynchburg *News & Advance* to disclose the name of the poster, stirring up the question of whether one person's right to a fair trial trumped another's right to free speech.

The *Roanoke Times* sent an email to the *News*'s city editor Caroline Glickman asking what the newspaper would do. She responded: "Lawyers are reviewing it and will respond as appropriate, as we would with any subpoena."

In less than a week, they did respond, sending a letter to the court identifying the anonymous author, who told the court that the jurors believed they were allowed to see the journals. "They brought them in on a table of evidence while we were deliberating . . . Some of us picked up a journal and went through it. As we found something interesting, we would read it out loud," adding that before they looked in them, "there were a couple of people on the fence because they didn't want to convict without a smoking gun."

The investigators worked hard to prepare for the second trial. They set up a situation room in the emergency EEOC room at the sheriff's department. They reinterviewed a number of witnesses, including Wesley's former co-workers, his landlords in the Tidewater area, Rick Keuhne at Kramer Tire, and Shameka Wright.

On Monday, July 26, Judge Updike tossed the guilty

verdict and set a new trial date for November 8, 2010. Sanzone announced his intention to file for a change of venue.

The prosecution team faced the direst consequences in this new trial. If the Commonwealth prevailed, the defense would be no worse off than they were before a mistrial was declared. If the outcome was different from the first trial, the prosecution would not only lose the justice they thought they had secured for Jocelyn, her family, and her friends, they would also look like bumblers. In life, as in football, the person with the most to lose is the one who made the last mistake.

TWENTY-FOUR

The prosecutors wanted the trial to remain in the Bedford County court system. The defense wanted the trial moved to another less media-saturated area but were concerned that bringing jurors from another locale to the trial site would taint their performance in the courtroom.

Neither one of them got what they wanted. Judge Updike moved the trial to the north side of Lynchburg, Virginia, to the Amherst County Courthouse. He also ordered that the jury pool be selected from Nelson County, a greater distance up Route 29 and even farther from Bedford.

On November 8, 2010, the second trial began, just like the first, with Wesley Earnest pleading not guilty and the first group of potential jurors entering the courtroom.

Judge Updike introduced the lawyers and the defendant and read the indictment against Wesley.

Choosing a jury from the pool was more of a challenge this time around—in addition to the usual issues of un-availability and bias, many potential jurors had heard varying amounts about the case and previous trial. Two exchanges during the selection process spotlighted the deep roots of the agricultural culture in the rural county in contrast to the creeping presence of progressive sensibilities.

When Sanzone asked if anyone's Thanksgiving plans would be disrupted if the trial ran long, one of the prospective jurors said, "We usually kill hogs Thanksgiving week. It's when I take my week vacation, but that's the only thing. If the weather's cold enough to kill [. . .] It's about a week's process time to get up the mess and everything."

When Sanzone threw in a question asking about their attitudes regarding Wesley's adulterous heterosexual affair and Jocelyn's romantic relationship with another woman, he got a blunt answer from one of the candidates. "To be very honest with you, Joey, I don't know. I am a lesbian, and I'm not sure how hearing the information would affect me given the circumstances." Definitely not an answer the defense expected to receive from a Nelson County resident.

But eventually, they were able to find twelve individuals to serve on the jury, plus two alternates. After sending them out of the room, names were drawn for the designated alternates. As usual, no one on the jury would know who those two people were until the end, in order to keep them focused on the trial.

This jury contained two nurses, an RN and an LPN, a civil engineer, a financial specialist, a retired thirty-year Air Force veteran with a degree in psychology, and two people with moderate hearing difficulties. At 6:10 P.M., the jurors were sworn and the players were all ready, waiting for the curtain to rise on a new day.

Before the jury got to work on the first actual day of trial, Judge Updike heard arguments concerning testimony and questioning that pointed to third-party guilt as presented in the first trial. Commonwealth's Attorney Randy Krantz claimed that all that the defense had presented the first time around was suspicion, suggestion, and conjecture. He argued that legal precedent indicated the evidence introduced must point directly to the guilt of a third person and the defense was unable to do that previously.

Defense attorney Joey Sanzone fired back that the presence of unidentified DNA from blood found at the scene, the stories the defense defined as "peculiar" from people who spent time with Jocelyn in the hours before her death, and the fact that the body was discovered by a person whom the defense claimed had an "odd explanation of what she did that day" clearly pointed to the possibility of a perpetrator other than his client.

The judge responded, "Considerable time was spent dealing with two women. And I never saw any evidence of motivation or ill will on the part of either woman towards the victim in this case [. . .] And I never saw the connection."

Krantz cited a ruling in another case saying that "proffered evidence that merely suggests a third party is not admissible."

"I didn't see any evidence that suggested that either woman committed it," the judge said, "other than some evidence that because they found the body that there was some opportunity, Mr. Sanzone."

The frustrated defense attorney said, "They're with the dead body."

"Right," the judge said. "Well, so were the police officers when they found her. I mean . . ."

"But the police officers didn't call friends before they called the police," Sanzone objected. He went on to mention Maysa's legal problem in Amherst on the day of Jocelyn's death and the erasure of Jocelyn's BlackBerry while in custody, saying that could only be done through the Genworth computer system and therefore had to have been accomplished by one of their employees.

"So you're intending to go through all that again, obviously?" the judge asked.

"I intend to go through it, yes, sir," Sanzone said with a nod.

"[. . .] I'm just being candid with you when I state I never understood that and I still don't," Updike said. "And it seems to me saying that that was a stretch is expressing it mildly."

The defense's case for reasonable doubt had hinged on the fact that someone else killed Jocelyn, but now it appeared as if the judge were about to shut that door. The defense team attempted to set that disappointment aside and focus on the opening statement of the Commonwealth.

The jury filed into their seats and the judge explained that they could take notes if they wished but that their notebooks would be collected each evening and returned to them the following morning. At the end of the trial, all of their writings would be destroyed. "Now, we're ready to begin with the opening statements. As for the Commonwealth, Mr. Nance . . ."

"Yes, sir. May it please the court," Wes Nance began. "Good morning, ladies and gentlemen."

"Good morning," the jurors responded in the manner of a well-behaved classroom on the first day of school.

"Wesley Earnest attempted to deceive law enforcement. He attempted to make the murder of his wife look like a suicide. He laid down a fake suicide note, and he left behind the gun that took her life . . .

"First, I'm going to prove to you, this was no suicide. Witness after witness, piece of evidence after piece of evidence will prove she did not take her own life. It was snatched from her by her estranged husband, Wesley Earnest."

Nance explained the discovery of the body by Marcy Shepherd, the findings of the medical examiner Amy Tharp, and the conclusions drawn from the blood analysis by Marjorie Harris. "So, ladies and gentlemen, we're going to prove this wasn't a suicide. And then we'll turn our attention to identifying the killer as Mr. Wesley Earnest. And there will be four main points in the Commonwealth's evidence identifying him as the killer. First of all, Wesley Earnest and Wesley Earnest alone is linked to the fake suicide note left at the scene. Wesley Earnest and Wesley Earnest alone is linked to the firearm, the handgun that took her life.

"Wesley Earnest will identify himself as the killer through his acts, his deeds, his statements, his lies, and even an inadvertent confession. And finally, Wesley Earnest is the only person with a motive to kill Jocelyn Earnest, a person who saw her as a problem or an obstacle that had to be eliminated."

Nance discussed the anomalies in the "suicide note" and Wesley's purchase of the handgun that caused Jocelyn's death. "At the time of his arrest at the home that he often shared on the weekends with Shameka Wright, law enforcement finds the gun box, the gun box that goes to the firearm that took his estranged wife's life."

Nance said that in December 2007, Wesley Earnest "was working at a school called Great Bridge High School. That school was a three hour and forty minute drive to Jocelyn Earnest's house. Now, on the weekends, he would often commute from Chesapeake to Shameka Wright's house near Concord or to the lake house. It was a trip he was used to taking.

"He had a new set of friends in Chesapeake. They knew some things about Wesley Earnest or thought they knew some things about Wesley Earnest. But there were some things that they had no idea about. His friends in Chesapeake didn't know that he was married, didn't know that he was going through a divorce. And it wasn't that he just didn't tell them. He actively denied it to them."

Nance noted Earnest's reaction to the condolences offered from those who'd heard about his wife's death. "Wesley Earnest responds by saying, 'I don't know what you're talking about' or 'how many times do I have to tell you I'm not married?' What did his friends know about him? They knew about that large lake house on Smith Mountain Lake. They thought that . . . he was independently wealthy. He told some of them that he was worth five million, others that he didn't have any debt, and that he didn't even need this job because he was independently wealthy.

"But when he is alone away from bragging to his friends you'll hear that he took a very different tone. He asked for spousal support from Jocelyn Earnest. He wrote one time that he was worth only one hundred and twenty-seven dollars. He had to borrow five thousand from his mother and twenty thousand from retirement just to pay his bills. What you'll find out is that he blamed one person for his financial problems, for his financial strife: Jocelyn Earnest. You'll see that he accused her of hoarding her higher income, of stealing tax returns and having one hundred thousand dollars in Genworth stock stored away somewhere.

"See, during the course of this divorce Wesley Earnest had been ordered to pay 75 percent of the mortgage on the lake house because that's where he was residing . . . So his financial crisis was looming. And there was a deadline looming. He had been unable to sell the lake house . . . And he even tried renting it for thousands of dollars a week without Jocelyn knowing. But at divorce . . . the house would have to be sold not a price that he wanted but at whatever the market would take . . . and have to split whatever was remaining, if there was anything remaining, with Jocelyn Earnest.

"So in December of 2007, specifically the week before Christmas break, the same week that Jocelyn Earnest dies, you will hear that he borrows a pickup truck from David Hall . . ." on December 17 and returns ". . . it on December twentieth, the day after Jocelyn is killed.

". . . Another unusual thing about Wesley Earnest on December nineteenth, the day that his wife is killed, is he was going to get his car cleaned before Christmas break by a fellow by the name of Jesse McCoy. Wesley Earnest tells him, 'I'm going to be out of town on December nineteenth, we can make it December twentieth, but I needed to be a little bit later in the morning because I'm not sure when I'll be at work.'

"Now, ladies and gentlemen, very early on in my opening statement I told you about an inadvertent confession by Mr. Earnest. And that's what you'll hear about. You see, law enforcement didn't tell anyone about the suicide note that they found or the details of it, the line about new love who would not leave the family. And they certainly didn't tell Wesley Earnest prior to his interview—or even during the interview—on December twenty-first, 2007, when he speaks to Sergeant Babb and Investigator Mike Mayhew. Wesley Earnest calls his boss, the principal at Great Bridge High School, Dr. Andrejco, who you'll hear from. She will tell you that she got a call from him—that ends up being about half an hour to an hour before he speaks to the police—and it's the first time she learns that he's married. And he said it looks like my wife killed herself based on a failed relationship. Ladies and gentlemen, he knew . . . how that crime scene was staged before he has any innocent reason for knowing it.

"I thank you ahead of time for your attention to this case. It will last several days but during the course of those days we will prove Jocelyn didn't take her life. And will prove that Wesley Earnest alone is tied to that fake note, is tied to that gun, is the only person with a motive to kill Jocelyn, and is the only person who identifies himself through his statements and actions as the killer of his wife."

TWENTY-FIVE

After a brief recess, defense attorney Joey Sanzone stepped in front of the jury to deliver the opening statement from the defense. "Ladies and gentlemen, thank you for your time and attention to all of us . . . In every endeavor in life, you need to know a little bit about boundaries. And let me say something about the boundaries of this case, because you need to know how to evaluate the evidence and sort over what we're trying to accomplish here. The first thing—the way we sit in the courtroom is important. The Commonwealth is nearest you because they have the burden of proof. And that's a very important concept. It's their job to put on evidence to prove their case to the proper legal standard.

"We have several legal standards. A civil case has a preponderance of the evidence standard, which is basically 51 percent of the evidence, the evidence it's more likely than the other. That's not the standard in a criminal case. And we can't put [. . .] a percentage on that, but it's a much higher standard than the civil standard because the standard is beyond a reasonable doubt. It's the highest standard that we have, because these are constitutional rights to be free in a free society [. . .] The Commonwealth [. . .] gladly accepts their burden of proof, but their burden of proof is a high one, and they have to prove their case beyond a reasonable doubt.

". . . There are two types of cases: there is a direct evidence case and then there's a circumstantial evidence case. A direct evidence case is: I saw Joey Sanzone run into that bus down there, he was the guy driving the car, I know him [. . .] There's no question about it, you saw what happened. This isn't a direct evidence case. This is a circumstantial evidence case. So instead of going straight to the point [. . .] this case is made up with a lot of little circumstances, a chain, if you will. And it's not enough in a case like this to have just two or three circumstances out there—things maybe you didn't like—they all have to be connected. All of the evidence has to be connected. All of the evidence has to be consistent with guilt and inconsistent with innocence, not just something standing alone. And that's where the problem comes in this case.

"If what Mr. Nance said was all there was in this case then I would sit down, Mr. Earnest would sit down, the case would be over, but it's not. And there are some very important details of this case that have been left out."

Sanzone talked about the couple drifting apart but insisted it was not a contentious divorce. They were not in direct contact and not angry with each other, he said. He went on to claim that it was normal for Wesley to request spousal support because Jocelyn had the higher income. "If there was a single person on this earth who needed Jocelyn Earnest alive and working, it was Wesley Earnest."

Sanzone discussed the ordinariness of Wesley's week and his shock at learning of Jocelyn's death. Then, he turned to Jocelyn's day, which began with a trip north to Amherst with her friend Maysa Munsey and continued with many text messages between Jocelyn and Marcy.

"There were literally more than one thousand text messages between Jocelyn Earnest and Marcy Shepherd during that month of December [. . .] Jocelyn Earnest was a mobile device chatterbox [. . .] And you can sort of track her life a little bit by these text messages, phone calls, emails. Well, they all stop at seven twenty-eight on the nineteenth. They stopped midstream of a conversation between Marcy Shepherd, the new love, and Jocelyn Earnest.

". . . At seven thirty the alarm at her house is turned off . . . It's an alarm that's set during the day. For who or what? Wesley's working at Chesapeake every day on the other side of Richmond, on the other side of Norfolk. Seven thirty-five [. . .] maybe she turned it off, maybe somebody else did [. . .]

"What's really interesting: the dog is locked up in the kennel all day long. When she gets home, she lets the dog out and takes it outside. When the police get there the next day guess what? The dog's still in the kennel. Never was let out the prior day. Pretty good indication . . ."

The Commonwealth's attorney spoke out: "Your Honor, I am going to object to him arguing what the indications are, Your Honor."

"I agree. I agree," said Mr. Sanzone.

"Sustained," said the judge.

"I'll withdrawal that," said Mr. Sanzone. "The dog was not let out, even though the keypad is located right next to the dog kennel." He pointed out that there is no way to know who turned the alarm off since no personal identification information is required to do so. Sanzone questioned why Marcy didn't go out to Jocelyn's house Wednesday evening and wait for her there.

"The next morning . . . she gets in the house, and she finds the body. And she calls her friend Maysa Munsey. Rather than call the police and report that Jocelyn is missing, rather than let the police go in and check out and see if she's okay, she chooses to get this key and go in the house. And that's when she says she finds the body."

He asserted that Jocelyn's body was moved that morning when Wesley was known to be at work—rather than at a time proximate to Jocelyn's murder, as the evidence he reviewed indicated.

"Now back to the chain, the unbroken chain. Reasonable doubts break the chain. And I'm going to point out all of the reasonable doubts. There are a lot of them."

Krantz interrupted with another objection. "Your Honor, we're not supposed to be arguing."

"I'm not arguing. I am . . ."

"Point out pieces of evidence," Updike said.

"And I'm pointing that out, Judge . . . I withdraw that . . . Let me say it this way . . ." He detailed the evidence he would present about the distance between Chesapeake and Forest, the time required to travel between them, and Wesley's lack of knowledge of Jocelyn's schedule and the alarm code.

Sanzone then turned to the murder weapon. "It's the smallest version of the .357. It's got a four-inch barrel. [. . .] It's a woman's gun [. . .] The gun was left at the house. And whoever did this knew either that it was Jocelyn's or maybe they even knew Wesley had bought it for her. But it was intended to be found."

Sanzone then called into question the basic science of fingerprint analysis. "They're going to tell you that in this case, they made their identification on fifteen or less of these points in the known area [. . .] You're going to hear from them that there is no such thing as a degree in fingerprint examination. In order to be certified as a fingerprint examiner, it takes less than a few days training, possibly as little as eight hours [. . .] They're going to tell you that there are no measurements taken to help make a match in fingerprints and they're not able to produce a catalogue of prints that match to one another . . .

"The last thing I'll tell you is this: This case is going to boil down to a battle between DNA and fingerprints. And you're going to hear two state experts on fingerprints for the prosecution and you're going to hear one state expert for the defense and one expert from the FBI on

DNA for the defense, because there is DNA evidence there at the scene . . .

"And then, lastly, the note itself is interesting because the Commonwealth told you that they say the writing is not Jocelyn Earnest's. I think you'll also find it's not consistent with Wesley . . . But it talks about two things that Wesley would not have known. First of all, it says Wesley left her with a ton of debt, though they paid off some debt earlier in the year because some things that needed to be paid were joint debts . . . And there's no way that Wesley would have known she had a new love because Wesley wasn't involved in her life and didn't know anything about it. The . . . context of the note is important. Who would know?

"And the last thing that was shown there—I promise this is the last thing. In the bathroom, right there on the toilet seat, was something that people from the south would recognize right away [. . .] There were towels sitting on the toilet seat. And that only means one thing: company's coming.

"So this is going to be the evidence. It is quite a bit of evidence. It's important to listen to each piece of it. And I know you will . . . I thank you so much. And at the end of the trial, I'll ask you to find my client not guilty."

TWENTY-SIX

The first witness called to the stand was Jocelyn Earnest's mother, Joyce Young. It is always disconcerting to listen to the testimony of someone with so intimate a connection to the victim. The job of the prosecution was to pull out all of that pain and make the jurors absorb the visceral sense of loss.

Joyce recited the outline of her daughter's life, from birth through childhood, her graduation from Hedgesville High and her four-year basketball scholarship from West Virginia University where she obtained a double major in economics and marketing. She recounted Jocelyn's move to Lynchburg, Virginia, and her work to earn her master of business administration from Lynchburg College. "She's been on the Dean's List. She's just wonderful."

She talked about Jocelyn and Wesley getting their home on Pine Bluff Drive and then marrying in 1995.

Sadly, she said, by 2005, Jocelyn was living in that home all alone. Joyce and her husband, Phillip Young, made the nearly two-hundred-mile trip to visit as often as every other weekend, and at least once a month, throughout Jocelyn's marriage and afterward.

When asked about firearms, Joyce said that she'd seen a rifle in the house when Wesley lived there but never saw it after he moved out and never once saw a handgun in the home.

The emotional stakes escalated when Assistant Commonwealth's Attorney Wes Nance directed Joyce to tell the jury about the last time she saw her daughter. It was the weekend before her death, Joyce recalled, and Jocelyn and Maysa Munsey had rented a van to transport her Christmas gift to West Virginia. They'd arrived at Joyce's home late Friday night, unloaded the van Saturday around noon, then left soon after because they didn't want to be caught in the ice storm predicted for that evening.

Joyce said that the last time she'd talked to her daughter was by phone on Monday night. "She was bubbly, laughing, very upbeat—just looking forward to finishing with work and having some time to relax."

Jocelyn had made many plans past December 19, Joyce said. "We had a joke with the stockings." She faltered and added, "Never mind." An overcome Joyce hung her head, struggling for composure.

Defense attorney Joey Sanzone had the most difficult job with this witness. He had to elicit information for his client without seeming to browbeat the victim's mother—an impression that could turn the jurors against the defense's case in a flash. He began his cross-examination carefully. He said, "Ms. Young, I apologize for your loss, but I need to ask a few questions. When it came to Jocelyn, she arrived that weekend with Maysa Munsey, not with Marcy Shepherd. And were you aware that Marcy and Jocelyn [had] a relationship?"

The answer was stillborn when Nance blurted out an objection. The jury was dismissed and Sanzone argued that it was relevant because unless Joyce knew about that relationship and the trip to the police with Maysa, then she didn't really have an intimate knowledge of Jocelyn's state of mind. "Judge, they are attempting to introduce this happy-go-lucky person having a wonderful time, and she's up here getting somebody arrested and out of jail."

"No," Judge Updike said. "She didn't get—there's no evidence that Jocelyn got Maysa arrested."

"She took—brought her up here, Judge, for the purpose of talking to the police so that she could be processed and released. And that's not a happy event. And we should be able to show this unhappy event," Sanzone insisted.

The judge, however, felt that Maysa's arrest was peripheral to the case and ruled that line of questioning inadmissible.

As far as Joyce's knowledge of the Marcy–Jocelyn relationship, Sanzone wanted to impeach the credibility of the witness; however, the judge ruled it "improper impeachment . . . This court finds that there's insufficient evidence and insufficient foundation, I should say, to relevance. Objection is sustained."

Sanzone brushed off that defeat and instead asked

Joyce about looking through drawers and closets. Joyce admitted that she didn't know there wasn't a gun; she just knew that she never saw or heard of one. She had also never seen condoms in the house and "I would not talk to [my] daughter about that."

When Joyce was asked if she had the security code and key to Jocelyn's house and if she knew of anyone else who did, she answered that she had both and thought that Jennifer Kerns would, as well.

The next witness was Jocelyn's sister, Laura Rogers. When Laura met her mother coming down from the witness stand, they hugged. Joey Sanzone objected to that display in front of the jury.

Laura described the rooms and layout of her sister's home, where she often visited, particularly after Jocelyn's separation from Wesley. While the couple was still living together, Laura had stayed in their home and taken care of their pets when they traveled to Canada to the Kernses' vacation cabin.

Laura told the jurors that there had been a gun safe in the bedroom shortly after the separation, but then it and other things were gone. After that the only firearm that Laura saw in her sister's home was the shotgun in the walk-in closet, sitting in the corner next to Jocelyn's sweaters. "Jocelyn and I weren't strangers to weapons," she said. "When we were growing up, our father took us out with a rifle to shoot cans and targets."

The last time Laura saw Jocelyn was the Thanksgiving holiday in 2007. She said that they had gone "nonstop shopping until we dropped" on Black Friday. "Jocelyn loved Christmas and loved the holidays . . . We had breakfast together the morning she was leaving—she was happy." She spoke to Jocelyn on the phone the weekend before she died, and they'd discussed last-minute shopping and plans to get together for the holidays.

Joey Sanzone handled her with delicacy, too, when it came time for cross-examination. He asked her about the condoms that had been found at Jocelyn's house. Laura said that she'd visited Jocelyn for her birthday in October and that when she'd opened that drawer, the prophylactics had not been there.

Before they left on lunch recess, the judge ordered an early return for the lawyers, to allow the defense to make a "proffer," an offer of evidence in support of an argument. In the courtroom, when one side is denied the right to introduce evidence, if that party wants to preserve the issue for appeal, he must introduce it into the record, out of the presence of the jury.

Joey Sanzone called Joyce Young back to stand. He questioned her about how many times she'd seen Marcy, but Joyce could not give a specific answer. When Sanzone asked her about Maysa Munsey, Joyce did know the last time she saw her was the weekend before her daughter died. She denied any knowledge about the criminal problem Maysa had had at the Amherst Sheriff's Office.

When her testimony was completed, Sanzone asked Judge Updike to reconsider his decision about that line of questioning. The judge still did not see the material as relevant.

TWENTY-SEVEN

When the jury returned to their seats, prosecutor Wes Nance called Deputy Jason Jones to the stand. "I arrived at the scene with a backup officer and I noticed two women standing on the front porch of the residence. And they appeared to be crying. We walked up, asked them what was wrong. They said that their friend was lying inside and they thought she was dead. We entered inside the house. I noticed when we entered inside—I was the first one that entered. I noticed that it was extremely hot. I looked to my right. I saw a white female lying on her back, appeared to be unresponsive."

The Commonwealth used Deputy Jones to enter photographs of the house exterior, Jocelyn's body, the thermostat, and the firearm into evidence as he described the pictures and his actions at the scene.

Joey Sanzone stepped up to cross-examine Deputy Jones. "Deputy . . ." he said, "if somebody is concerned about the safety of an elderly person, a friend, a husband in a house and they're not responding to the door—you get called in to those kinds of situations fairly frequently, don't you?"

"Yes, sir."

"In fact, doesn't the sheriff's department encourage people to do that sort of thing so that you can assist? You're professionally trained?"

"We provide a service," Jones said. "It's called welfare check and—just to go and check on the well-being of people. They may have a family member that lives maybe in another jurisdiction. And we go by if they can't, make contact with them, just do a well-being check and make sure they're okay."

Sanzone continued, "Now, on the day that we're talking about here, December twentieth of two thousand seven, no one called you that morning to ask that you go by and check on this residence, did they?"

"No . . ."

"And the first . . . you heard about anything at Jocelyn Earnest's residence was a call when you went there and these two women were there."

"Yes, sir."

"Once you assessed the situation you really wanted to preserve the scene of whatever was going on there, didn't you?"

"Yes, sir, because I didn't know what I had at the time."

Sanzone prodded, "But you couldn't control what happened before you got there."

"No, sir."

"And when you got there the house was open. You could get in."

"Yeah."

"And you have no idea of your own personal knowledge, what may have gone on in that house concerning the body and those two people before you got there."

"At that time, I didn't know."

"Could not have protected that crime scene."

"Not before I got there, no, sir."

Sanzone asked if he checked identification to be certain that Maysa Munsey and Marcy Shepherd were who they claimed to be.

"I did."

". . . Did you ask them to remain until the investigators got there?"

"I did."

"Because that's just standard operating procedure."

"Yes, sir."

Sanzone went on to the point that was pivotal to the defense strategy. "Were you informed of any romantic relationship?"

"No, sir."

"And when it came to the two of them, after you arrived, they weren't restricted from making phone calls or anything of that nature, were they?"

"No, sir."

When Sanzone had no further questions and Nance had nothing on redirect, Deputy Jason Jones eased out of the witness box with great relief.

———

Investigator Gary Babb stepped into the witness box next. He had served in law enforcement for more than twenty years, starting in Bedford County investigations in 1999. Babb talked about his conversation with Deputy Jones when he arrived at the scene. Then, he moved on to the suicide note. "There was a white sheet of paper, copier paper size, laying facedown. Any writing would have been facedown because it was just white on the outside.

"Before I entered the house I had put on gloves. And I told him," he said, referring to Jones, "that's probably the note there. And when I did, I reached down, picked it up by the edges, and turned it like this," he said, demonstrating how he'd handled the paper. "Looked at it, read it, and placed it back so it would be in the exact position for the forensic guys once they got there."

Prosecutor Wes Nance used Babb to introduce photographs of the crime scene and the position of the note on the floor, and Babb read the contents of the note to the jury.

Investigator Mike Mayhew was the next to testify. He had twenty-one years of experience with the Bedford County Sheriff's Office and had been an investigator for seven years of that time.

He told the jurors that he arrived at 12:48 that Thursday afternoon. "It's a really pretty neighborhood. Each house is—they keep their yards nice," he said, noting that

In 2001, Jocelyn Earnest *(left)* and her sister, Laura Rogers *(right)*, traveled to Antietam National Battlefield in Sharpsburg, Maryland, with their father.

Bill Branham

Jocelyn was the matron of honor at her sister Laura's wedding, on October 4, 2004.

Bill Branham

Jocelyn with her beloved dog, Rufus, who was found in a kennel in the Pine Bluff house on the day Jocelyn's body was discovered in the living room of her home.

Bill Branham

Four friends gathered together during good times in 1997 *(left to right)*: Bob Kerns, Jennifer Landis, Wesley Earnest, and Jocelyn Earnest.
Jennifer Kerns

Wesley and Jocelyn Earnest at the wedding of Bob and Jennifer Kerns in 1998.
Jennifer Kerns

Jocelyn and Wesley on a hike at Crabtree Falls in Montebello, Nelson County, Virginia, in the summer of 2001.
Jennifer Kerns

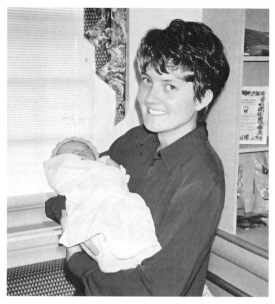

Jocelyn holding Bob and Jennifer's son at the hospital, shortly after he was born in 2002.

Jennifer Kerns

Friends planned an "Almost 40 party" for Jocelyn while she was out on an excursion with her sister. Jennifer *(left)* and Jocelyn *(right)*.   *Jennifer Kerns*

The Kerns's rustic cabin in Canada, where Jocelyn Earnest spent time nearly every summer in the last ten years of her life. *Jocelyn Earnest, courtesy of Laura Rogers*

The boat the Kerns used for fishing and puttering about on the lake when they were staying at the cabin.
Jocelyn Earnest, courtesy of Laura Rogers

Jocelyn in a contemplative moment by the fire on the shore of the lake in Canada.
Jennifer Kerns

Wesley and Jocelyn showing off the fish they caught one summer at the lake at the Kerns's family cabin.
Jennifer Kerns

Jocelyn in a lighthearted moment teasing Wesley with a fishing-bait earthworm beside the lake.
Jennifer Kerns

The three-bedroom-two-bath home on Pine Bluff Drive located in a woodsy community in Forest, Virginia, where Jocelyn and Wesley Earnest lived together after their marriage, and where Jocelyn was found shot dead just beyond the front door in December 2007.   *Diane Fanning*

On Smith Mountain Lake, Wesley Earnest's $1.3 million dollar testament-to-his-success lake house was fully engulfed in the flames of a suspicious fire in March 2009. Arson was suspected, but no charges were ever filed.   *David Wilson*

Detective Gary Babb, on December 20, 2007, at the crime scene on Pine Bluff Drive on the morning that Jocelyn's body was discovered—his first stop in an investigation to put Jocelyn's killer behind bars.

Bedford County Commonwealth's Attorney Office

Inked Print

Latent Print

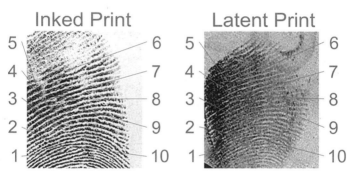

The chart used in the courtroom to demonstrate to the jury the comparison between the known fingerprint of Wesley Earnest *(left)* and the unknown latent print *(right)* found on the "suicide note" at the scene of the crime.

Bedford County Commonwealth's Attorney Office

The Smith and Wesson .357 short-barrel revolver—registered in Wesley Earnest's name—that investigators found on the body of Jocelyn Earnest and later identified as the weapon that fired the shot that ended her life.

Bedford County Commonwealth's Attorney Office

Mike Mayhew, Bedford County Sheriff's deputy, one of the investigators of the Jocelyn Earnest homicide.
Diane Fanning

Joey Sanzone, one of Wesley Earnest's defense attorneys.
Joseph A. Sanzone

Assistant Commonwealth's Attorney Wes Nance led the prosecutions of Wesley Earnest for the murder of his estranged wife, Jocelyn Earnest.
Diane Fanning

the homes were all about three hundred feet apart on both sides of the road, and that the neighborhood was separated from another nearby neighborhood by a little bit of wooded area.

Mayhew described the Earnests' home, with its wooden front porch and rounded picture window in the front and the swimming pool and toolshed behind it. He took photographs of the exterior of the home and the surrounding landscape before moving inside.

The next morning, November 10, 2010, Mayhew again took his place in the witness box as Wes Nance continued his direct examination. Mayhew had ended his testimony the day before with a discussion of finding firearms and ammunition in the walk-in closet of the master bedroom and elsewhere in the home, but today picked up with a description of Jocelyn's green Honda, backed into the driveway. From the trunk of her car, he collected a Toshiba laptop for forensic analysis.

On cross-examination, defense attorney Joey Sanzone directed the investigator to three documents: one showing the purchase of the murder weapon on July 14, 1999; another showing that Wesley completed the requirement to get that permit on April 24, 1999; and a third dating Wesley's concealed weapons permit on April 30, 1999. Then he said, "So both the permit and the passage of the pistol safety course occurred before this pistol was purchased."

"That is correct," Mayhew said.

"So, it would have been impossible to use this pistol to pass that course."

"That's correct."

"And that would mean that he used another pistol to pass that course," Sanzone said, attempting to create distance between his client and the murder weapon.

"That's what it would lead one to believe, yes."

". . . In your conversations with him, you're aware of him . . ." Sanzone began.

"Objection, Your Honor. That's hearsay, Your Honor."

"Well, it's from the defendant, but that's fine," Sanzone said. Turning back to the investigator on the stand, he continued: "You said there were two empty cartridges in that handgun."

"That's correct."

". . . And you only found evidence of one bullet being fired there at the scene."

"That is correct."

"So you don't know if the second bullet was fired after that or before that."

"No, sir, I do not."

". . . And you really looked around that house to see if there was any evidence anywhere of another bullet fragment, another hole in the wall . . . You all looked very carefully."

"Yes; me and several other investigators, that's correct."

Moving on to the victim's body, Sanzone established that Jocelyn was dressed for the outdoors and said, "You took care to make sure that no one did anything with her body until it had been examined by the medical examiner."

"That is correct."

"Including taking care to make sure that the area of her hands was preserved . . . so there wouldn't be any contaminants."

"That's correct."

". . . There's been a lot of evidence gathered in this case but in the course of the gathering of that evidence did you collect Marcy Shepherd's or Maysa Munsey's cell phones?"

"Yes, it was collected."

"But not on the day you found them there at the house."

"No, sir."

"You would agree with me that if somebody . . . tells you that they've been in communication with a person who's now lying there dead that you would want to see that communication or hear it if you could."

"Later, after the thing, yes, you would want to do that."

". . . And you agree with me also that as time passes, your ability to get that evidence may not be there."

"There is that possibility," Mayhew admitted.

". . . Did Marcy Shepherd tell you on that day that she had text messages on her phone to and from Jocelyn Earnest?" Sanzone pressed.

"No, on that day, she did not."

"And . . ."

Commonwealth's Attorney Krantz popped to his feet, objecting to the line of questioning. Judge Updike cut him off and sent the jury out of the courtroom.

When the room was cleared, Krantz objected to "any reference or innuendo by Mr. Sanzone that Marcy Shepherd or anyone else is a suspect or wrongdoer in this case, unless or until he meets the legal threshold of establishing with particularity as established by the Supreme Court to enter third-party guilt in this case [. . .] And to suggest that to the jury, Your Honor, is not within the scope of the Supreme Court's ruling. We're just asking Mr. Sanzone to follow that law."

"I intend to follow the law, Judge, but I don't agree with their characterization," Sanzone shot back. He argued that Marcy was the only person scheduled to meet with Jocelyn at the time of death.

Krantz countered that by citing the complete cooperation of Marcy and Maysa with law enforcement and added that the defense was not offering any evidence of actual guilt by either woman.

Sanzone disputed the women's cooperation, pointing to Maysa's plea of ignorance of details in the Amherst County case and Marcy for not revealing the romantic relationship or text messages at the scene.

"So, all of these facts, Judge, and the fact that people are present, that they are doing things to impede the investigation—and now I think that those very acts impede our ability to look back and accurately determine what happened."

"Last comment," Krantz said. "Nothing plus nothing equals nothing . . . There is nothing that Mr. Sanzone can point to that shows the actual guilt of anyone else. It is just intended to confuse and mislead the jury."

". . . Well, I guess since it's the Commonwealth's motion, they get the last word," Sanzone said.

"Y'all finished?" the judge asked. When the lawyers agreed that they were, he stated that it would not be fair to prevent the defense from offering evidence that someone other than the defendant killed Jocelyn Earnest. "But any evidence has to be admissible evidence, has to be relevant evidence . . . Guesswork or speculation has got no place in a court of law." He continued, "If the Commonwealth puts these women on and asks them about finding the body and being there before the police officers . . . if Mr. Sanzone wants to ask either one of them, 'Did you kill Jocelyn Earnest?', you can ask them. You can ask the police officer if you want . . . Anybody who was there because anybody who was there and had the opportunity, you can ask them. That's cross-examination."

The judge cautioned, "This business of the relationship . . . between Ms. Shepherd and Ms. Earnest, as far as whether that proves anything concerning the death, I don't even really have to get there. I've already got in evidence a note that talks about a new love. And if she gets on the stand and testifies . . . she loved Jocelyn, then the nature of the relationship is going to come out as far as bias, prejudice, motive, fabrication."

However, Updike warned the defense, "Now, Mr. Sanzone . . . if you want to proffer evidence on your own . . . you're going to have to show . . . it clearly points to some other person . . . But if it's might have, could have, should have, or that kind of stuff, possibility, then that to me just becomes an issue of letting the jury guess or speculate. They're not supposed to guess or speculate. Neither am I. Neither is anyone else in the courtroom."

After the jury returned, Joey Sanzone focused his questions back on Marcy's phone, forcing Investigator Mayhew to admit that he had not seized her cell until two weeks after the murder, and that during that time, Marcy had had the ability to alter or delete any messages.

The defense then turned to the possibility that one of the policemen could have moved the body before Mayhew arrived at the scene. All the investigator could say with any certainty was that they told him they had not.

Using crime scene photos, Joey Sanzone asked a series of questions about what the investigator had found there. "Has anyone come forward and said, 'I was using the bathroom on the day that or on the day before the blood and hair were found'?"

"No, sir."

"Has anyone come forward and said, 'That's my blood in the sink'?"

"No, sir."

After a break for lunch, Nance conducted his redirect examination, asking the investigator about Maysa's and Marcy's demeanor the day the body was discovered.

"Very upset, crying, upset of the whole situation," Mayhew said.

On recross, Sanzone asked if Marcy had, on that same day, revealed anything about her romantic relationship with Jocelyn.

"Not to me, she didn't."

TWENTY-EIGHT

The next witness to testify was Jennifer Kerns, a registered nurse and good friend of Jocelyn Earnest's. "We became friends pretty much right away. We had a lot in common to begin with—we both played college basketball and had a lot of similar interests. I would say the friendship began immediately and just continued to strengthen each day through the next twelve years or more until her death."

Jennifer said that they saw each other several times a week, meeting at her house, at Jocelyn's house, or meeting for lunch. She added that she often came with her children to use the swimming pool at Jocelyn's home.

Prosecutor Wes Nance asked about the firearm that Jennifer saw in Jocelyn's house in late 2005.

"There was a shotgun propped up inside—right inside the doorway of the master bedroom walk-in closet,"

Jennifer said. Nance followed up by asking if Jennifer had ever seen the firearm after that one incident.

"No, I did not," she replied.

"Did you ever see a handgun in Jocelyn Earnest's home after Mr. Earnest moved from the residence?"

"No, I did not."

Nor, Jennifer said as she was questioned further, had she ever seen a handgun anywhere in Jocelyn's possession or in her vehicle, which Jennifer rode in frequently.

"Now, in your frequent contact with Jocelyn Earnest, were you able to observe her demeanor and reaction . . . to the separation from Wesley Earnest?"

"Yes."

Sanzone rose again, "Judge, we object to this. It calls for speculation on the part of this witness."

After a brief argument, the judge overruled his objection. It only took one more question and answer before Sanzone objected again when the witness described what the two of them did together. This time the judge sustained it, instructing Jennifer to describe what she observed, not offer conclusions or interpretations or opinions.

Nance started, once again, asking about Jocelyn's state of mind immediately following her separation from Wesley. "What predominant emotion did you observe from Jocelyn Earnest during that time period?"

"Sadness."

"Was there an incident that you were personally present for in March of 2006 that appeared to change her general demeanor?"

"Yes."

The defense voiced another objection. "Your Honor, we object because it does not reference my client and his attitude towards Ms. Earnest."

"Objection of relevancy," said Judge Updike. "I'm not going to comment at this point other than to say that the objection is overruled."

Nance asked, "Ma'am, I'm going to turn your attention to March of 2006 . . . Were you aware of a lake house on Smith Mountain Lake built by the Earnests?"

"Yes."

"And in March 2006, did you go with Jocelyn Earnest to that lake house?"

"Yes."

". . . Could you explain to the jury . . ."

Sanzone interrupted, "Judge, I have a motion outside the presence of the jury."

Updike sent out the jury and Sanzone continued. "Judge, I assume what we're going to hear is that Ms. Earnest went and watched through a window and saw an interaction between Mr. Earnest and a female. Mr. Earnest didn't say anything to her that day, didn't do anything. And this is all about Ms. Earnest. Doesn't have anything to do with my client. And, in order for them to show some sort of contentiousness, motivation, something of that nature, they need to show something regarding Mr. Earnest, not Ms. Earnest."

"Isn't the possibility of suicide also an issue in this case?" the judge asked.

"Judge, we are not arguing suicide at all," Sanzone said.

"Is he conceding that it's not a suicide, Your Honor?" prosecutor Krantz interjected.

"Judge, I don't know. I don't have the burden of proof."

"That's true," the judge agreed. ". . . I'm just asking a question that because of the note that was found in the area of the body and the nature of the note, does not the Commonwealth have the burden of proving beyond a reasonable doubt that this death was not a suicide?"

"The only reference to my client in that note is having to do with finances," Sanzone argued.

"There have been objections as far as the state of mind of Ms. Earnest is concerned," Updike said. "I feel that such evidence is relevant to the issue of whether or not she died as a result of suicide. That's my ruling and my feeling . . . Let me just ask this question out of the presence of the jury: What is this testimony, Mr. Nance?"

"Your Honor, this is evidence on marital infidelity on the part of Mr. Earnest," Nance answered, adding, upon question of relevancy from the judge, "Your Honor, I believe the relevance is two-fold. First of all, its impact on Jocelyn Earnest—we would anticipate Ms. Kerns's testimony is that she went from being sad to more determined and ready to move on past this marriage. But also, the relevance of marital infidelity is relevant pursuant to the marital disharmony . . . and lack of bliss . . . *Cantrell versus Commonwealth* . . . states: in the prosecution of murder of one's spouse, the Commonwealth may introduce evidence of marital infidelity to show marital disharmony."

"But, Judge, in those cases, they're talking about somebody that gets mad because the spouse is over here having an affair with somebody and the incident is related to that affair. That's not the case here at all," Sanzone said. "And for them to say . . . she became more determined and ready to move on and abandon the relationship, I don't think even fits the theory that the court has cited here. It's just simply intended to show a bad act. It's nothing more than some sort of prior bad act on the part of my client regarding fidelity and intended simply to cast him in a bad light and create sympathy."

"Okay, Counsel," the judge responded. "I understand the argument. The objection is overruled. The evidence will be presented. Objection's noted and preserved."

The jury returned to the courtroom, and Nance returned to his line of questioning. Jennifer described the day that she and Jocelyn observed Wesley and Shameka Wright engaged in an intimate act at the Smith Mountain Lake house. When she said, "Jocelyn got angry and said, 'This is it. I'm done. I'm over this,'" she brought Joey Sanzone to his feet.

"Judge, now I object: hearsay. And they know we object."

"Your Honor, it's not offered for the proof," Nance said. "I believe explanations are merely a verbal act, and they're not coming in for the truth of the matter asserted."

"The court understands the objection is on the grounds of hearsay. The objection is overruled," Updike said.

Amidst repeated interruptions from the defense, Jennifer continued to describe Jocelyn banging on the window, waving and shouting into the house.

Wes Nance also had Jennifer give her testimony regarding the night in February 2007 when she encountered Wesley outside of Jocelyn's home dressed in dark clothing with a hood pulled tightly over his head.

The witness told the jury about the last time she was in Jocelyn's home on December 7, 2007, after volleyball practice. Nance asked, "Were you able to observe her demeanor in December of '07?"

"Yes."

"What did you see? Tell the jury."

"She was excited, looking forward to Christmas, anxious to give my children the Christmas presents that she had purchased for them."

"Judge," Sanzone objected again. "That's not a proper response. Demeanor is not—that does not deal with demeanor."

"I think it does," Updike said. "Overruled."

"If you could finish the thought that you had," Nance said to the witness.

"Looking forward to seeing them open their gifts—happy, excited, jovial."

On that remark, the direct examination ended and Blair Sanzone, Joey's daughter and co-counsel, began the cross. "Ms. Kerns, you and Jocelyn were such good friends that you had the alarm code to the Pine Bluff home; is that correct?"

"Yes."

"And you were an authorized user through the actual alarm company; is that correct?"

"Yes."

". . . And you had a key to that home on Pine Bluff; is that correct?"

"Yes."

"Who else had a key to that home that you know of?" Blair Sanzone asked.

"Maysa Munsey."

"And who else had the alarm code to the Pine Bluff home?"

"Maysa Munsey."

"And anyone else that you know of?"

"No."

"You would often spend the night at Jocelyn's home on Pine Bluff; is that correct?"

That was not correct; Jennifer replied that she had spent the night once in 2006, but not at all in 2007 or 2005.

"The last time you had any contact with Wesley Earnest was in the winter of 2007; is that correct?" Blair Sanzone continued.

"In the driveway, yes."

"And the last time you have any personal knowledge of Jocelyn Earnest and Wesley Earnest having any contact face-to-face with one another was that [. . .] night [. . .] is that correct?"

"They did not have face-to-face contact that night."

"Then, when was the last time that you personally know of that they had face-to-face contact? What was the date of that or approximate date?"

"The last time that I know of was the day I went to court with Jocelyn, one of their last hearings."

"And that was December 2006, was that correct?"

"I guess."

"Now, you said that you know that Jocelyn and Wesley separated from one another in 2005. That's when you would consider them to be living in two separate households."

"Yes."

"And when you and Jocelyn were spying up at the lake house in Moneta in March of 2006, they'd been separated since 2005 by that time. Many months had passed, correct?"

"They were not living together at the time."

"Right," Blair Sanzone said with a nod. "And he was living in Chesapeake, Virginia, working down there. Did you know that?"

"I did not have personal knowledge of where he was living."

"And did you know at that time, that night in March of 2006 when you were up at the lake house spying that Jocelyn was romantically involved with Marcy Shepherd?"

Both members of the prosecution team jumped to their feet with objections, and the judge sent the jury out of the courtroom once again. After hearing from both sides, the judge ruled in favor of the prosecution, saying, "Putting aside whether there was or was not a relationship, it's my ruling that whether this witness knew or did not know of such relationship, if it did exist, that is irrelevant. Objection is sustained."

Blair Sanzone switched to another line of questioning. "In December of 2006, you and Jocelyn went to the lake house in Moneta, didn't you?"

"Yes, we did."

"And you two actually took a big van that afternoon that you went; is that correct?"

"Yes."

"And when you were there at the lake house property, you two entered that property and you essentially cleaned out the lake house of all content that you two could fit in that van, is that correct?"

"No, that is not correct."

"Did you two remove furniture from the lake house property?"

"We removed some items of furniture but not all the furniture."

"And you removed all sorts of personal items, anything you could fit in that van, isn't that correct?"

"No, that's not correct."

"What did you put in that van?"

"We put in the van a chest coffee table, a tan-colored sectional sofa, a tan colored love seat, a twin mattress that was still in the package. We put in the van a tool belt and toolbox and some tile that was leftover from tiling of the bathroom and the kitchen. We took a few silk plants, a television, a DVD player, and a blue and white rug and a bedspread."

"And you, of course, didn't take inventory of that; write down exactly what you took that day."

"I know what we took that day [. . .] Those items were

stored in my home for six to eight months after that. So I know what we took because it was stored in my home."

"And Ms. Earnest took some of the property back to her place, didn't she?"

"No, she did not, not until months later."

Blair Sanzone badgered her about that day a bit longer and then asked, "Now, up until December 2007, you said you were able to go to Jocelyn's house whenever you wanted to. She gave you sort of unfettered access to her home; is that correct?"

"Yes, as she had to mine."

Blair Sanzone asked whether Jennifer went "snooping through [Jocelyn's] drawers," which Jennifer denied. "I actually went into her drawers and cabinets and cupboards to clean, straighten, rearrange, and organize her things."

"And you didn't go through every single drawer with the purpose of looking to see if a handgun was there or not, at any point, up until December nineteenth, 2007."

"I would have no cause to look for a handgun. She didn't have one."

"And when you were going through those drawers, did you come across condoms?"

"After they no longer lived together, no. There were none in the bedroom."

"So as far as you know in December of 2007, there were no condoms in drawers in her home to your personal knowledge."

"I did not look in her drawers in December," Jennifer said.

Blair Sanzone asked a few other questions about

whether the shotgun was too big to fit in a drawer, and what sports Jocelyn played, then turned her attention to Jocelyn's street.

"You can park along Pine Bluff, isn't that correct? There's a space for you to pull over, you know, on either side of the road and park down the street or up the street . . ."

"Yes."

"Who else did you know who was also staying in [Jocelyn's] home, if anyone, in December of 2007?"

"I do not know of anyone."

Blair Sanzone passed the witness over to Wes Nance for redirect. He asked just two questions. "Ms. Kerns, Ms. Sanzone made reference to your ability to park on Pine Bluff Drive. And it's a residential neighborhood, isn't that right?"

"Yes."

"In the winter of 2007, though, did you see the vehicle that Mr. Earnest was driving when you had that conversation with him that night?"

"There were no vehicles on the road at all on either side anywhere near Jocelyn's home," Jennifer said.

Robert Kerns took the oath to testify after his wife stepped down from the stand. He said, "I originally met Wes in the mid-nineties when playing golf in Bedford County . . . We became friends through playing golf. Also, we played a lot of volleyball together. And through volleyball, I met Jocelyn. And then our wives [. . .] became best friends at that point."

He said that then they spent a lot of time together

doing couples' things. "While the marriage was intact, I was closer to Wesley. After it was dissolved, closer to Jocelyn because she spent a lot of time at the house and Wesley was living outside of Lynchburg."

In response to the Commonwealth's questions, Bob told the jurors about the breakfast meeting he'd had with Wesley in the fall of 2007. He explained Wesley's concerns regarding his credit, financial obligations, and being forced into an untimely sale of the lake house.

On cross, Joey Sanzone jumped right into that meeting. "He explained to you that [. . .] they were paying the bills, didn't he? He explained to you that the bills were being paid."

"Yes."

"And he told you that they were selling the rental house."

"I don't recall that. He may have. I don't recall a discussion of the rental house."

"If I told you that the rental house was sold and they received . . . a hundred and thirty-seven [thousand] dollars from the sale of that house, you wouldn't disagree with me, would you?"

"All I know is he communicated to me that he was desperate enough for cash that he took things from the house basically to sell."

"Well, I know that's your claim here today. What did he sell? Tell the jury what he sold."

"He did not tell me what he took," Bob said. "I know through other sources what was taken from the house." When pressed on this point by Sanzone, Bob admitted,

"After four years, I do not recall specifically what he told me he took from the house to sell." Nor did he know how much money Wesley might have gotten for any of those items, nor from the sale of the rental house.

"You don't know any of the specifics of any of the other financial amounts that they were dealing with," Sanzone said.

"Specific amounts, no, sir."

"And essentially, the entire nature of the conversation was he just wanted you to talk to Jocelyn to make sure that his opinion that they try to sell the . . . lake house and realize the most from it was what he wanted you to convey. That's the only specific you recall about financial detail."

Bob started to talk about Wesley's credit, and Sanzone cut him off, but Krantz objected. "He's allowed to answer his question."

"All right," Judge Updike said. "Sustain that. Allow the witness to answer."

Bob continued, "He described what his finances were and that his credit was being destroyed and that he was strapped because of [. . .] his obligations to the lake house mortgage and trying to meet other financial obligations and that's why he took items from the home."

"Well, I'm not asking you to repeat your narrative every time I ask you a question."

"Now, Mr. Sanzone . . ." the judge admonished.

"I'm asking . . ."

Updike cut him off. "Mr. Sanzone, don't instruct the witnesses. Now if [. . .] any counsel has a problem with the conduct of a witness [. . .] ask me to address it. Okay?"

"Judge, then, I would ask that the witness be instructed to be responsive to my questions."

"All right, sir. I feel, at this time, that instruction is not necessary, not appropriate."

"All right," Sanzone said and then asked the witness, "What specific credit matters were causing any trouble?"

"He just mentioned that, in general, his credit was being damaged."

"So my original question was . . . what specific detail you can recall about the finances of the lake house?"

"His credit was being damaged because of the lake house, yes, sir."

"And you have no . . . knowledge of any of the specifics about the credit."

"No, sir."

"You have no knowledge of any of the specifics about how much he made a month, how much was being spent a month."

"He did share with me the mortgage on the house . . . Forty-seven hundred, somewhere in the forty-sevens, mid-forties."

"And they were splitting that?"

"No. I think he had a larger share of responsibility for the lake house. It was not an even split."

"Mr. Kerns, are you confusing what took place with a December hearing before the Bedford County Circuit Court and an escrow agreement with the conversation that occurred before December of 2006?"

"I was not party to that hearing."

"Well, the seventy-five, twenty-five comes out of that . . . Did you know that?"

Bob said he did not.

"As far as your relationship with Wesley, you were on Jocelyn's side of their disagreements after 2005."

"Not necessarily. From a financial standpoint, what he told me that morning made sense. And that's why I communicated it to Jocelyn . . . I think anyone with any sense of economics would say that if they sold the lake house quickly, they were due to lose money. If they waited until the market turned, they'd make money. And I believed him when he said he was financially strapped."

When asked, Bob said that he'd seen Jocelyn at least once a week but denied knowing either Marcy Shepherd or Maysa Munsey and was not aware of his wife spending any time with either woman. He also did not know about any phone calls to or from Marcy or Maysa to his home.

He also denied ever having seen condoms in Jocelyn's drawers, telling Sanzone, "I never looked in drawers." Nor did he know of any people other than Wesley's brother, Tyler, who might've been living at her house in 2007.

"My last question is: do you know if any of these financial problems or all of these financial problems we're talking about was solved with the sale of the rental property?" Joey Sanzone asked.

"I have no idea." To Bob's great relief, neither attorney had any further questions.

TWENTY-NINE

Shari Irving, an employee of Genworth Financial for twenty-five years, was the next witness for the prosecution.

"When did you start to work for Jocelyn Earnest?" Assistant Commonwealth's Attorney Wes Nance asked.

"In early 2007."

When asked about Jocelyn's demeanor, Shari replied, "She was very upbeat. She smiled all the time. She was very encouraging. I appreciated her management style. She was a people person. She cared about the people who worked for her. She had a plan for us for our professional development. And she cared about our personal life, our families. She always asked about [. . .] my family, my grandchild. She just helped all the people that worked for her in any way she could professionally. She was a big fan of the Life is Good merchandise. And she had a lot of us in the office buying that merchandise. You would see cups and little signs pop up on people's desks that said 'Life is Good.' And that's just the kind of person she was," Shari said, noting, "I did very much enjoy working for her. She was one of the best bosses that I've had in the twenty-five years with the company."

"Did you ever see her outside of work or was it strictly at work?"

"I did see her occasionally outside of work, usually for work functions. She did invite some of her direct reports to her home once or twice for an occasion."

"During the entire time that you interacted with Jocelyn Earnest did you ever see her in possession of a handgun?"

"No, I did not." Shari also told the jury that Jocelyn did not bring a purse to work but did carry a laptop bag back and forth. On multiple occasions, she had seen Jocelyn packing and unpacking that bag and she never saw a weapon in there, either.

Shari discussed the meeting they'd had late afternoon on December 19, 2007. She stayed at work afterward to retrieve documents, and later that night at 6:53 P.M. sent Jocelyn an email requesting overtime pay, as per procedure. Nance produced the reply Shari received from Jocelyn at 7:28 P.M., approving the overtime.

In response to defense attorney Joey Sanzone's questions, Shari explained Genworth's management structure and said that she'd had no contact with Jocelyn on the morning of December 19, 2007, but that afternoon there had been a system failure that ultimately caused the overtime work.

Sanzone noted that Jocelyn Earnest had "worked with y'all on it until quarter to six."

"Yes."

"But then she had to leave."

"Yes."

"And she never indicated that she was going to come back that evening, did she?"

"No."

"Now . . . if she had an appointment, she could have returned—she would have been able to get into the office and work on the problem, couldn't she?"

"She could," Shari said.

"Did you know Maysa Munsey?" Sanzone asked.

"I know who Maysa Munsey is, yes."

"Did you ever see Maysa Munsey over there visiting with Jocelyn in her office?"

"Yes . . . once or twice a week maybe."

"Do you know Marcy Shepherd?"

"Yes."

"How often would Marcy Shepherd be over there?"

"About the same time."

"Do you know Jennifer Kerns?"

"No."

"Have you ever seen Wesley Earnest prior to December nineteenth . . . 2007?"

"No."

Other colleagues of Jocelyn's from Genworth Financial were called to the stand and had similar memories of her positive attitude.

Lisa Cawthorne described her as "very happy [. . .] very upbeat, very excited. And towards the end of the year, she was more excited about the holidays and being able to spend it with her family." Lisa told the jury that she'd had a late afternoon meeting with a very upbeat Jocelyn on the day she died.

Blair Sanzone conducted the cross-examination, eliciting that Lisa had never seen Wesley before December 2007 and, although she knew of Maysa Munsey professionally, they worked in different offices; ditto Marcy Shepherd, although Marcy had collaborated on a project that brought her out to Lisa's office about once a month.

Blair asked about December 19, "And did she [Jocelyn] tell you she had dinner planned with Marcy Shepherd that evening?"

"She did not."

"Did she tell you anything about her evening [plans] on December the nineteenth?"

"No, she did not."

Pam Gillespie, another Genworth Financial employee, described Jocelyn as "very friendly and always was interested in how you were doing after work and if you had problems at work."

Pam had helped organize the Christmas dinner on

December 18, 2007, and recalled Jocelyn as "very happy, glad to be there, went around, talked to just about everybody."

On cross-examination, Blair Sanzone determined that Pam had never seen or heard from Wesley Earnest, nor had she witnessed Jocelyn receive any phone calls or text messages from Wesley.

After Pam Gillespie stepped down, a fourth Genworth staff person took her place. Gary Brandt had only begun working there a couple of months before Jocelyn died.

Wes Nance used Gary's presence on the stand to enter into evidence a photograph from his camera taken of employees at the Christmas party, the night before Jocelyn was murdered. On cross, Blair Sanzone asked if Gary ever saw Wesley Earnest or received any phone calls or emails from him. Brandt said "no" to all three. Then she asked if he knew Maysa Munsey or Marcy Shepherd. He said that their names sounded familiar but that was about it.

Following the Genworth employees was Wayne East, an installation design manager for Allied Security systems. He testified that on December 29, 2007, the sheriff's department had called him out to Jocelyn's home to retrieve a history of the times that the system had been turned off. He discovered that the time and date were off, either because the installer had not set it properly (a common occurrence with those systems) or possibly due to a power outage.

Wayne said that he then removed the panel from the

house system and took it back to the office. Then he adjusted the date and time with the computer—the settings were fourteen hours and eleven minutes ahead of actual time, and the year was set at 2000. From that, he knew that on December 18, the system had been armed at 8:18 A.M. and disarmed at 7:38 P.M. On December 19, it went on at 7:34 A.M. and off at 7:35 P.M.

On cross, Joey Sanzone established that that pattern was the typical one for use of the system—armed during the day while Jocelyn worked, unarmed after she came home.

THIRTY

D r. Susan Roehrich, a licensed professional counselor and a marriage and family therapist for thirteen years, with a PhD from Virginia Tech, a master's from Virginia Commonwealth University, and a bachelor of science degree from Penn State, was accepted as an expert witness by the court. Jocelyn Earnest was her client. They had their first meeting July 13, 2005, and continued to meet until their last session together, on the day of Jocelyn's death.

During the initial session, Dr. Roehrich focused, as she did with all of her clients, on providing information on the limits of confidentiality and making an assessment of the risk of homicidal or suicidal ideation.

"Did you ever have concerns that she would harm herself?" prosecutor Wes Nance asked.

"No."

Dr. Roehrich recalled that when they first met, Jocelyn

"was overwhelmed by the change in her marital relationship and the changes that would ensue for her personally when that relationship would end. So, she was what I would consider mildly depressed and anxious because this was a very unexpected event in her life." Dr. Roehrich described how she asked Jocelyn to do an exercise she used with many other clients, "what is called a self-concept inventory . . . to answer a series of nine questions based on how they have seen themselves for the past two weeks. That just gives me a snapshot. And it goes anywhere from how they describe themselves physically to what they think their strengths and weaknesses are, to how they function, the daily tasks of living, how they perform on their job, things like that. So I normally ask that as one of the first things just to kind of get a snapshot of them so that we don't spend a lot of time in sessions going through those same questions. They kind of do it for homework and then they return it, and then we go over it."

"Were there other tools or other homework that you would have given Jocelyn Earnest?" Nance asked.

"Yes, yes. What I also asked Jocelyn to do was something called journaling, which is a very powerful therapeutic tool which allows people to pretty much talk about or process through writing what their day's event were, whether there was a significant event that was upsetting or not [. . .] allowing them to speak freely on a day-to-day basis to keep a record of what's going on in their thought process [. . .] The other tool that I used was something called a timeline [. . .] from birth [. . .] They have to ask other family members to kind of help them out with memories or associations, if you will, and go all the way through to that time period that they're dealing with right now, looking for significant events in their life or issues that might have arose that would create in them, you know, the way they make decisions now." Jocelyn, she noted a little later, "was very engaged in the journaling process."

"I'll begin with the timeline," Nance said. "Is that something that Jocelyn Earnest took your advice and participated in?"

"Yes, she did."

"How do you know that?"

"Because Jocelyn would bring in the timeline and periodically we would then go through that as part of our session. We would go through what she had written on each of the years [. . .] and we would basically talk about what was written. And if there was a question mark that she had then we talked about who she might be able to talk with." Dr. Roehrich described the timeline as being handwritten on butcher paper, a large piece of rolled-up white paper, and Jocelyn's journals as spiral-bound notebooks, "like you might get for your children to go to school with." The handwritten entries covered various topics, from basic descriptions of her day, or "if there was a specific event that occurred that was upsetting her or if she was working on a particular topic that we were talking about in therapy, she might journal what she had thought about throughout the week."

Nance asked whether Dr. Roehrich had noticed any

change in Jocelyn's demeanor over the years they worked together.

"Yes, I did," the therapist replied, stating that "the initial couple of months that I worked with Jocelyn, she vacillated between wanting to save her marriage—"

Defense attorney Joey Sanzone broke in. "Judge, I object. This is hearsay."

"Agreed. Sustained," Judge Updike said.

Nance continued, instructing her to limit herself to discussing "just the change in [Jocelyn's] demeanor or emotions," not anything specific.

"Okay," Dr. Roehrich said with a nod. "So, her change was from a sad, depressed individual who was anxious to an individual who eventually was very excited and embracing life."

"You said that you met with her on December nineteenth, 2007."

"Yes, sir."

"And what time was her appointment on that evening?"

"Her appointment was from six to seven." When questioned, the therapist described Jocelyn as "very happy. She was very upbeat. She was looking forward to Christmas and the New Year and having a good year." Dr. Roehrich had no concerns of Jocelyn harming herself.

On cross-examination, Joey Sanzone asked whether Dr. Roehrich knew Maysa Munsey, Marcy Shepherd, or Jennifer Kerns before Jocelyn's death.

She said she did not.

"In the course of your profession, you deal with people who have different types of problems," Sanzone noted. "Do you deal occasionally with people who find out that instead of being heterosexual, they're homosexual?"

"Yes. I have in the past."

"And is that often an anxious, traumatic situation?"

"That would depend upon lots of other variables, on whether they perceived it to be anxious and traumatic. It's a very peaceful reckoning and—"

Sanzone cut her off. "But it can be traumatic."

"It's possible, sure."

"And if you're hiding that [. . .] is that usually a sign of a traumatic situation?"

"From other people is it a traumatic—not really—"

Sanzone interrupted, "Did you know that Jocelyn was having a relationship with Marcy Shepherd?"

"No, sir. Not until after her death."

The final Commonwealth witness of the day was Investigator Mike Mayhew. Nance brought out testimony regarding the wills of Jocelyn and Wesley Earnest, and their references to the murder weapon. Pointing to the document prepared for Wesley, Mayhew quoted, "'I want my three-fifty-seven caliber stainless steel Smith and Wesson handgun and all fishing rods with tackle to go to Robert Franklin Kerns.'" In contrast, he testified that Jocelyn's comments about that same gun did not use the possessive pronoun "me" at all.

When Joey Sanzone conducted the cross-examination, he directed the investigator to the box for that weapon that law enforcement had secured at Wesley's girlfriend's home in Concord, Virginia. "As far as you know, this was out in the open."

"To my understanding, it was in a closet—"

Sanzone broke in, "Easy to see?"

"If you open the closet, correct."

"And there's nothing's been tampered with here," Sanzone said, holding up the box.

"No, sir."

"And when we look at this from on the inside, it seems to be just like brand-new."

"Appears to be," Mayhew agreed. Sanzone took him through the packaging in some detail, then said, "There's no evidence in your possession that says that this gun remained for any period of time in this case after it was purchased, is there?"

"No, sir."

Sanzone moved back to the topic of the will, pointing out that "when it comes to his will, Mr. Earnest's will, it says right here in number three, if she survives him, he wants her to have everything."

"That is correct."

"And the only specific mention of the three-fifty-seven comes later in those paragraphs about what happens if she dies first, then he dies, where his things go."

"That's correct."

"And he talks about it being his three-fifty-seven after her death."

"It says, I want my three-fifty-seven caliber stainless steel Smith and Wesson, yes, that's . . ."

"That's what it says but he wants that to happen if she died first and then he dies."

"That's the way I interpret it, correct."

"And you read her will, which says that if she dies first, everything, including the three-fifty-seven, went to Wesley."

"That's correct."

The defense bounced back to the cardboard gun box, making note that it was "not a particularly unique box. Smith and Wesson put them out for these size weapons of all types."

"That's correct," Investigator Mayhew agreed.

"And if a person wanted to hide the fact that they had this box that related to that three-fifty-seven, all they'd have to do is peel this paper piece off the bottom."

"That would be one way, yes."

"And that would be an easy way, because once that's gone nothing about this box relates to the three-fifty-seven."

"That is correct."

Sanzone continued on with Mayhew about how nothing on the box appeared to have been defaced.

"No, sir, it doesn't appear to be."

On redirect, Nance worked to discredit the defense's line of questioning. "Investigator Mayhew, you were just testifying that there was no damage to the identification of this gun box; is that correct?"

"That is correct."

"Did Wesley Earnest know you were coming to arrest him on February twenty-seventh, 2008?"

"No, sir, not that I know of, no."

"Did he have any idea you were going to be executing a search warrant at his girlfriend's house on February twenty-eighth, 2008?"

"No, sir. As far as I know he didn't, no, sir."

When Nance finished, Sanzone said, "Judge, I do have a question, just brief follow-up to that." Turning to the investigator, he said, "But you knew that's where Mr. Earnest was staying."

"Yes, we knew he was staying there."

"And you talked to him several times about his wife's death."

"I did talk to him once with you, that's correct."

"And, you'd taken his fingerprints."

"Yes, that's correct."

"And despite all those things, this was right out in the open as if he had nothing to hide."

"It was in a closet, yes, sir."

With that answer, the proceedings ended for the day, and the judge turned to the jury and reminded them that the next day, a Thursday, was Veteran's Day, and the courts would be closed. The extra day gave the attorneys on both sides time to review their respective strategies and plan for upcoming witnesses—but left family members and friends of Jocelyn Earnest interminable hours to agonize and fret over the delay in progress toward justice for their loved one's death.

THIRTY-ONE

Marcy Shepherd's name had arisen again and again; now she finally took the stand on Friday, November 12, 2010. After the first trial, where the defense strategy had been trying to paint her as Jocelyn Earnest's killer, Marcy's anxiety level was high.

"When did you start working for Genworth?" prosecutor Wes Nance asked.

"I started working for them at the end of August in 2005."

"During the course of your employment did you get to know Jocelyn Earnest?"

"I first met her a couple of weeks after I started." Marcy described how they'd become friends while working on a company-wide project that Jocelyn was running. "And as the training leader, I had a significant role on that project. And so just through interaction and time and working a lot of long hours, we got to know each other." They saw each other every day at work, and would also occasionally go out to dinner or grab a drink.

"Did you ever see Jocelyn Earnest with a firearm?"

"No. Never." Nor, she specified upon questioning, had she ever seen one in Jocelyn's car or home.

"In 2007, what were your feelings toward Jocelyn Earnest?"

"I loved Jocelyn Earnest."

"What was it that you loved about Jocelyn Earnest?"

"Jocelyn was one of those people who was special to those that knew her. And she could be the person that you needed her to be, whether it was fun and joking, or whether it was a confidant. She had incredible character and integrity, and a lot of people admired her. I was one of those people. She was . . . smart and she was generous and she was helpful. And she would give whatever she could to others. And she didn't have to be super close to them to make them feel like they were important to her. She was, gosh, just one of those good people."

"Ms. Shepherd, what would you describe Jocelyn's demeanor to be generally speaking when you first met her?"

Sanzone objected that the question was general, remote, and irrelevant, but Updike overruled him. Marcy tried to answer the question when Nance rephrased it but had difficulty getting out an answer that Sanzone did not interrupt. Finally, Nance asked, "Did you see a change in Jocelyn Earnest's demeanor . . . in the second half of 2007, compared to 2005?"

"Absolutely. She was taking care of herself. She was working out. She was trying to learn how to eat in a healthy manner. She was making plans. She was excited to be with her family. Whereas previously, she was avoiding contact with many people. And, then in 2007 . . ."

Sanzone came to his feet again. "Judge, again . . . these are statements about activities, not demeanor."

"I'm going to allow that particular comment as descriptive. Overruled. Proceed," the judge said.

"So, she was excited to spend time with her family and friends that she had previously isolated herself from," Marcy said.

Nance elicited that Marcy had last seen Jocelyn on Sunday, December 16, 2007, when they went shopping together. "What was her demeanor on that date?"

"She was looking forward to [. . .] giving the kids their presents, because they were—well, you know how kids are at Christmas. And they were toys. And she was really excited to see them open them on Christmas Day and play with them. And her team's Christmas party was coming up and she was looking forward to sharing that time with them."

"Did you have any contact with Jocelyn Earnest between that December sixteenth date and noon on December twentieth, that Thursday?"

"Only through text messaging."

Marcy told the jury about the messages she'd exchanged with Jocelyn, and her friend's abrupt end to their conversation. She explained watching television with her son and waiting for a response from her friend. She told them about going to CVS and to Genworth to drop off Jocelyn's wrapped Christmas present. "I bought her outdoor lighting because she was fixing up her home." She went on to explain her drive out to Jocelyn's home out of concern for her friend's continued lack of communication. She then discussed the events of the next morning when she returned to Jocelyn's house and discovered the body.

Joey Sanzone started his cross-examination by probing into Marcy's home life. "Ms. Shepherd, back in [. . .] December of 2007, you and your husband were separated; is that right?"

"Yes."

"And you had entered a separation agreement with him at what time? When did you do that?"

"In April of 2006." She went on to explain that they were, nonetheless, still living in the same house to care for their young children.

"But you don't know Wesley Earnest, never met him."

Marcy shook her head.

Sanzone then began to question Marcy about how often she'd met with the prosecution pretrial. "How many times have you met with the Commonwealth or [. . .] witness coordinator to prepare for your testimony here today?"

"Once. How many times have I met with them before the trial? Once."

"Prior to today, you've only met with them one time in the past?"

"To prepare for this trial. That was how I understood the question."

"All right. Let me put this a different way. How many times have you talked to them about the substance of your testimony here today [. . .]?"

"I'm guessing three or four."

"My point is this: you've gone over a lot of things in preparation for today. People have asked you a lot of questions from the Commonwealth's side."

"No."

"You don't think so?"

"I don't think so."

Sanzone dropped that line of questioning and instead began asking Marcy about the telephone call when Marcy had asked Jocelyn about kissing. "All right. Tell me how you worded it," he asked when she objected to his phrasing.

"Well, gosh, the exact wording is difficult to remember this many years later, but it was something to the effect of asking her if I kissed her, would she kiss me back—something like that." That phone call, Marcy said, took place in autumn of 2005.

"And then you ultimately did kiss her."

"Yes."

"And where did that take place?"

"That took place at her home," Marcy said, adding that it was after their work Christmas party.

"Had y'all been drinking?"

"Not really."

"So you went to her house and you kissed her. About what time of day or night was that?"

"I'm guessing. I don't know. Maybe ten o'clock."

". . . The two of y'all were there together and no one else was around. No one came over that night."

"Correct."

Commonwealth's Attorney Krantz objected, and after much confused arguing back and forth between the lawyers and the judge, and references to testimony that had appeared in the earlier trial, Sanzone finally asked Marcy, "Did you [. . .] say it was a romantic relationship you were in?"

"It was an emotional relationship."

"I want to turn you now to page one-thirty-one of your testimony previously given. And the question from Ms. Sanzone was, was it a romantic relationship. And what was your answer?"

"I said it was."

"And you said that under oath [. . .] didn't you?"

"Yes."

"Now you went to great pains to keep the fact that you were romantically involved with Ms. Earnest secret, didn't you?"

"No."

"So you say that you and Jocelyn communicated, but most of the time it was by text, wasn't it?"

"Correct."

"And there were a lot of texts between you and Jocelyn, weren't there?"

"Yes."

"Would you agree with me that there were generally

more than a thousand texts between you and Jocelyn on a monthly basis?"

"I really don't know."

"Do you contest that? Do you say . . . that's not true or are you just saying you don't know?"

"I'm just saying I don't know."

"But you certainly were in communication often with her, and it was the vast majority text."

"That's correct."

"Could it have been, say, for instance during May, seventeen phone calls and fifteen hundred texts? Could that be true?"

"I don't know."

"But you did start calling her on the weekend that she went with Maysa to West Virginia, didn't you?" Sanzone asked. "Didn't you call her and talk to her at five o'clock on that Friday for a good long while as she was going to West Virginia?"

"It's possible."

"Didn't you talk to her a little bit longer at about six thirty as she was going to West Virginia with Maysa?"

"I don't remember."

"You weren't invited to West Virginia."

"I didn't go."

"And Maysa and Jocelyn went together, not you."

"Correct."

"And you were upset about that."

"No."

"And on Sunday when she got home, that was when you made some plans to go out on Wednesday, you say."

"Yes. No. We didn't make plans on Sunday to go out on Wednesday. We made plans on Monday to go out on Wednesday."

". . . You had taken the whole week off."

"Yes."

"You were going to spend time with Jocelyn."

"No."

". . . You being her new love, being in a romantic re-lationship, you weren't planning on spending more than just a tiny bit of time with her on Wednesday on the week that you had taken off?"

"That's correct."

"And you talked on the phone. You generally would text her during the day, wouldn't you, as well as in the evening?"

"We texted a lot. I'm sure there were texts during the day, yes."

"And texts in the evening?"

"Uh-huh."

"And you knew you had been talking to her, you had been texting her late on Monday, late on Tuesday, hadn't you, into the evening?"

"I don't remember when we texted . . . precisely."

"Haven't you said that y'all always said goodnight to one another? Isn't that true?"

"Yes."

"So you don't remember the specifics of the texts?"

"True, that's right."

Sanzone badgered her on specific messages and times. Marcy tried to answer, but finally she protested, "It was a long time ago." The defense attorney then pushed her about whether she'd reviewed documents before she took the stand. She admitted she had but said they were her own notes, not anything official. He moved on to ask pointed questions regarding her ability to leave her children with her husband at any time, the accessibility of transportation to drive to Jocelyn's house, and her freedom of movement that entire day. "And your testimony here to the jury today is that you went to Jocelyn's for the first time that night when?"

"That I went there after I left Genworth."

"After Genworth, after nine thirty in the evening . . . But that's not what you told Investigator Babb on December twentieth at the crime scene, is it?"

"That's right."

"And you remember what you told him, don't you? You told him that you had gone there closer to eight forty before you went to Genworth, before you went to CVS."

"Yep."

"You told him the next morning, the day that you called the police and were there with the body. You were talking about the events of the night before. It should have been fresh in your mind. And you told him that you went there before you went to CVS or Genworth. And now you're telling the jury something different under oath."

"I told him previously that I had made a mistake and that I had gone there after I had left Genworth."

"But you didn't tell him the truth the day you were

right there at the scene, did you? Your very first statement to the police about when you were there was eight forty, wasn't it?"

"I don't remember the exact time."

"But you didn't correct your statement before you left Jocelyn's house on the twentieth, did you? You're saying today that you weren't there at eight forty. You weren't there before you went to Genworth. You weren't there before you went to CVS. You never told them that day, did you?"

"I'm not sure what [. . .] question [. . .] you're trying to ask me."

"It's a real simple question," Sanzone insisted. "On the twentieth when the police come to the house and Jocelyn's body is there and you are, too, you tell them that you went to Jocelyn's house at eight forty the night before."

"Yes."

"You never corrected that statement on that day. Is that right?"

"No, I didn't."

"It was a long time after that that you talked to them again and told them something different. When did you talk to them and tell them something different?"

"I don't know."

"How many interviews did you have with police?"

"I don't remember."

". . . And when you went to the house at eight forty or before you went to CVS, you didn't notice any lights on in the house, did you?"

That question raised another objection from the prosecution that caused the judge to say, "I'm confused myself."

Sanzone reworded his query, continuing along with that line of questioning in an obvious attempt to trip up the witness and destroy her credibility.

"And your testimony here today is that you were at the CVS right next to Jocelyn's house, two or three minutes away, and instead of going to Jocelyn's house, you drove all the way to downtown Lynchburg to Genworth, then drove all the way back out past that CVS again to get to Jocelyn's house. Is that what you're saying?"

"Yes."

The defense then questioned Marcy's movements inside of Genworth and asked her about the gift for Jocelyn that she left in the office that night. "There was no reason you couldn't have left that present in your car, was there?"

Marcy explained it was a large box and she didn't want her children to see it, but Sanzone countered, "What you were trying to do was create a timed record so that you could later come back and show where you were that evening at nine twenty-eight and at nine o'clock with CVS. Isn't that true?"

"That's not true."

"You knew you'd been seen over at Jocelyn Earnest's house and you knew what happened to Jocelyn."

"No."

"When was the last time you were in Jocelyn's house?"

"The last time I was in her house was Sunday, the sixteenth."

"Do you know anything about the condoms there at the house—that were found in various places throughout the house?"

"No."

"Do you know anything about the hair that was found at the house?"

"No."

"Anything about the blood that was found at the house?"

"No."

The next question led to a semantics battle between the defense and prosecution, and then Sanzone continued. "You had been in the house with Jocelyn's body before the police arrived."

"Yes."

"When the police arrived, you and Maysa were standing at the front door."

"I was standing in the doorway, and she was standing on the front porch."

"Both doors were unlocked at that time, the back door and the front door?"

"I don't know if they were locked or not. The front door was open because I was standing in the doorway."

"And you'd opened the back door and come in through it."

"That's correct."

"Now, do you have anybody who can verify [. . .]

when you got to Jocelyn's house? Was there someone with you when you arrived at Jocelyn's house?"

"No."

"Did you see anybody when you were there at the house before the police got there?"

"No."

"Did you attempt to call the police for a welfare check?"

"No."

"Now, you didn't turn your phone over to the police that day, did you?"

"No."

"And there were text messages on your phone from Jocelyn to you and from you to Jocelyn: is that correct?"

"Yes."

When asked, Marcy admitted that the first time police asked her for her phone, she demurred.

"I told him that I didn't want to be without a phone."

"Well, you have a home phone, is that right? You have a land line at home."

"I do have a land line."

"And at work you have a land line."

"Yes."

"And your husband who is still there in the house with you has a cell phone, doesn't he?"

"Yes."

"And you're saying that under those circumstances to further the investigation of your close friend, you did not want to give up your phone?"

"I was afraid and I did not want to be without a phone."

"The phone was issued by your company, wasn't it?"

"Yes."

"Did you ask your company if they could issue you another phone while you let the police look at this phone . . . ?"

"No."

"You told them that you didn't want to be alone in the dark. Isn't that what you told the officer?"

"I don't remember if I said I didn't want to be alone in the dark. I knew that I didn't want to be without my phone."

"And you wouldn't let him pick up your phone and return it to you at the end of the day on December twenty-second."

"I don't remember refusing to provide my phone. I expressed my concern about being without a phone and he said it was okay."

"He said he'd pick it up later?"

"That's what we agreed to."

"And during that period of time from that day forward, you had every opportunity to erase messages on that phone, didn't you?"

"I wouldn't have."

"You had every opportunity to, didn't you?"

"I had the phone."

Sanzone produced the Commonwealth's evidence that detailed the findings on Marcy's phone. Then, he ran her through all the text messages she had with Jocelyn on December 19 including at 6 P.M. "When your phone was turned over there's no message from her at six o'clock, is there?"

"There's not."

"And you had that phone in your possession the whole time from December twentieth to January the third when you turned it over to the police."

"That's correct."

"And that missing message from Ms. Earnest is not among these records. You deleted that, didn't you?"

"If I did, it was unintentional. I did not delete it on purpose."

"Well, do you just delete things? You know the police want to see your phone. You know they're interested in this period of time. And you're saying you just unintentionally deleted it?"

"It's not there. I didn't mean to delete it is what I'm saying."

Sanzone questioned her about specific times, engaged in a squabble with the prosecutors and the judge, and then asked, "Ms. Shepherd, you deleted messages on this phone, isn't that true?"

"I did not intentionally delete messages off that phone. I do not know of any messages that I deleted after I spoke to the police. And I'm sitting there showing them my phone. We're looking at it together. I'm interpreting the messages."

"But you didn't let the police have the phone so they

could look at it themselves and interpret the messages. Instead, you're reading it to them; isn't that true?"

An exasperated Marcy said, "What's the question?"

"You didn't turn your phone over to them that day. You're holding on to the phone and telling them things about what's on the phone."

"I was being helpful by operating that phone [. . .] They were looking at it with me."

Sanzone continued to hammer her on not immediately releasing her phone, then harangued her about changing her story of her movements the night Jocelyn died. Then, he moved to questioning her about her knowledge of a condom at the crime scene. He wrapped up his cross with a final question. "Even though you didn't want anybody to know about the relationship before Jocelyn's death, you did call Susan Roehrich after Jocelyn's death and told her about your relationship, didn't you?"

"Yes," Marcy said.

On redirect, prosecutor Wes Nance established that Marcy's husband was aware of her feelings for Jocelyn before December 19 and that she'd volunteered the information to the police about her text messages with Jocelyn. Then he asked, "Why were you afraid to give them your cell phone on that particular night?"

Sanzone bounced up. "Judge, I object to that."

Nance started to plead with the judge, but Updike cut him off to send the jury out of the courtroom. When they were clear, he said, "All right, Counsel. I think I know where we're headed, but I'll hear it . . . repeat your question, please."

"Your Honor, my question is why she was afraid to turn over her cell phone," Nance said.

Updike turned to Marcy and said, "Outside of the presence of the jury, you can answer that."

"Based on what Jocelyn had told me about Wes, I was afraid. Should I say more?"

Nance asked, "What did she tell you?"

Sanzone spoke up, "Judge, we . . ."

Updike interrupted. "Now, the jury's not in here, Mr. Sanzone . . . For me to do my job, I have to know what the answer is. Proceed."

"And ma'am," Nance asked, "what was it that Jocelyn told you about Wes specifically?"

"She told me that if he didn't get what he wanted that he would kill her and then kill himself and that if he ever found out about us, he would kill us both. I didn't walk my dog for a year."

When Nance said that was all of his questions, Joey Sanzone argued, "Judge, first of all, we say it's hearsay. Secondly, we say that it's speculative. Thirdly, we say it's improper evidence. This is a questionable claim being made by her."

". . . All right, I'm going to consider this," Updike said. "But I'm going to tell you, I have some concerns here. Of course, I have some concerns about the nature of the response, but Mr. Sanzone, I also have some concerns because you've gone to great lengths suggesting during your cross-examination that the reason she did not turn over her phone in December [. . .] was for some untoward, dishonest purpose. Now, to just say she has a reason in her mind why she didn't turn it over and not allow her to say anything in response in my view is not fair. That leaves you to make your argument and does not allow the Commonwealth to respond as to her explanation of why she didn't turn it over."

After back-and-forth with the defense, Judge Updike asked Marcy to repeat her answer.

She said, "Based on what Jocelyn had told me on numerous occasions, that if [Wesley], you know, didn't get what he wanted, he was capable of murder and that she suspected that would be how she died, that he would kill her and then himself."

"Okay," the judge said. "Stop there a minute and let me get that. And then there was something else about finding out."

"And that if he found out about the two of us that he would kill us both."

"As a consequence of these statements, you were afraid of whom or afraid of what?"

"I was afraid of Wesley Earnest. And if you want observable behaviors, I could give those."

"What bearing, if any, does that have on your decision of your actions as to your cell phone in December and whether you would or would not give that to the police?" Judge Updike asked.

"Well, I never refused to give my cell phone. I expressed a deep concern about being without my cell phone simply because I thought he was hiding in the shadows,"

Marcy said, adding that Jocelyn "was not someone who just made things up. And when she expressed fear, I believed her. She had a couple of examples that I thought were worthy of her fear. Thus, when I found her body, worthy of my fear as well."

The judge ruled, "The essence of it, as I see it, is that this witness is saying [. . .] she had fear for her personal safety [. . .] I'm going to allow her to say that."

Marcy did just that when the jurors returned to the courtroom. An emotionally drained Marcy was finally allowed to step down from the stand.

THIRTY-TWO

The Commonwealth called their next witness, Richard Van Roberts, a firearms examiner for Virginia Department of Forensic Science with thirty years' experience. In that time, he had performed five thousand to six thousand examinations of guns.

He identified the murder weapon as a .357 Magnum caliber handgun with a short two-and-an-eighth-inch barrel with a five-shot capacity and an internal hammer. He walked the jury through the operation of the gun, the function of the safety mechanisms, and the loading of the ammunition.

He told them that he'd verified that the weapon was firing properly and concluded, "The two cartridges and the large jacket fragment were fired in and through this weapon. The other small pieces of lead and jacket were too small [. . .] for any identification."

On cross-examination, defense attorney Joey Sanzone used the witness to establish that the gun was very similar in size and function to one marketed by Smith and Wesson as a "Lady Smith"; that a gun did not have to be stored in its case or box; and that there was "no way to tell the time span between the first shot firing from the gun and the second one."

On redirect, prosecutor Wes Nance questioned the firearms expert about the brand of the weapon, establishing that it was not the Lady Smith model. Sanzone, on his recross, reiterated the point that it was extremely similar to the Lady Smith, inferring that it was a gun a woman would use, not a man.

The next witness for the Commonwealth was forensic pathologist Dr. Amy Tharp, assistant chief medical examiner for Roanoke. With her bachelors' in zoology and neuroscience, medical degree from New York Medical College, specialized training in anthropology at Wake Forest University in Winston-Salem, an additional one-year fellowship in forensic pathology, and her experience in performing more than 1,300 autopsies, her qualification as an expert was a foregone conclusion.

Dr. Tharp testified that Jocelyn Earnest's body had arrived fully clothed in a body bag, and that she'd conducted her examination on December 21, 2007.

First, Dr. Tharp said, she'd opened the bag and took a photograph, observing that rigor mortis was passing and the victim's head was tilted to the right side. When

UNDER COVER OF THE NIGHT   233

Nance showed her a crime scene photograph and asked if the angle of the head was the same as it was when the body arrived in her facility, Dr. Tharp said, "Yes."

"Did you make notation of the dried blood on Jocelyn Earnest's face?"

"Yes."

"And was there anything in particular that drew your attention to that?"

"The position of Mrs. Earnest's head tilted to the right—she appeared to have blood actually running uphill over her left cheek against gravity, which did not appear consistent with her position as I saw it in the scene photos and in the body bag."

Prosecutor Nance projected a photograph of Jocelyn's face on the screen and instructed, "Explain to the jury what the significance was to you about these dried blood streams."

"As you saw in the first photograph, her head was originally tilted to the right. And she had dried blood going off to the right down the right side, but there's also blood going over to the left cheek and across the left side of the face, which would be going against gravity," Dr. Tharp reiterated.

"What was the significance of that to you as a doctor and pathologist?"

"That her head had at some point been not completely tilted over to the right for the entire time that she had been dead from the time the injury occurred."

Nance took the pathologist through the steps of undressing and examining the body, and she described for the jury the x-rays taken. Introducing a number of autopsy photos, Nance pointed at one and asked, "And you were describing this as the entrance wound, is that correct?"

"Yes."

"And how do you make that determination?"

"One of the things that we learn in all that training is how to distinguish an entrance wound from an exit wound. When a bullet enters skin, it's spinning like a football and it tends to scrap the edges of the skin as it goes in before it actually punches through the skin into the skull.

"In addition, there are these little red marks all around the wound. It's not just the bullet that comes out the end of the gun. You'll also have bits of burning and unburned gunpowder and smoke and flame. And depending on how close the gun is to the skin, you might actually get some of those other things striking the skin as well. In this case, the gun was close enough that you'd get some of these little bits of gunpowder striking the skin and creating what we call stippling. It's sort of almost a sandblasting effect from the bits of gunpowder.

"I know it is not a contact wound because of all the bits of gunpowder. If it was, if the gun was pressed tight to the skin, it should have gone through the entrance itself and not have been deposited on the outside on the skin."

Nance introduced a photograph of the exit wound on Jocelyn's left temple and said, "Ma'am, we can see Jocelyn Earnest's left eye in that photograph. There appears to be discoloration."

"Yes. She has what we call preorbital ecchymosis or

basically a black eye. However, that's not because she was struck in the eye. When there's any kind of fracture of the base of the skull over the eyes, blood will leak down into the soft tissues around the eye. And in her case, the bullet fractured, I believe, every bone in the back of the skull including the bones over the eyes and blood leaked down around the eyes and caused that effect."

"Generally, what is the shape of this exit wound versus the entrance wound we saw earlier?"

"This wound is a little more irregular. It's not a nice, round, crisp hole like with the entrance wounds, because once the bullet has gone in and it's struck bone, it's no longer spinning in a nice, tight spiral like a football. It's tumbling end over end. And in this case, it probably came out somewhat sideways."

Dr. Tharp described the internal examination of the skull, clarifying the damage to the brain. "The bullet actually came through the right side of the brain, came across the brain stem and then out the left side of the brain and out the left temple, effectively killing her immediately."

"So, she not only lost consciousness, this would be an immediately fatal injury?"

"Yes," said Dr. Tharp, going on to add that Jocelyn "would have collapsed immediately."

Nance directed the pathologist to the pivotal point of her testimony. "Do you have an opinion to a reasonable degree of medical certainty whether this is consistent or inconsistent with a self-inflicted gunshot wound?"

"Yes, I do."

"And what would that opinion be?"

"This is inconsistent with a self-inflicted injury."

"And why do you reach that result?"

"For several reasons. One is the location. When people shoot themselves, they don't typically choose a location that would be difficult to reach. Behind the right ear . . . would create a slightly awkward angle. They're going to use a place that's more comfortable for them. Under the chin, in the mouth, and the temples or forehead are more common places, again not just because it's easier to reach, but they also want to make sure they hold the gun tight because they don't want to miss. The purpose is not to injure themselves. They're trying to get the job done. So they're going to make sure they hold that gun tight. And holding it at an awkward angle back here and away from the skin enough that you have that stippling . . . people don't shoot themselves that way."

Joey Sanzone focused on the time of death and the scientific impossibility to pinpoint with any precision after twelve hours. Dr. Tharp spoke of livor mortis, a settling of blood after death where a push of a finger on the skin causes it to blanch and leave an impression, occurring about six to eight hours after death, making it useless in this case where the body had remained undiscovered for much longer. She also said that she could not pinpoint time by undigested food in the stomach since she did not know what or when Jocelyn ate before she died.

Sanzone questioned her about the open wounds on the body. "Does blood continue to come out of those from time to time?"

"[. . .] It depends on whether there's been any drying or anything of the injury before. Occasionally, you can get clotting and congealing of blood at the injury, which will help prevent some of that."

"But if you turn a body [. . .] sometimes blood will flow that has not been previously flowing, is that correct?"

"It can."

Sanzone moved on to question the doctor's opinion on the distance the gun was from Jocelyn's head, suggesting that it was impossible to determine because the victim's hair would block some of the stippling.

Dr. Tharp disputed that, insisting that any blockage would be minimal. "I would still think that it would be unlikely to be any closer than two inches because you would expect, at closer than two inches, you'd be getting flame. There would be burning of the hair from the flame of the gun."

"And you described the wound back here as being in the back of the head, but [. . .] if she was turned sideways, for instance, then that becomes more along the line of her shoulders, the path of the bullet, doesn't it?"

"Yes, but she would still have to have her hand almost even with her shoulders to still get that angle."

"Right. But that position is possible."

"It is physically possible."

On redirect, the prosecution established that regardless of the position of the body, the position of the gun, as relative to the head, remained the same. The relationship between the two was pivotal to the trajectory and the official ruling of homicide.

THIRTY-THREE

Marjorie Harris, a forensic scientist with the Virginia Department of Forensic Science with expertise in blood stain pattern analysis, was accepted as an expert witness before the court. She first explained her specialty to the jurors. "It's based on some of the basic sciences: physics, mathematics, fluid dynamics. What I do is look at deposits that have been left at a dynamic event that's happened to a blood source that allows blood to either fly into the air or fall onto the ground. I look at three things. I look at their sizes. I look at their shapes. And I look at the way the stains have been distributed."

Nance introduced as evidence the carpet sample Harris had analyzed in the laboratory. She pointed to it where it lay on the floor as she explained, "So we see that initial blood drops begin here. They continue to travel this way. This is a large volume that's now beginning to pour out of her body." She noted how the spatters showed "that this is a volume that's being released from the distance above the carpet, pouring out of her body if you will."

"So, at this point, is the origin of the blood flow above the carpet?"

"Yes . . . and then there is a dragging through this that actually leaves pieces of hair within the stain." She then detailed the information in the patterns indicating that the body had been moved after death, and the absence of blood stains on Jocelyn's clothing showing she'd been leaning forward when she was shot.

"Now if you look at the stains, especially lower in the middle portion of her back, there's nothing that relates to a blood source in her hand that would put that blood directly there. So that blood was what we call transfer from [. . .] And I believe that blood to be the blood that was on the carpet as her body was moved across that. And then that transferred the blood from the top of the carpet onto the back of her jacket."

Nance asked, "Do you have a conclusion to a reasonable degree of scientific certainty as to the series of events that are reflected in both this blood stain pattern and the blood stain patterns or lack thereof on her clothing?"

"Right," the expert said. "Initially when she received her injuries, blood began to flow or pour from those injuries and potentially from her nose, her mouth, and her left ear. She was in a leaning forward position because nothing was dripped on the front of her. We see that the head [. . .] continued to drip and pour blood onto the carpet here, here, here," she said, pointing at the sample. Pointing to another spot, Harris said, "This was a heavier volume that poured out. As a matter of fact, when it hit, it broke into pieces of what I call the 'Mc-Donald arches' where they come out and then they come back down. And when you see this, you'll see the little stains all around this central pattern. And that tells me that a volume of blood was dropped from a height above the carpet.

"Now, once that happened, and she was on her back, she was pulled across to where her head was stationary here," she said, pointing to another stain. "And there are bits of hair that are actually still . . . here in the carpet that were stretched out as her head moved across that wet, tacky blood. Then as her head maintained . . . here and blood leaked out of the entry wound and the exit wound, it flowed here and created almost a small pool that left coagulation and clotting."

Joey Sanzone did the best he could to discredit Marjorie Harris's testimony on cross-examination. "Ms. Harris, you said that you knew that the initial blood flow started at some point when she was above the ground . . . not lying on the ground."

"Yes, that's correct."

"But you can't tell how far above the ground, can you?"

"No."

He then questioned her ability to tell whether blood came from an entry or exit wound. She agreed with him, except in the case of spatter at the moment of the shot.

". . . And you can't tell the difference between dripping blood from a few inches above the ground and dripping blood from a higher height, can you?"

"In some instances you can, but it would take experiments with different volumes and . . . the same type of surface. And I did not do that in this case."

"So in this case, you couldn't say whether those twin drips came from her just lying on the ground and the blood dripping down."

"Oh no. They came from a [. . .] height above the floor. In particular when the volume fell and hit the carpet and then created the secondary spatter that had to be from a distance greater than what would just drip off her hair."

Sanzone moved on to the larger areas of blood. "If a person falls and remains still you expect to find one pool, don't you?"

"Yes."

"And that's not what you found in this case, is it?"

"Actually it is."

"You found one pool and you found trails to the pool."

"There were trails from where the bleeding initiated and blood dropped or poured out of her body. And then there was pooling where her head remained stationary and created the [. . .] compression area. If you want to say there's two pools [. . .] but just because her head was in the way and blocked them from connecting."

"You said there was hair that had been stretched across . . ."

"Yes."

"You have said that you think the body moved after it initially came to rest on the ground."

"Yes."

"Is it fair to say that it moved twice?"

"I don't . . ."

"You talked about changes in the blood flow on her face. These changes in blood flow clearly occurred before all the blood had dried, wouldn't you agree?"

"Yes."

"So that happened fairly early on after she hit the ground."

"Well, again, you yourself said that if there's a hole in the body and the body is moved then blood could leak out of it. So not necessarily," she said.

"There's no hole in her nose," Sanzone said.

Krantz rose to his feet. "I think they call those nostrils, Your Honor."

Sanzone continued as if the prosecutor had not spoken. "There's not a wound. There's not a gunshot wound to her nose, is there?"

"No, sir, but there is clearly blood being released from her nose and flowing out of her nose."

"Oh absolutely. But my point is, it changes direction . . ."

"Yes, but if I can clarify that. It doesn't necessarily mean that her body has to move in conjunction with that. If you think about your head, your head's on your neck and it pivots. So even though the main part of my body is stationary, I can move my head in a variety of ways and actually change the position of my face and head. And my body doesn't have to really move to do that."

"Oh, I agree. But you can't do it after you've been shot through the brain. You would agree with me on that."

"Well, I don't think she's doing it of her own volition, no."

Sanzone tried to pin Harris down on the time it takes blood to dry solid, but she testified that it was all dependent on the variables: the surface, the air flow, and the temperature. She also insisted, "When her jacket moved across the blood, it was wet. And I would say that her head and her jacket moved across the blood at the same time."

"But you can't say that with a reasonable degree of certainty, can you?"

"Yes, I can. On her jacket I can."

"On her jacket that moved across when her head moved across? What is it that scientifically connects those two things?"

"Because her head is attached to her body."

A squabble broke out between attorneys on opposite sides over the questioning. The judge did not directly address the point of either man but did say that the questioning was getting repetitious and needed to wrap up.

The back-and-forth between Marjorie Harris and Joey Sanzone continued with the forensic expert refusing to agree with any conclusions drawn by the defense. The cross-examination was followed by redirect and recross sessions that turned into sparring matches between the legal teams rather than the delivery of useful evidence.

The last person on the stand that day was Lieutenant Michael J. Harmony, a computer forensics expert, who testified about retrieving Jocelyn's laptop from Genworth and making an image of the hard drive.

Prosecutor Nance asked, "And what's the purpose of making an image versus doing the forensics on the original computer and its hard drive itself?"

"Once the computer is fired up, once the operating system has started, it actually starts changing data and time stamps and basically alters the original evidence. We make a forensic copy of it so that we don't tamper with the original evidence," Lieutenant Harmony explained. He told the jury that a keyword search of Jocelyn's work and personal computers demonstrated that the suicide note had not been written on either one of the devices.

On cross, Joey Sanzone asked if Lieutenant Harmony had examined Marcy's or Maysa's or Jennifer's computers or BlackBerrys. Harmony said that he had not.

THIRTY-FOUR

The first witness of the day on Monday, November 15, 2010, was James Fitzgerald, a criminal profiler and forensic linguist with the Academy Group in Manassas who had worked for the Federal Bureau of Investigation for twenty years. He was accepted by the court as expert in forensic linguistics.

He began by explaining the term "idiolect" to the jury. "It's simply a term linguists came up with to describe a personal dialect. And all of us have a personal dialect. It is a combination . . . of one's entire life experience that has to do with your age, your gender, your socioeconomic status, certainly your profession, your education, and how you were educated, how far, what kind of school you went to," Fitzgerald explained, later noting, "If we're speaking about looking at someone's writing style or written communications prepared by an individual, be it known or unknown, and comparing these features, many of which could be considered part of the speaker' or writer's idiolect, that process would again be authorial attribution."

Fitzgerald testified that he'd analyzed 77 pieces of communications written by Wesley Earnest and 253 separate communications by Jocelyn Earnest in order to compare to the note found at the crime scene. "The particular writing style reflected in these eighty-three words—my overall opinion was that it was not then consistent with the writing style of Jocelyn Earnest."

He went on to describe the basis of that belief: "Jocelyn was a prolific writer and usually, there was more substance to it than we find here in this particular communication. In addition, virtually all of Jocelyn's communications . . . were handwritten. As you notice, this one is computer generated. In Jocelyn's known writings, various names are referenced throughout [. . .] However, as you notice in a particular communication found at the scene of her death, there is the name 'Mom' and the name 'Wes' [. . .] and that's it. Again [. . .] that's not consistent with the known handwriting style of Jocelyn Earnest." Plus, he added, the supposed suicide note was only "a few sentences in a static form and I would also say unemotional or detached. And that varies greatly from the known writings of Jocelyn."

Fitzgerald also said that another point that bothered him was that her journals did not reflect any concern with finances that was "life shattering or life altering. Yet, in that short note, she wrote, 'Wes has buried us in debt.'

That line appeared to have no context in any of her other writings."

Lastly, Fitzgerald said, "And this is a nerdy linguistic thing, but punctuation can be important in helping to identify possible writers. And in the particular note you [. . .] have a comma, just one time. We don't really count after mom, basically the greeting for the person. But there's a comma split just there near towards the end of the first paragraph. And then the rest is periods." This was inconsistent with Jocelyn's typical writing style.

On cross, defense attorney Joey Sanzone asked if Fitzgerald had evaluated the writings of Marcy or Maysa, or anyone other than Jocelyn and Wesley. He said he had not. Sanzone also wanted to know if Fitzgerald had examined any writings on the BlackBerry and got a negative response to that question, too.

Then Sanzone asked about the nature of the analysis performed. "There's a statement here about 'my new love.' You don't attempt to match content to the note, do you? You don't attempt to find out who might know about the new love?"

"The request I had of me at the time by the Commonwealth's Attorney's Office and the Virginia State Police—that particular request was not made of me."

"So you can do a content connection in these linguistic reports . . . ?"

"That's possible, yes, depending on the circumstances of the communication involved, of course."

"Sometimes people ask you to do that, but you weren't asked to do that in this case?"

"My request was to do a linguistic analysis [. . .]"

Sanzone then questioned him about the phrase "the family" found in the note at the crime scene.

Fitzgerald said, "It reads sort of unusual in that one would expect . . . from one's learning language experience that there would be a pronoun of some sort in there or a modifier, most likely 'his,' 'her,' or 'their.' For whatever reason, the author of this communication chose to make it the definite pronoun . . ."

Sanzone honed in on Fitzgerald's conclusion. "You can't say that was written by Jocelyn Earnest. That's your statement here today . . ."

"It's my opinion that [. . .] the writing style reflected in this communication is inconsistent with the overall writing style of [. . .] Jocelyn Earnest, yes."

"And as far as Mr. Earnest: it's not Mr. Earnest's writing, either, based on your opinion."

"I have no professional opinion in that regard . . ."

"But certainly your decision is not a statement that [. . .] this was written by Wesley Earnest."

"That's correct."

Attorney Jennifer Stille, the lawyer whom Jocelyn had retained for her divorce in November 2005, was the next witness for the Commonwealth. She talked about drafting an agreement of proposed settlement and presenting it to Wesley for consideration.

Joey Sanzone voiced his objection to testimony about

events from 2005 being part of the record because of remoteness. Judge Updike overruled him.

Stille continued to tell the jury that in June 2006, she had, on behalf of Jocelyn, filed a complaint for divorce in the Bedford Circuit Court on the grounds of adultery, cruelty, desertion, and separation in excess of one year. After asking for and being granted an extension, Wesley eventually filed a counterclaim. At Nance's direction, Stiles read alternately from the complaint and counter-complaint, covering Jocelyn's allegations and Wesley's responses to them. She followed that by telling the jury about the motion for relief filed by Wesley Earnest asking for exclusive use of the lake house, spousal support payments, and one hundred thousand dollars to resolve the loan made to the couple by Wesley's father.

Stille listed all of the debt she knew to be existing for the couple as of December 2007, and noted that after Jocelyn's death, Wesley Earnest owned the deeds to all the couple's properties.

"Now when you talk about these debts, you've got a few credit cards that are owed by Wesley, but the bulk of this debt is joint debt owed by Jocelyn and Wesley: isn't that right?" Sanzone countered.

"Certainly, if you include the joint deeds of trust."

"You know that Wesley had been doing work fixing up the lake house."

"I know that he had submitted some bills to Jocelyn for work he said he did at the lake house," Stille replied. When asked by Sanzone about specifics, she said, "I had no knowledge about work he was doing on the house [. . .] He had submitted a list of work he wanted to do and that was subject to discussion."

Sanzone pressed her on the disagreement between the parties on when they began living apart and for the reason why no divorce trial date had yet been set. Stille said that the four-month difference in dates was irrelevant since by either measure, they met the twelve-month separation period required by Virginia law. As for the finalization of the legal end of their marriage, there were still several items in the settlement requiring agreement by both parties.

Sanzone then took Stille through a long list of joint monthly expenses and the combined incomes of the two parties with Jocelyn earning $106,000 per year and Wesley making $77,600, questioning their inability to pay their bills before dramatically switching gears and asking: "Did Jocelyn Earnest ever tell you that she had a romantic relationship with Marcy Shepherd?"

"No."

"That is information that can be used against a person in a divorce, can't it?"

"If somebody has evidence of a romantic relationship and they're trying to prove adultery, certainly, that can be used."

"And if people are alone at night and they're there by themselves and they're kissing by their own admission, that's evidence that can be used against a person in a divorce proceeding, can't it?"

"Certainly, if those witnesses will come and testify to that, that's evidence . . . you would want to put on," Stille agreed, though she denied having any knowledge of Jocelyn being involved in a romantic relationship with Marcy Shepherd, or anyone else.

The jury took a lunch break, and after much squabbling by the lawyers over whether or not Sanzone could ask about what Wesley's divorce attorney may have asked Jocelyn regarding her sexual partners, the judge ruled that any statements made by Jocelyn were inadmissible because they were hearsay.

When the trial recommenced with the jury in their places, Stille responded to Sanzone's questions by saying that although in the interrogatories, Wesley denied committing adultery on certain dates, he did admit committing adultery in general in the December 2006 hearing.

"And there was no knowledge on your part about any sexual relationship or romantic relationship that Ms. Earnest was having with Marcy Shepherd or any other person."

"That's correct."

"That wasn't an issue in this case? Mr. Cunningham [Wesley's divorce lawyer] and Mr. Earnest weren't pressing you hard to discover a female . . . sexual, romantic relationship . . . ?"

"Not at all. Never came up."

After redirect by Nance, Sanzone used his recross to push Stille to agree that the day Jocelyn died her salary ended and Wesley assumed all of the debt.

She said, "Yes and all of the equity, too."

THIRTY-FIVE

After various witnesses testified about the materials obtained during the search of Wesley Earnest's girlfriend Shameka Wright's home, including the gun box, personal photo albums of Wesley and Shameka, and various documents (particularly those relating to bills and delinquent loans), real estate agent Johnny Maddox of Country & Mountain Realty next took the stand and told the jury that he'd met the defendant in June 2007, and that on June 15, 2007, Wesley had verbally authorized Johnny to sell the lake house for $2,150,000, but Wesley never showed up to sign the document, and that no sale ever happened.

When the jury entered the box on the sixth day of the proceedings, their first witness of the day was Neil Phillips. Neil said that he'd first met the defendant in August 2005 when Wesley rented a room in his home. The tenant told him that he was taking a new position in Chesapeake and his wife would be joining him soon.

Neil said he'd evicted his boarder after Wesley said, "Bitches like my wife and your wife should be dead."

Joey Sanzone started his examination of the witness with a question about the criminal activity of Neil's son. That prompted an objection from the Commonwealth. This time, not only was the jury sent out of the courtroom but so was the witness. Sanzone argued that the real reason Wesley had gotten into an argument with Neil was because of the son's activities, but Nance countered, "I'd be afraid this would open a Pandora's box, because from my understanding from Mr. Phillips, the reason for him asking Mr. Earnest to leave had nothing to do with that arrest, but a whole slew of actions by Mr. Earnest that we're attempting not to go into."

Sanzone objected again saying that the end of the tenancy agreement was not a disagreement about Neil's wife. The judge, however, decided that the defense could not bring up testimony about the son's arrest.

Sonya Stevens, a teacher at Oscar Smith Middle School, stepped into the witness box. She said that she'd met Wesley during the 2005–2006 school year. "He patrolled the hallways and helped out in various capacities [. . .] he kind of did everything.

"I'm one of the coaches," she said, "and he had an

interest in marathons and just athletics in general [. . .]
My track athletes were fond of him, and he would stay
after. And then after I was done coaching, we would run
occasionally. And then at that time, we would just talk
about life in general, mainly his life because it was more
interesting." She noted that he told her he wasn't married,
and had never been married, because he'd "'never found
the right one.'" She'd seen Shameka Wright from afar at
a work Christmas party but had never met her or Jocelyn.

"Did Mr. Earnest speak of his finances at all?"

"He did while running. He talked about mainly some
of his properties. He had this wonderful estate [. . .] on
Smith Mountain, some land [in] California." Sonya recalled, "He said he did not have to work [for a living] . . .
He chose to do that because he likes the children."

Nance asked if, after Wesley left after the end of the
academic year and went to Great Bridge High School,
she'd had any further contact with him.

"Several times," she said. "He would show up sometimes at my track meets because we shared a track, called
every now and then. He would call and say, 'Hey, coach.'
And he would call or text 'I'm getting together,' 'I'm
doing this,' 'you're invited.' It was just kind of an all call
type of thing where he just invited old friends."

"Now, I want you to turn your attention to late December 2007 to early January 2008. Did you have occasion
to reach out to Mr. Earnest during that time period?"

"I did . . . I heard through the grapevine that his
wife was killed. I heard it was a car accident. And I texted
him and just said I'm sorry to hear about your wife . . .

I got a response back that said, 'What are you talking about?'"

On cross-examination, Joey Sanzone established that the witness was only a casual friend of Wesley Earnest and that they did not have the type of relationship that encouraged deep conversations or the exchange of confidences.

The next witness, Molly Sullivan, was also a teacher at Oscar Smith Middle School who knew Wesley in that same time frame. Her retelling of what Wesley said to her was nearly identical to Sonya's testimony.

On cross-examination, Joey Sanzone tried to get Molly to say that her relationship with Wesley was shallow and none of their conversations were deep or personal. Molly, however, would not agree with that assessment.

Chesapeake Police Department detective Wade Satterfield sat in the witness box next. He was the youth services officer at Oscar Smith Middle School the year that Wesley was there and they became friends. With him, too, Wesley had indicated he was a "small-time millionaire" and had never married because he'd never found the right woman.

"I asked him what the right one was [. . .] The type of person he described was an African American female."

Joey Sanzone began his questions of the witness. "Detective Satterfield, you and Wesley went fishing together. You did a lot of things together down at the beach in Chesapeake, didn't you?"

"Yes."

"And y'all would joke around; tease each other, things of that nature, too?"

"Yes."

"And the term 'small-time millionaire' sounds a little bit like a comedy term [. . .] Did you know whether he was being serious or kidding with you . . . ?"

"He never showed me his financial records," Satterfield said.

"That's my point."

Officer Wallace Chadwick with the City of Chesapeake was the school resource officer at Great Bridge High School for about seven years. "We routinely worked together with him being the assistant principal and me being a police officer at the school. We worked together on cases, discipline-related. Some of them reached the criminal justice category. We would get involved together, interviewing kids and things of that nature."

"And pursuant to working together, did you come to know Mr. Earnest's interest in law enforcement?"

"Yes, we talked frequently, you know, about things about my job and things like that. And he was also involved in some of the community things that our police department offered [. . .] We had a program set up called the Citizen's Police Academy [. . .] where citizens come in and kind of get a feel for what police officers do. For example, I'm on the dive team [. . .] we taught a section on what the dive team does."

"Did you ever have occasion to meet Shameka Wright?"

"One time . . . It was at a retirement party that both of us had attended—most of the school staff was there— for one of the principals that retired . . . I didn't physically meet her. I saw her."

"Did you later ask Mr. Earnest who she was?"

"Yes [. . .] He just said it was a chick he had met in the mountains, and he called her a mountain chick."

Joey Sanzone wanted the witness to tell the jury about an incident at the school that happened on December 20, but Chadwick could not remember it, saying that after ten years of doing the job, individual events and the dates when they happened were not something he could specifically recall.

Investigator Mike Mayhew returned for a repeat performance on the stand. The first item covered was the interview that Mayhew had with Wesley on December 21, 2007, at 6:15 P.M.

"And that would be the day after the discovery of Jocelyn Earnest's body?"

"That is correct."

"And who was present during the course of that interview?"

"Mr. Earnest, his attorney Mr. Sanzone, myself, and Investigator Babb."

"Now, prior to speaking to Mr. Earnest did you disclose to him or any other person the discovery of an alleged suicide note?"

"No, sir, I did not."

"Or did you discuss the themes contained within that suicide note?"

"No, sir, I did not."

"Either before or during that interview did you discuss with Mr. Earnest how Jocelyn was killed?"

"No, sir, not during the interview. It was later that I was asked and it was told how she was killed."

"And what did you tell him at that point?"

"That it was a gunshot wound."

"Did you discuss the date you believed she was killed at that time?"

"No, sir, I did not, except that she was found [on] Thursday, December twentieth at twelve o'clock noon." Nance took Mayhew through how the investigators had asked Wesley what his schedule had been like that week, and about the truck he'd borrowed.

Joey Sanzone, on cross, attempted to establish that Wesley had many sources to learn facts about the case before his initial interview with law enforcement: news accounts, his conversation the night before with Investigator Babb, and other people who might have been interviewed before him about the case. Mayhew acknowledged that some of the information could have been legitimately obtained, but other details could not.

Sanzone asked, "Now when he came in, it was perfectly voluntary."

"Yes."

"He didn't have to."

"Correct."

"And he agreed at that point to provide fingerprints or any other information or any other samples you might need."

"Yes, he did."

"The conversation you had with Mr. Earnest, you [. . .] asked if she was ever suicidal, didn't you?"

"Yes. It was asked if she [had] ever spoken about suicide or [. . .] harming herself [. . .]"

"And he told you [. . .] years ago . . ."

"No [. . .] He said the year before [. . .] I think his correct wording was 'several times she has stated to me she wanted to commit suicide.'"

Sanzone pulled out the document of the interview and asked him to read from it. "And then what did he say?"

Mayhew read the question and its answer: "'When is the last time she told you that?' 'I guess it would have been right after the summer of 2005 when I left and went to Chesapeake.'"

After some back-and-forth about the truck and the holster found in the gun safe, Sanzone handed the witness over to Nance for redirect. Nance said, "Mr. Sanzone asked you about media reports and your knowledge of them."

"Uh-huh."

"Are you aware of any that referred to this being consistent with suicide?"

"No, sir."

"Or the finding of a suicide note?"

"No, sir."

"Or the themes that may have been contained in that suicide note?"

"No, sir, there was not."

Sanzone now stood for recross and asked: "But you do know what may have been rumored in the general public?"

"No, sir, it's general public."

"And you don't know what rumors Mr. Earnest may have heard?"

"No, sir."

THIRTY-SIX

The Commonwealth called Dr. Janet Andrejco, who'd been the principal of Great Bridge High School for four years until her retirement on August 1, 2010. Her presence on the stand spawned another defense objection, which led to a round of questioning outside of the presence of the jury.

After a lengthy argument, the judge ruled Dr. Andrejco's testimony was admissible and the jury returned to the courtroom. She reviewed the schedule for the school, demonstrating that Wesley had not been responsible for overseeing any school activities on December 19, 2007, and that he'd been at work on December 20, the last day the school was in session before beginning their holiday break on December 21. In response to the prosecutor's questions, she told the jury that there were approximately 350 computers and 150 printers at Great Bridge High.

Nance asked, "Did he [Wesley Earnest] return after the winter break?"

"He did." However, Dr. Andrejco testified, he did not return after law enforcement appeared at the high school on January 24, 2008, pursuant to the investigation into the death of Jocelyn Earnest.

On cross, Dr. Andrejco testified that the school walkie-talkie system had about fifteen people on it, including the assistant principals, and they could all be reached immediately at any time they were at the school.

Next, the Commonwealth called Jesse McCoy's uncle to the stand, where the Baptist pastor testified about helping out his nephew—Wesley's former student—by performing the detailing on Wesley Earnest's car on Thursday, December 20, because Wesley said he'd be out of town on Wednesday.

On cross, Joey Sanzone asked, "Sir, you say this was a brand-new business. When had it started up?"

"It never officially materialized," he said. Wesley Earnest was their only client.

Sanzone asked the preacher if he could, without any reference to his notes, tell the jury when was the first time anybody asked him to go back and revisit the conversations with Wesley Earnest.

"I had no reason to until Dr. Earnest called me the following May asking me for a receipt."

". . . You hadn't even thought about these conversations for six months at that point, had you?"

"That's correct. Well, I take that back. That's not entirely true. Earlier that year, my nephew called me [. . .] and said [. . .] had I heard about Dr. Earnest being indicted? And at that time I did not. But that made me think, do I need to be aware of anything. So I certainly started to replay some things in my mind to make sure that I had what I had clear."

"But you had no notes?"

"No, sir."

"And all of this is just done just sitting around thinking back over a few months?"

"Well, he would have been our first official customer. And you always remember your first and [. . .] with much more clarity than others."

"Well, but he was your only customer. Y'all weren't in business."

"That's true. And that's all the more reason for me to remember that a little clearer."

"You didn't call him up on Wednesday and confirm that he was out of town anywhere, did you?"

"No, sir."

"You didn't talk to him on Thursday about returning from town anywhere, did you?"

"No, sir."

"In fact [. . .] all you needed was a day when he was going to be at school from eight o'clock in the morning to four o'clock in the afternoon so you could pick up the car and detail it."

"Essentially."

"And with him being at school on Wednesday from eight to four, you could have done it that day."

"We talked about that day, but . . ."

"You couldn't do it that day."

McCoy explained that Thursday worked better for him anyway. "Being a Baptist pastor, Wednesdays are heavy church days [. . .] I told him that would not be a good day for me and if we could avoid that day that would be best, but if it absolutely had to be that day, I could make an exception."

"And he certainly didn't insist on it being Wednesday, did he?"

"At one time he did. That was the best day for him at one time [. . .] but he changed it because he had other commitments."

Erik Goodrick hopped into the hot seat saying that he lived in Virginia Beach and Wesley was his neighbor in 2007. When Wesley moved, they still kept loosely in contact by telephone.

Erik told the jury that he was in Chicago in between Thanksgiving and Christmas installing a printing press. Wesley called him twice while he was gone, but since his phone was dead, he did not retrieve any messages until after Christmas. In the first message, Wesley simply asked that Erik call him back. In the second one, Wesley said he needed to borrow Erik's truck. When he got the messages, Erik returned the calls and left a message but Wesley never called him back.

In response to questions from the defense, Erik said he knew nothing about Jocelyn Earnest and never saw her. He did, however, see Wesley's girlfriend, Shameka Wright.

Erik said that he was not surprised by Wesley asking to borrow his truck because he'd done so once before when he had needed to move some furniture. On that occasion, Wesley had cleaned the truck before returning it, something Erik never did himself. He and his wife used to joke about needing to get Wesley to borrow the truck again so it could get cleaned.

David Hall, a teacher and coach with the stocky body of a wrestler, took Erik's place before the jury. He said that he struck up a friendship with Wesley, who was teaching him how to hunt. The two of them went out together as much as they possibly could. He said that Wesley never mentioned Jocelyn, and they never discussed finances.

Before Christmas break, he and Wesley exchanged vehicles after school during the week of December 17. David said that Wesley wanted to move furniture to a trailer but asked him not to say anything about that to any of the administrators because he was trying to establish a residence.

When Nance asked about the condition of the tires on his truck, Dave said, "Oh, they were in great shape. They were about a year and three months old, but I rotate them every three thousand miles." He then told the jury about Wesley borrowing the truck again in January and returning it with new, but inferior, tires.

Like Wesley Earnest, Jim Clevenger was a public school administrator working as an assistant principal at Great Bridge High School. While he and Wesley worked together, they formed a professional friendship. "There were times that we would go out and get dinner before a football game or something, you know. That was the extent of the social activity. But, yes, we did [. . .] Wesley actually volunteered some information about his financial status [. . .] He indicated in his first year that he didn't necessarily have to work, that he was not like most administrators who could limit how much they could invest, that the folks downtown were investigating how to coordinate the paperwork so that he could invest a portion of his money."

"Did he say the status of his debts? Anything like that?" Nance asked.

"He indicated that he didn't have a lot of responsibility."

Jim told the jury about Wesley Earnest's stressed reaction to the arrival of two men in dark suits at the high school on January 24. He said that Wesley specifically asked if Dave Hall had spoken to them and that Wesley appeared preoccupied all day.

Joey Sanzone did his best to make Wesley's inquiry about David Hall appear innocent or coincidental. The question, however, hung in the air. It had made a lasting impression on the witness; would it weigh as heavy with the jury?

THIRTY-SEVEN

After brief testimony from a clerk at the Chesapeake Campground, noting that it was Wesley Earnest's mother who rented him the space for a trailer on December 26, 2007, the next witness was the store manager for Kramer Tire in Chesapeake, Rick Keuhne. His qualifications as a tire expert were accepted by the court. He told the jury about his January 10, 2008, transaction with the person calling himself Tom Dunbar.

At the sound of that answer, Joey Sanzone asked to approach the bench and the jury and witness were sent out. He and the judge had a lengthy discussion about the vacating of the first verdict and the standing of the motions filed for that trial and this one. It all boiled down to an objection by the defense that the tire evidence was irrelevant and unduly prejudicial.

"The court feels that this is probative as far as circumstantial evidence . . . and that probative impact is not overcome or overwhelmed by prejudicial impact," Judge Updike ruled.

When testimony resumed, Rick Keuhne related the circumstances of the sale and his inability to find anything wrong with the man's tires.

"Mr. Keuhne, are you familiar with emergency tire repair substances such as Fix-a-Flat?" Nance asked.

". . . Fix-a-Flat is nasty stuff that individuals put in their tire if there happens to be a hole . . ."

"When a tire is changed is the evidence of the use of Fix-a-Flat apparent?"

"Very apparent . . . If anyone has kids and watches Nickelodeon when you see the green slime that's what Fix-A-Flat looks like inside of a tire. It not only gets inside the tire and completely coats it and also does the same thing to the rim. And tire changers hate it because it takes an additional . . . ten to twenty minutes to clean the rim to get the Fix-A-Flat off."

". . . Did you observe any evidence of the tires that were driven in on this vehicle having Fix-A-Flat or a similar substance in them?"

"No, sir."

On cross, Sanzone attempted to undermine Rick's standing as an expert witness. Then he raised questions about the validity of the receipt since it had not been signed by the customer. Rick said that was not unusual when a customer pays cash, since the store only required a signature on charge purchases. Sanzone came close to badgering the witness over a small point, whether the document presented was a work order or an invoice. Then, the defense cast aspersions on his inspection. "You never looked at the rims of the vehicle after the tires . . ."

"Yes, I did. Yes, sir, I did," Rick insisted, clarifying that while he did not inspect the insides of the tires, he had checked out the outsides.

"Were you inside your showroom ringing up these sales?"

"When?" Rick asked.

"On the day these tires were sold. You don't ring up tires from outside in the shop, do you?"

"I . . . did the original work order inside . . . the showroom. I then carried the ticket out into the shop, and then I went back out to the store. The only customer I really had at that time that evening was Mr. Dunbar."

Investigator Gary Babb was recalled as the final witness of the day to testify about the false address on the Kramer Tire work order. He told the jury that there was no Silver Spoon Drive in Roanoke; in fact, no road by that name anywhere in Virginia.

As for the zip code, 24131, the closest number that he could find was 24121, which is the zip code for the lake house. The phone number given had area code, 304, that he said was a West Virginia area code—the area code where Wesley's mother and stepfather lived.

The seventh day of the proceedings, November 17, 2010, began with more legal huddling. Joey Sanzone requested that his proposed fingerprint expert, Jennifer Mnookin, be allowed to be present during the Commonwealth's testimony on fingerprints. Wes Nance objected primarily because Mnookin was not an expert in the purported field, but a law professor who taught and researched evidentiary issues, but when pressed by the judge, Nance relented.

The prosecution case continued with Kenneth L. Riding, a retired employee from the Department of Forensic Science at the State Crime Lab in Roanoke, where he'd worked for ten years as a forensic scientist specializing in latent prints. Prior to that job, he was a latent print examiner for Arlington County Police Department in northern Virginia and spent five and a half years examining prints at the FBI in D.C. He testified that throughout his forty-one-year career, he had examined around 4 or 5 million prints, and had testified about 310 times. He was accepted as an expert by the court.

First, Riding explained his methodology. "The fiction ridges . . . have what are known as Galton's details . . . These characteristics consist of bifurcations where a . . . single ridge will work into two ridges. They are known as ending ridges, dots and enclosures or islands where a ridge will bifurcate and come back together forming an enclosure."

"And in doing fingerprint comparison and this differentiation is there a methodology that you use?"

"Yes, there is," Riding said. "It is called ACEV, which is an acronym for the process used in [. . .] doing fingerprint identifications and comparisons. It stands for analysis, comparison, evaluation, and verification."

Riding testified that he did not find any fingerprints of value on the shell casing or the murder weapon; however, although there were no visible prints on the alleged suicide note, his luck changed when he used a chemical called ninhydrin to process it. "The chemical reacts to the amino acids that are given off by the fingers," he said. "Two latent fingerprints were developed on the suicide note."

"And where were those fingerprints in proximity to the paper and the printing on the paper?"

"One was on the front and one was on the back of the paper."

"Once you develop those latent fingerprints do you document that in some form or fashion?"

"The note is actually sent to the forensic photographer there at the state lab."

Nance presented an exhibit to Riding. "Do you recognize that?"

"It appears to be enlargements of the fingerprints that were developed on the suicide note." Riding then demonstrated the manner that the note could be held to leave the prints where they were: one as if the paper were pinched from the top, the other as if the note had been grabbed on the side.

"Sir, once those two latent prints were developed, what do you then do with it?"

"I eventually compared them against some elimination

fingerprints, which were submitted to the lab." He then explained that he'd had to obtain Jocelyn Earnest's fingerprints by going to the morgue and getting them himself. Then, he said, "It is a matter of looking at the latent print and picking out points of similarity or characteristics in there and comparing them with the fingerprints of Jocelyn Earnest [. . .] The latent prints developed on the note were not identified as Jocelyn Earnest's." He testified that he also got a negative result when he compared the unknown prints to Maysa Munsey, Marcy Shepherd, and Dora Farrah, another of Jocelyn's co-workers known to have been in Jocelyn's house in 2007.

He then described his work with Wesley Earnest's prints. "The comparison is made by placing the latent print side by side with the inked print, using . . . a microscope as a magnifier and picking out points of similarity . . . And you move back and forth between the latent print and ink print looking for similar points of identification in both prints in a relative area on both prints and trying to find . . . a sufficient number of points to effect an identification."

"Did you find points of similarity?"

"Yes, I did."

"Did that allow you, based upon your training and experience, to reach a conclusion as to the origin of the fingerprints on the front side of that note?"

"Yes, it did."

Joey Sanzone made another of his many objections during this testimony, this time based on speculation. The judge overruled him.

"Mr. Riding," Nance said, "what was your conclusion regarding your analysis of the front side of the note?"

"That the latent print on the front side of the note and the inked fingerprint card . . . [of] . . . the left thumb were made by one and the same person."

They went on to discuss the latent found on the back of the note, which Riding also identified as being from the left thumb of Wesley Earnest. Using an exhibit with enlarged photographs prepared for the trial, Riding then pointed out the similarities to the jury over many objections from the defense.

Sanzone began the cross-examination by putting Riding's training, certification, and proficiency testing under the microscope. "You didn't use any sophisticated graphic program available on a computer to make your comparisons in this case?"

"No. I didn't have to. The print was good enough [. . .] to use the magnifying glass and naked eye."

"But my point is, you don't have any training on those programs, is that correct?"

"That's correct."

Sanzone's next questions contained a thinly veiled criticism of Riding for accepting what he received from the Bedford County Sheriff's Office and not going outside of that to obtain other prints for comparison. Then he said, "When we talk about the print, you said that the left [. . .] thumb print was the one you identified both times."

"That's correct."

"And are you familiar with the term reciprocating print? And by that I mean, if I put my thumb on my paper right here I use my other fingers to balance . . . or to complete my grip. Are these sometimes called reciprocating prints on the back of the paper?"

"Yes, they are."

"Did you find any reciprocating prints for the first thumb print that you said was at the top . . . ?"

"No, I did not."

Sanzone repeated the question for the other print and got the same answer. The defense attorney then directed him to marks on the paper that could have been from other fingers.

Riding said, "Well, they could be but they're not clear enough, but they also may not have had any friction detail or been of any value for comparison purposes."

"Can you tell me for the first print or the second print when those prints were made?"

"No, I cannot. There's no scientific way to tell when the print was left."

"Did you receive any latent prints, any partial prints, any smudged prints, any possible prints from the alarm pad in Jocelyn Earnest's home?"

"No. I did not receive those."

Sanzone asked Riding the same question about the thermostat and the light switch and got a negative response to both. Then he said, "Would you agree with me that oftentimes a surface such as a plastic surface . . . on an alarm pad, a doorknob, a thermostat, a light switch . . . can often be good places to find fingerprints?"

"Yes, they can be."

After establishing that the prints recovered from the

note were partials, Sanzone asked, "And by your identification [. . .] here, you're passing judgment on the unknown area of the full print, aren't you? Aren't you passing judgment there?"

"No, I'm not."

"Aren't you saying that if you had this partial print, if you could see the whole thing, it would match the full print?"

"I don't need the full print to make an identification."

"Oh, I understand, but what I'm asking is, when you say that this interior part matches, aren't you also saying that if you could see the outside here you believe that matches?"

"Yes, I do."

"And you have never seen, don't know, can't know what this outside portion of the partial print looks like actually, can you? No way to look at it by looking at the partial print."

"No, I can't."

"If there is one point of dissimilarity in this unknown portion that we've talked about between the known print and the partial print—if it had been extended out there would be no match; isn't that true?"

"But the print has already been proven from the partial latent."

Sanzone complained the answer was not responsive but the judge urged him to continue. Sanzone said, "You said the print has already been proven to your satisfaction, is that what you're saying?"

"Through the science, it's been proven."

"Well, now, let's talk about the science [. . .] When you start examining fingerprints you know whose finger-prints you're . . . seeing, don't you?"

"Most of the time, yes."

"This isn't a blind study. It's not something where you're submitted a set of prints and you don't know who they belong to and you're submitted a second set of prints and you don't know who they belong it; isn't that true?"

"That's correct."

"You look at each set individually. Wesley Earnest's name was written on one card and Jocelyn Earnest's was written on another, isn't that right?"

"Yes."

"Do you know what 'expectation bias' is?"

"No. Can you explain it to me?" Riding retorted sharply.

An objection from the prosecution prevented Sanzone from doing just that. He asked the witness about the points of similarity in one of the prints. Riding testified that there were sixteen.

The defense led the questioning through the points of similarity, questioning every decision. Riding repeatedly insisted that the size differences were irrelevant because that would vary with the pressure applied and the size has no bearing on the ability to match one ridge to another.

"And in this case, from a percentage point of view you had . . . 20 percent of the possible points of similarities in the lowest number of a full fingerprint. You would agree with that, wouldn't you?" Sanzone asked, referring to how a whole print could have up to seventy-five points.

"Yes, but the print can be identified with as little as seven or eight points."

"According to your system?"

"Yes."

"Now, do you have a particular document that you can rely on to say how many people in this room have fifteen points of similarity in their thumb print?"

"No, I cannot, but in my forty years of experience, the most . . . points of similarity that I have noticed in the millions of prints that I have looked at, the most I've been able to find that were similar was five . . . maybe six points of similarity."

". . . You're aware of other people finding points of similarity between two people up to fifteen points?"

"Objection, Your Honor," Krantz said. "Assuming facts, not in evidence, Your Honor. He's testifying."

From there, the questioning went in fits and starts as the prosecution objected, the lawyers argued, and the judge got exasperated and ended up sending the jury out of the courtroom. After more back-and-forth with the attorneys, Updike ruled that the question was improper and would not be asked in front of the jury. Sanzone used his remaining questions to inform the jury that although there have been massive changes in technology since the 1960s, there have been no fundamental alterations to the way law enforcement performs fingerprint identification.

Andrew Johnson, another forensic scientist who worked with the Commonwealth of Virginia assigned to the

Western Laboratory in Roanoke for seventeen years, followed Riding. Johnson specialized in fingerprint analysis as well as impression analysis—such as shoe prints, tire treads, other impression evidence. His extensive training came from a variety of sources including the FBI and Royal Canadian Mounted Police.

After going through the long list of trainings, teaching experiences, and honors that qualified him as an expert, he answered questions about measurements. He explained that because people apply variable pressure and that changes the flatness and width of the fingerprint, that any documentation of width and height of ridges or patterns would be meaningless.

Nance took Johnson through a long discourse on the biology and history of fingerprint identification. Then the witness testified to his examination and confirmation of the print identification made by Riding.

Joey Sanzone made a major issue over the fact that Johnson did not bring his notes to the courtroom. Prosecutor Krantz objected to the innuendo that the defense was raising, leaving the impression that the Commonwealth had something to hide. The judge clarified the situation as well as he could to the jurors, but likely many were left with some concern over what had not been revealed.

On redirect, Johnson explained that he'd also found fifteen to sixteen points of similarity to Wesley Earnest's prints on the suicide note. At a later date, he examined the prints again using an uncropped photo and found two additional points of identity.

With Johnson's testimony, the prosecution closed its case. In traditional response, the defense made a motion to strike the Commonwealth's evidence. "Judge . . . in support thereof, I say that there's no evidence that anybody physically saw my client at the scene. There's evidence that the gun had been possessed and ownership had been claimed within a will by Ms. Jocelyn Earnest. There's evidence also in this case, Judge, that no one can establish the timing of the fingerprint." Sanzone cited a Virginia Supreme Court case that ruled "that the mere existence of a fingerprint at a crime scene is not enough to make a sufficiency argument . . . And for all those reasons, we would submit that the case is not proper at this point to go forward."

"Viewing the evidence in the light most favorable to the Commonwealth as required at this stage, the motion is denied," Judge Updike said. "The court feels this is a circumstantial case and there is circumstantial evidence other than fingerprint. Denied. Objections duly noted and preserved."

The Commonwealth's case was made. It was now up to the defense team of Joey and Blair Sanzone to present testimony to free Wesley Earnest. If they failed to do so, the high school administrator could spend the rest of his life behind bars.

THIRTY-EIGHT

On November 17, 2010, defense attorney Joey Sanzone called his first witness, Susan Cropp, a forensic mitochondrial DNA examiner for the FBI with a bachelor's in biology from Ohio State, master's in zoology from Ohio State, and PhD in Population and Evolutionary Biology from Washington University in St. Louis. The judge qualified her as an expert in DNA analysis.

She explained that mitochondrial DNA is related to maternal inheritance; it is not unique to an individual because all maternal relatives would have the same sequence. She testified that current databases have identified 5,071 different mitochondrial DNA types. In other words, there are that many known matrilineal genetic lines in the world.

She performed a mitochondrial DNA analysis on six hairs submitted by Bedford County. She compared them to seven reference points: Joyce Young, Maysa Munsey, Shameka Wright, and several male acquaintances known to have been in Jocelyn's home in the past, Leon Hill, Keith Whitted, Wesley Brian Earnest, and Charlie Carol Boyd III. No match with any of those individuals.

On cross, the Commonwealth simply established that in addition to DNA analysis, the FBI lab also relied on fingerprint analysis to counter the defense claim that the science in that field was inaccurate.

After a break, Joey Sanzone called Dr. Jennifer Mnookin to the stand. Krantz immediately objected to her testimony. The jury was sent out and the voir dire examination began.

In his introduction of the witness, Sanzone said that Dr. Mnookin was an expert in fingerprint identification, its history, and its use. The Commonwealth stated that they had no objection to the defense laying out her background for the record but that their objection was that she was not a fingerprint examiner, and thus *not* an expert in the field. Because of that, they argued, she should not be allowed to render any opinion regarding the analysis done on the fingerprints.

Outside of the presence of the jury, the judge wanted to hear about her qualifications and testimony before making a decision. The defense walked him through her impressive credentials, a social science degree from Harvard, a law degree from Yale, and a PhD in history and the social study of science and technology from MIT. She was currently working as a professor of evidence at

UCLA's law school and served on various national and statewide organizations.

"Have you published articles relating to fingerprint identification?" Joey Sanzone asked.

"Yes. I have published around half a dozen or so academic articles on various aspects of the adequacy of the research foundation and scientific basis for latent fingerprint identification [in] peer-reviewed academic journals."

Sanzone spoke of her national affiliations and asked, "The National Institute of Justice is what type of organization?"

"It is a research arm of the Department of Justice essentially, and it funds research into the criminal justice system. I along with some co-investigators applied for a set of competitive grants and [. . .] I'm the primary investigator [. . .] Our study is endeavoring to develop some objective measures of difficulty for latent print comparison. And then we are hoping to be able to determine some useful information about error rates as a function of difficulty."

"Are you aware of the method for fingerprint evaluation in this case that was talked about, the ACEV method?"

"Yes, I am not a fingerprint examiner, but I do—"

Krantz interrupted, "Your Honor, I know he needs to make out the record and the Court's ruled, but that's the exact issue right there."

The judge allowed Mnookin to explain that although it was out of her expertise to "make a statement about whether or not two prints did or did not match," she expounded on her study of other methodologies. Updike asked for a response to the interview from the prosecution. Krantz said, "At the end of the day, she's a law professor. There can be but one judge in this courtroom. And nothing that she offered overturns . . . the underlying reliability of fingerprints. And I'm not sure what she'd be testifying to. And as she very candidly stated . . . she is not a fingerprint examiner. She would not be rendering an opinion on whether any particular fingerprints matched. She is not a scientist." He argued that the law clearly stated, "'Being an expert in one field does not qualify one to speak as an expert in another field even if the field is closely related,'" and said, "I have no questions about her knowledge base and the usefulness of the endeavors she's engaged in, but I paid careful attention to what she said . . . They're hoping to develop, trying to create, would like to try to develop. So even with her stated research, it's tenuous at this point."

Judge Updike agreed, ruling that in his opinion, such testimony "requires someone who qualifies as an expert in the field of fingerprint analysis . . . Though this witness quite obviously is an expert in many fields, extremely well educated, extremely intelligent, I'm certain, but the issue of whether she's qualified to offer evidence that I feel is of the nature requiring expertise in the field of fingerprint analysis, it is my ruling that she is not."

The next witness, Rodney Wolforth of the Virginia Department of Forensic Science, possessed expert qualifications in his stated field of DNA analysis: a bachelor of science degree in biology and a master's degree in forensic chemistry from the University of Pittsburgh along with working experience since 1976 with the Michigan Crime Lab and as the unit supervisor in the forensic biology section here in Virginia. Adding to his background was his stint as a visiting scientist at Quantico where he worked on the short tandem repeat project, which was the type of analysis he did now.

After receiving the swabs of the sample from the sink, Wolforth testified that he'd compared that unknown to samples from Jocelyn Earnest's family and friends, as well as from law enforcement known or suspected to have been in the house. None were a match. He did determine that the blood came from a male, but nothing more than that.

The profile of that sample was now a permanent record entered into the Combined DNA Index System, which is the federal, state, and local DNA database, and could still be matched on any sample that came through in the future, but as of that day in the trial, no matches had been found.

Krantz conducted the cross-examination with an attitude, as if he were offended by the existence of an employee of the Commonwealth as a witness for the defense. "I'm assuming at some point in time, after DNA analysis began being used in the forensic sciences labs in Virginia, including Roanoke, they shut down all the other parts of the lab; is that correct? I mean, there's no longer a toxicology lab since we have DNA?"

"No, that is not correct."

"Oh. Is there no longer any fingerprint department since you have DNA?"

Sanzone broke into the interchange. "Your Honor, I'm going to ask that I be allowed to revisit some prior testimony if we keep going on this line."

"All I can do is rule on things as they come in," Updike said.

"I object to the questions and the way they're being asked," Sanzone said.

Krantz jumped back into the fray. "My point, Mr. Wolforth, is just because there's now been DNA since 1996, that didn't shut down all the other parts of the lab, did it?"

"No, it did not at all."

"You as a forensic scientist would acknowledge that all the other parts of the lab are reliable sciences and are depended upon?"

"Judge, I object to that," Sanzone said. "We can't testify about anything other than the DNA."

With the judge's permission, Krantz rephrased the question. "These other departments still exist."

"Yes, they do."

After an inordinate amount of legal squabbling, Krantz moved on to the area of touch DNA and asked the witness about the testing of the murder weapon and ammunition.

Wolforth explained, "A swabbing from the barrel, cylinder, and frame of the firearm was done, and no DNA results were obtained. The shell casings and cartridges were also swabbed, and no DNA results were obtained."

"You didn't find anything there belonging to Jocelyn Earnest?"

"I found no DNA," Wolforth responded.

The next witness was Roger Earnest, father of the accused. He dragged a heavy emotional burden into the witness box. He testified that he had a good relationship with his son Wesley, and that he'd had a good one with his daughter-in-law Jocelyn as well. They'd visited each other's homes, and Roger said that he'd helped the couple out when he could, such as with the loan he made to them for $100,000 when they bought a rental property.

"With regard to the one hundred thousand dollars, are you still owed that money?" Sanzone asked.

"Yes. I allowed them to pay it monthly, you know, a stipend. I guess you could call it interest. I considered it principal."

Sanzone asked him about target shooting at his home in 2002, and Roger said that Jocelyn had proved to be a better shot with the .357 than his son.

Exhibiting the murder weapon, Sanzone asked, "Who had this gun or one like it on the day that y'all were up there?"

"Jocelyn."

"Did she bring it down to where you were shooting?"

"Yes, sir."

"Did she keep it with her when she was down there?"

"Except during the time that Wesley fired it, yes. After that, she kept possession of it."

Krantz asked Roger about the loan and payments. Roger said he'd received $18,000, which they called interest, but that he didn't want to earn interest off of them, so he'd given the money back to Wesley. To date, he had not received any payment on the principal.

Krantz said, "Would it surprise you to know then that Wesley had told Jocelyn that you had consulted two attorneys who were intending to sue her over the hundred thousand dollars? Would that surprise you?"

"I wouldn't have any knowledge of that," Roger said.

"Did you ever have any plans to sue her?"

"I had no plans. I did consult an attorney . . . just for advice and he told me I would have to sue. And I wasn't going to do that."

Roger testified than he had only known Shameka Wright for two years or less, or since 2008 or 2009, so Krantz asked, "Would it surprise you to know that your son was having an affair with Shameka as far back as 2004?"

"I don't know."

Sanzone objected and the judge responded, "My ruling is going to be the same as earlier rulings I made in a different context. This witness's knowledge of any relationship between the son and Ms. Wright I find irrelevant. Objection sustained."

The prosecution attempted to enter into evidence a letter of claim against the estate of Jocelyn Earnest for the one hundred thousand dollars, signed by Roger Earnest. Krantz argued that it proved an inconsistent statement and went to the credibility of the witness. Sanzone countered that it was collateral and irrelevant because it was a

claim, not a lawsuit. The judge sided with the defense—
the letter was not admitted and the witness was dismissed.

Joey Sanzone called Investigator Mike Mayhew back up
on the stand to identify photos of the gun safe in the
basement of Jocelyn's home and of the holster found inside of it. Then he produced the actual holster along with
the murder weapon and asked, "Will you stand and see
if that gun will go into that holster?"

Mayhew slid it in and said, "Yes, sir, it does."

On cross-examination, Krantz asked, "What did you
have to do to get to that gun safe?"

"Actually, there were [. . .]bed frames and headboards
and bed mattresses and boxes stacked up. We actually had
to move . . . a lot of stuff to get in there."

"The gun safe wasn't accessible?"

"No, sir, it was not."

"It was locked, wasn't it?"

"Yes, it was."

"And do gun holsters have serial numbers?"

"No, sir. Not that I am aware of."

"Did you find any ammunition at the house associated
with that firearm?"

"No, sir, I did not."

Cindy Dawn King, a teacher at Great Bridge High School,
stepped up to the stand next. She testified that Wesley had
supervised and critiqued her teaching methods, providing

her with his report on her performance on the afternoon of December 20, 2007.

When it was Wes Nance's turn to question the witness, he said: "You made some observations about Mr. Earnest during the time that he was evaluating you that morning, correct?"

"Yes, sir, I did."

"You noticed that he wasn't paying much attention to you."

"Yes, sir, I did."

"And you thought, 'This is going to be the easiest evaluation I've ever had.'"

"I thought that." Cindy went on to mention that Wesley had left the classroom at one point because, according to her students, he had to answer a call on his cell phone. After an objection on hearsay grounds, Nance wrapped up.

Al Ragas, technology liaison and technical support specialist at Great Bridge High, testified that he'd known Wesley for five years and thought he was efficient and conscientious.

He said that he had seen Wesley throughout the day on December 19 and met with him at 3:30 that afternoon to discuss a student's misuse of the computer. When they finished dealing with that matter, Al said, he punched out, a little bit after 4 P.M. On December 20, he told the jury that he had seen Wesley at the school at 7:35 in the morning.

On cross, Krantz asked, "On the nineteenth, you didn't notice anything unusual about Mr. Earnest [. . .]?"

"Yes, sir."

"Nothing?"

"No, sir."

"And did Mr. Earnest ever complain of being ill that day to you?"

"No, he would not have."

"What time did you punch out?"

"I believe it was four-something that I punched out."

"You didn't punch out at three twenty-six P.M.?"

"Three-twenty-six P.M. for lunch break [. . .] I was called at three thirty where I went to see Dr. Earnest."

"So if we look at your time sheet, it will say you punched out at three twenty-six, correct?"

"Exactly."

Krantz moved on to other topics, then asked, "Did you go to his house?"

"I've been to his house."

"Did you go there for fun?"

"No."

"Did you go there for work?"

"Yes."

"What did you do at his house?"

"I did trim for him," he said, referring to the carpentry work he did at Wesley's lake home.

"And where was the house located?"

"At Smith Mountain Lake."

"So he was your employer?"

"Yes."

"He paid you?"

"No."

"You did it for free?"

"No."

"Well, did he pay you or did you do it for free?"

"He didn't pay me and I didn't do it for free."

"How were you compensated?"

"He said that if I worked on the house then my wife and I would be able to maybe use it one time for a little getaway."

"I understand. And did you do that?"

"No."

THIRTY-NINE

The thought of the next day of the trial on November 18, 2010, sent many observers into a state of heightened anticipation. The defense had promised that Wesley Earnest would enter the witness box. Would they honor that commitment?

The day started with the defense calling Jack Tymchen of Verizon Wireless. At the time of crime, he was working at Alltel as an operations manager for the wireless network in central Virginia. Jack testified that when a call came from Rustburg to Wesley's phone, the phone registered at the Portsmouth switch, which covers the whole eastern part of the state. He told the jury that there was nothing in the records to indicate that the phone ever left that area.

Assistant Commonwealth's Attorney Wes Nance used his questions to establish that the only occasion Wesley had actually answered his phone during that time period

was on the morning of December 19 and the morning
of December 20, 2007. Any calls that came to his phone
in between those times went unanswered. Nance said,
"That phone could have been sitting on a nightstand the
entire time, couldn't it?"

"Yes, sir," Jack said.

"And there's no way to prove otherwise?"

"That is correct."

On redirect, Sanzone had the witness explain that
there were a lot of reasons why the phone might not have
been answered: it could have run out of charge, been out
of the service area, or been turned off. Nonetheless, the
damage had already been done.

The prosecutors were not happy when a young man named
Wayne Stewart stepped into the witness box. He was in
the courtroom to deliver an alibi for Wesley Earnest.

Wayne worked a 4 to 8 P.M. shift at Taco Bell on Grass-
field Parkway in Chesapeake, located close to Great Bridge
High. He had not testified in the first trial because when
investigators questioned him earlier, he'd gotten confused
about dates and had not been certain of which day Wesley
had been there. But now he testified that on December
19, 2007, he saw Wesley come through the drive-in
around six o'clock and place an order for a Grande Meal—
ten hard tacos and ten soft tacos. He said he remembered
Wesley's visit there that night because it had been a bit of
a hassle to take care of him.

On cross, Krantz came right to the point: "Do you

recall telling the members of the Bedford County Sheriff's Department you . . . remembered him coming in, but you didn't know what day it was? Is that right?"

"Yes, sir."

"And you also told them that Mr. Earnest came back to you and tried to get you to remember, isn't that correct?"

"Yes, sir."

Sanzone fired back with questions on redirect: "Mr. Stewart, did Mr. Earnest come back and see you . . . the following week?"

"Yes, sir."

Sanzone produced a document containing a prior consistent statement that he was preparing to hand to the witness. That set off objections from the prosecution that led to the jury being removed from the courtroom. The defense claimed the paper contained Wayne's recollection about Wesley's visit the week after Jocelyn's death. Sanzone said the witness would testify that the store manager wrote and signed it immediately after that visit and before Wayne was ever interviewed by Bedford County. The prosecution insisted that because someone else wrote it, it was hearsay; and furthermore, there was no foundation to verify the date of its creation.

The judge said, "The statement is not barred by the hearsay rule because it is not being offered as proof of its content, but rather, it's being offered as proof that the statement was made. It is not, however, substantive evidence. It relates only to credibility . . . That's my understanding of the law and that will be the understanding that I apply here." Updike ruled the paper admissible, but not its contents.

The defense elicited testimony that Wesley came in on Christmas Eve or Christmas Day to ask Wayne to write a statement about his visit the prior week.

Then, Krantz nibbled at him again: "You remember Mr. Earnest coming through and ordering that meal?"

"Yes, sir."

"You don't know whether or not it's on the nineteenth, though, do you, sir?"

"Not really, sir."

"Do you remember being interviewed by the Bedford County Sheriff's Department?"

"Yes, sir."

"In fact, you told them that you probably shouldn't have signed that statement: isn't that correct?"

"Yes, sir. I thought I was helping him out because I thought he was losing his job or something like that. If I would have known it was anything like this . . ."

"You wouldn't have signed it, would you . . . ?"

"No, sir."

On further redirect, Sanzone asked Wayne if he'd told the investigators that he'd signed the document and believed it to be true and then asked: "And did it scare you when the police came?"

"Yes, sir, because I thought I was in trouble, you know. That was the only thing."

"Does it scare you being here today?"

"Yes, sir. I've never really been in court for real." Wayne went on to tell the jury that to the best of his recollection, Wesley did place that order on December 19 and he had no intention of deceiving anyone.

Wayne seemed to be trying to please everyone, but it was obvious that all he really wanted was to get off the witness stand and go home. After a bit more back-and-forth with both attorneys, the miserable experience was finally over.

It is difficult to comprehend the living nightmare faced by the mother of the accused, Pat Wimmer, but she took the stand seemingly firm in her belief in the innocence of her son. After establishing her identity, Joey Sanzone asked, "Did you know Jocelyn Earnest?"

"Yes, I did."

"How did you and Jocelyn get along?"

"We got along real well."

"And you knew her for many years?"

"Yes."

"When Wesley separated from Jocelyn, did you meet Shameka Wright?"

"No, I did not."

"Have you met Shameka Wright at some point after the separation?"

"I have, yes."

"And do you get along with Shameka?"

"I do."

"Would you say your relationship with Wesley has continued to be good all these years?"

"Absolutely."

"Back when Wesley and Jocelyn were separated did there come a time when you went to the lake house [. . .] and saw the lake house in a different condition inside?"

"Yes, the furniture had been removed."

"Can you tell the jury a little about what you saw inside the house as far as how much had been removed?"

"[When] you first walked in, the kitchen was on the right, and there's a big, what I call, a great room in the front. And so when I first went in my first impression was that it was empty, it was bare . . . I believe there was like two couches in there, maybe a love seat before, about a week or so before we were there, an oversized recliner chair, coffee tables, end tables, a big screen TV—I don't know how big but bigger than the one we have—a couple scatter rugs . . . That was gone. There were bunk beds . . . office supplies—that sort of thing was gone."

"Bare is the word you used?"

"Yeah. The front room, like I said, it was bare. Now, there was some things still left in some of the bedrooms, but the front room itself was void or bare of furniture."

"You said office supplies were gone?"

"What I noticed was the computer paper . . . Also, cleaning supplies, including, like, toilet paper, that sort of stuff was gone." She went on to describe the furniture she and her husband had given to Wesley to replace what had been removed.

Sanzone asked, "Did there come a time later when Wesley told you that he needed to change his living arrangements in Chesapeake?"

"Yes, he did."

"And did you have a suggestion and an offer as to what he could do for a few months until the next year?"

"My husband and I have a travel trailer. And so I made the suggestion—"

"A recreation vehicle?"

"It's twenty-seven foot long [. . .] I made the recommendation that he stay in that because we had noticed around about in different campgrounds they have provisions that you can leave it for a few weeks, a few months. And we found the Chesapeake Campground [. . .]"

"And did you put any limitations on how long he could use it or anything of that nature?"

"Well, we were shooting for April, if he could find something before spring, but we figured that it could also go to June when school was out. So it was not a set limit [. . .]"

"Did you also help him out by going down and making the arrangements?"

"Yes, we did."

"Were you there when that was done?"

"[. . .] When we went down there on the twenty-sixth of December and we checked in the original check-in registration, it was under my husband's name, Michael Stephen Wimmer [. . .]"

"Did you check in the first time . . . for him?"

"Absolutely [. . .] We checked in as Michael Stephen Wimmer, our address, our phone number, our credit card, of course. And Liz or Mrs. Satterfield, she asked would there be anyone else staying with us [. . .] And I told her that after a while my son would be coming in. So she wanted to know what his name was so she could put it on as another person because that campground has a security gate [. . .] So I told her Wesley Earnest. She said Wesley Wimmer, and she was typing the name [. . .] And I said, no Wesley Earnest. And we went back and forth like that several times, and she kept saying, 'He's your son.' I said, 'Yes.' So, she just wasn't understanding the different names [. . .] I just turned to my husband and said, 'I hope he doesn't mind being called Wesley Wimmer Earnest because I think that's what she did.'"

After an excessive amount of legal wrangling over whether or not the defense would be allowed to introduce Jocelyn's BlackBerry call history (ultimately denied by Judge Updike), David Wilson, who lived next door to the lake house on Clearwater Drive, testified about his observations in December 2006, when he said he saw two women come to the lake house in a large rental truck, then witnessed the women carry out beds, tables, chairs, and TVs, but said that he didn't know how full the truck was, couldn't see inside of it. The Commonwealth had no questions for the witness.

Investigator John Tetterton of the Amherst County Sheriff's Department was the next person in the witness box. He told the jury that on the morning of December 19, 2007, he'd met with Maysa Munsey and that Jocelyn Earnest had been there with her.

Commonwealth's Attorney Krantz said, "Your Honor, we don't dispute this officer's testimony."

The lack of any questions from the prosecution frustrated Sanzone, who'd anticipated having the chance to ask additional questions on redirect. He asked the judge if he could pose the questions anyway, but Updike said, "There can be no redirect if there's no cross-examination."

Maysa Munsey was next on the stand. She said that she'd met Jocelyn in 1997, and answered that she did know Jennifer Kerns through Jocelyn, but hadn't socialized with her. Maysa said that she and Marcy Shepherd worked in the same building, but in totally different departments with no crossover.

Sanzone asked about the drive to West Virginia that Maysa took with Jocelyn.

"We left Friday night and came back Saturday morning. There was an ice storm so we were trying to beat the storm."

When asked about when they'd seen each other next after that trip, Maysa replied, "It could very well have been Sunday. I saw Jocelyn all the time."

"After Sunday when was the next time you saw her?"

"It could have been Monday."

"Did you know when you saw her next?"

"No."

Sanzone asked if she had the key to the house and the code to the alarm. She said she had both and had entered the house in the past using them. She testified that she'd met with Jocelyn at customer service at 7:30 on the morning of the nineteenth and sent her texts the evening of that day but did not get a response. Then Sanzone wanted to know if she called Jocelyn at 3 A.M. that night, and she said that it was possible but she didn't remember.

Sanzone said, "I'm going to show you a document and . . . see if it refreshes your memory."

The judge stepped in and explained further. "The document will be taken away. If your memory is refreshed, you may testify from your refreshed memory. You may not, however, just say what is on the document."

After Maysa looked it over, she said, "I didn't specifically remember giving her a call, but, like I said, we're friends . . . If I couldn't sleep, I probably called her."

She testified about the time she spent with Jocelyn on the morning of the nineteenth and calling Jocelyn at 3:15 that afternoon.

Sanzone asked, "Were you frequently at Jocelyn's house?"

"Yes, I was."

"Who else was staying there at Jocelyn's house . . . [on] . . . December nineteenth or twentieth or around that time?"

"Nobody."

"Did you see condoms in the house?"

"I did not."

Nor did Maysa know anything about the blood in the sink. She did say that she, her son, and her then-boyfriend had all stayed over at Jocelyn's house over the summer, while dog-sitting for her.

"You had no personal knowledge about the relation-ship between Marcy and Jocelyn, did you?"

"No, I did not."

"And on the nineteenth or anytime that week, you'd not seen Wesley Earnest, had you?"

"No."

Prosecutor Wes Nance started his cross-examination by asking Maysa if she'd ever seen Jocelyn with a handgun in the ten years that she knew her or if she'd ever seen one in Jocelyn's home. She answered that she had not to both questions.

On redirect, Sanzone asked again if she'd ever seen condoms in the house or blood or hairs in the bathroom. She responded in the negative to all three. Maysa stepped down, relieved that this had been a far less confrontational experience for her than it had been during the first trial.

FORTY

The most suspenseful question in any murder trial is often whether or not the defendant will take the stand. Since Wesley Earnest had testified in the first trial in which he was found guilty, there were a lot of doubts that he would run that risk again. Nonetheless, the courtroom observers got their hearts' desire. Wesley Earnest took the oath and sat in the witness box to testify on his own behalf.

His lawyer, Joey Sanzone, took Wesley through his life history, including his marriage to Jocelyn. When the talk turned to the time of construction of the lake house, Sanzone asked, "Would it be fair to say that you did more of the work than she did?"

"Absolutely."

"But did you complain about that? Did you have any problem with that?"

"No, in fact, I found the construction work to be almost like therapy."

"Did it bother you in any way that you were doing a little bit more of the work?"

"No. In fact, after I finished the workday working as an assistant principal, I would go there and work with my hands. I loved it because it just really took any kind of stress out of the day."

"In the beginning, would she go there a lot with you?"

"We started building in 2004. And I know her work schedule, at that time, was working a lot of hours. So, I don't know how much time she was able to be up there."

"And just tell the jury about her work schedule back then and what was going on in that regard."

"She was doing an excellent job with work, but as such, she got one of those senior management levels. And with that required some eighty-hour workweeks, weekends, lots and lots more hours [. . .]" Between her work schedule and his work on the lake house, Wesley said, "it was rare to see each other [. . .]"

He said that although he requested she spend more time at home with him, Jocelyn "couldn't tear herself away from work. So I think my last effort was the anniversary of August 19, 2004 [. . .] Tried to put together some dinner and trying to welcome her home and have [. . .] a little social time together [. . .] It was somewhere close to midnight before she came home. Hadn't gotten a phone call. Hadn't heard anything from her."

". . . And that was just one of similar instances that had been going on for a while?"

"It had been. It just had been very disappointing all along. And we had gotten the occupancy permit for the lake house during that summer as well, but she refused to make that drive to work. So I was staying at the lake house by myself [. . .] Both insurance and mortgage required . . . [that we] . . . occupy the house as the primary residence. So you just can't leave it empty."

"As far as the intimacy goes, had that stopped at some time before?"

"Yes [. . .] Maybe early 2004."

"Had there been a problem with that even before that?"

"Yes [. . .] The very first year of marriage, she actually told me to go sleep with other women and come home to her, which was very hard because your first year of marriage is supposed to be the honeymoon time [. . .] I didn't want to do that. I just kept hanging in there with her refusing to see anybody else [. . .] And those requests to see other women and come home to her and just not sleep in the bed there at Pine Bluff Drive with anybody else was repeated over and over in 2002, 2003, going into 2004 period."

Friends and family who'd experienced Jocelyn's emotional devastation when she learned of Wesley's infidelity scoffed at these statements, calling them self-serving, arrogant, and outright lies.

Wesley said they separated in the summer of 2004, "and we saw less and less of each other and just kind of [. . .] started diverging."

"Did you ultimately meet someone else?"

"I did. I met Shameka Wright." Wesley went on to describe meeting her at Big Lots where she had been working at the time.

"And have y'all been happy?"

"We've been very happy."

"Can you tell us why you chose to move to Chesapeake?"

Wesley described the larger size of the school division and what that meant to his career, and said that he'd been looking for a fresh start. He also said that he "hadn't talked to [Jocelyn] face-to-face in a conversation without attorneys since—the best I can recall was June of 2005." He claimed to know nothing about her life after June 2005. "And I knew very little from the summer of 2004 to the summer of 2005," he added. At Sanzone's questioning, Wesley said he no longer had a key to the house on Pine Bluff, and not only did he not know the alarm code, "I didn't even know there was an alarm system there."

Sanzone asked his client about the December 2006 removal of furniture from the lake house, and Wesley confirmed his mother's earlier testimony. After that, Sanzone also had him back up his mother's testimony about the travel trailer and the campground.

Moving on to David Hall's truck, Wesley contradicted Dave's testimony, claiming that he'd returned the vehicle on Wednesday morning, December 19, 2007, before Jocelyn had died. He followed that testimony by verifying Al Ragas's timeline, which put Wesley at the high school until after four o'clock that afternoon. When Sanzone asked where he went after his conversation with Al, Wesley said that he went home.

"Why did you go home?" the defense attorney asked.

"Much as the same right now, I've got this problem in my throat because my seasonal allergies have been acting up . . . Throat was sore, scratchy. And [I] went home to take a nap and get a little rest in."

To undermine the prosecution's testimony that placed his cell phone in Chesapeake during the evening of December 19, he claimed that he did not have adequate cell coverage at his house, and missed a lot of incoming calls because of it. He added that he hadn't gotten a signal at the Taco Bell, either. From there, Sanzone easily transitioned his line of questions to confirm the testimony of the fast food restaurant's employee, Wayne Stewart.

After covering Wesley's story about going out to pick up food that evening, Sanzone asked him what he did when he returned home.

"Just did some reading and organizing some things, packing up, getting things ready to finish my move," he said, referring to his upcoming change to the campgrounds.

"Did you ever leave Chesapeake that evening, that day, the morning, the next day, anything?"

"Not at all."

Wesley further said that scheduling his car detailing for Thursday had taken some time.

"But it was not because you were out of town any of those days?"

"No."

Sanzone took Wesley through the events of December 20, 2007, from his activities during the last day of school before the holiday to his drive west. "So you go to Shameka's house," Sanzone said. "And it takes you about three and a half hours to get there at Concord. What happened when you got to her house?"

"Well, I just unloaded the car with all the Christmas goodies and things that the teachers and kids had brought in. And I gave it to them [. . .]"

"Did you hear some news?"

"I did. Shameka's mother informed me of what, I guess, was on the news, that Jocelyn had died."

"And how did you take that?"

"It hit me hard. It was devastating. In fact, my knees buckled [. . .]"

"Wesley, what did you do after that?"

"We just talked for a little bit and tried to kind of take it all in. Then I contacted the sheriff's department."

"Why did you contact them?"

"I figured being next-of-kin, there might be something I needed to do or talk to them, see what was going on."

"Did you ultimately meet with them the next day?"

"I did."

"And prior to going to meet with them, did you talk to a number of people [. . .] about what may have happened or did people talk to you?"

"Yes. There were rumors of all kinds [. . .] going around. I know that Shameka worked for Campbell

County and heard rumors from the Campbell County first responders and people talking about this and that, all kinds of things."

This testimony was the first accusation that Campbell County emergency personnel, who had not even responded to the crime scene, had been spreading stories about the event. And frankly, there is no indication that the statement was true.

"Now when you went up and met with the sheriff, were you informed that if there was anything that you could do to further clarify what was going on with you on the nineteenth and twentieth that you should do it . . . ?"

"Yes," Wesley said, going on to state that it was the sight of his Taco Bell leftovers a day or so later that reminded him he'd been there on Wednesday, and said he went back to the place while it would still be fresh in the fast food employees' minds.

Sanzone then questioned Wesley's second occasion of borrowing David Hall's truck in January. Wesley testified that when he'd borrowed the vehicle in December, he had run over boards with nails hiding in tall grass by his mom's trailer. He said he'd stopped the leak with Fix-A-Flat, then replaced the tires the next month.

"Now with respect to Dave, when he called you to talk about the tires on the truck, he actually wanted his old tires? He liked the type he had before rather than what you put on there?" Sanzone asked.

"He was very happy to get the new tires," Wesley insisted. "In fact, he called me Santa Claus."

Next on the defense agenda was a discussion of guns.

Wesley testified that he bought the Smith and Wesson .357 as a gift for Jocelyn and confirmed his father's story that she was a better shot than he was.

Talking about the couple's wills, Sanzone asked, "And the portion where it talks about the three-fifty-seven being yours, is that after the portion that you would get everything if Jocelyn died first?"

"It is after that portion," Wesley said with a nod.

"Was it your intention through that will to ever say that the gun was your gun?"

"Not at all."

"After the writing of those wills, and before that, who did the gun belong to?"

"It always belonged to her."

"Did it ever in your mind come to a point where you thought it was yours . . . ?"

"No. It was a gift to her. It was going to be hers all along," Wesley said, adding that—unlike any of the other witnesses questioned—he'd often seen Jocelyn with it.

"When she was walking, she had it in [. . .] her jacket, sweater. She would have it in her right pocket or it would be in the glove compartment of the console of the Honda Accord," he claimed, saying, "Downtown, she worked those late-night hours and it's not the best neighborhood."

Sanzone geared up for his finale. "The bottom line in this whole case and this whole matter: did you kill Jocelyn Earnest?"

"No."

"Did you go to that house that night as she was returning from someplace?"

"No."

"Did you even know what time Jocelyn would be home or what her schedule was on the nineteenth?"

"No."

Holding up the note found at the crime scene, Sanzone asked, "Did you compose this note and leave it?"

"No."

"Did you, of your own knowledge, even know that Jocelyn had a new love?"

"I had no knowledge of anything."

"The first time you heard of that from Marcy Shepherd was when?"

"The preliminary trial."

Joey Sanzone had asked the last question of the direct examination. He could only hope that his client would hold up well under any prosecution attempt to throw him off his version of events.

FORTY-ONE

Before the jury returned to the courtroom after their break, Joey Sanzone raised an issue with Judge Updike. "The Commonwealth gave me a copy of a letter from my client to Shameka Wright's brother yesterday. And I think they [. . .] intend to use that to cross-examine him today [. . .] This was something that was part of his mail from the regional jail to his friend. And there was no search warrant acquired for the acquisition of this letter."

"What's the Commonwealth's response?" the judge asked.

"Judge, to help the court, this was a letter that the defendant wrote from the jail to a civilian," Commonwealth's Attorney Krantz said. "He did not write this letter to his lawyer. And in this letter, the defendant purports to script testimony during his trial, even to the point of coaching witnesses on unallowable hearsay: that it's okay, because once the jury's heard it, it's too late. Now [. . .] we gave the defense advance notice, but we waited until the defendant testified. And, Judge, I can tell the court, he followed the exact script that's in this letter [. . .] The Commonwealth's position is: there is no expectation of privacy in the jailhouse mail. The mail was seized. When it was found that these sorts of statements were in there that could have included, Judge, the suborning of perjury, the obstruction of justice, it was turned over to the Commonwealth's Attorney office, Your Honor."

Krantz argued that prisoners were advised that their mail was screened for security risks, and that they'd had a legitimate reason to look into Wesley's mail; Sanzone countered that since his client had not yet been convicted of a felony, he still had certain civil rights.

"I'm trying to do some research," Updike said. "And I found a case or two that I'd like to read." He opted to table the issue for the time being. "Let's bring the jury in. And just don't address this issue please in the presence of the jury."

Krantz began his cross-examination by introducing ten pages of handwritten material Wesley had prepared for his divorce attorney. Once Wesley had positively identified it, Krantz switched gears and said, "Mr. Earnest, when you moved to Chesapeake, you lied to your friends down there about being a millionaire and not having to work and being independently wealthy, didn't you?"

"Shared some successes and exaggerated some others."

"You lied to them, Mr. Earnest, didn't you?"

After an objection from Sanzone was overruled by the

judge, Krantz continued, "Mr. Earnest, did you tell them the truth?"

"About?"

"Were you, in fact, a millionaire?"

"No."

"Were you independently wealthy?"

"No."

". . . Were you wealthy enough that you did not have to work?"

"As far as, like, working in education [. . .] or construction or . . ."

"Mr. Earnest, my question to you [. . .] did you mislead your friends that you were independently wealthy enough that you did not have to work?"

"I did some exaggerating. And I've often said that I could retire from education and then work in the construction field and be happy."

"Mr. Earnest, let me repeat my question to you: Did you tell your friends the truth or not?"

"I exaggerated some things."

"And do you consider exaggerating things to be the truth or a lie?"

"Less than truthful."

"Do you consider less than truthful to be a lie?"

"Sure."

"So let me repeat my question: Did you lie to your friends?"

"Like I said, there were a number of different conversations."

"Mr. Earnest . . ."

"There were some exaggerations."

"Did you deceive them, Mr. Earnest?"

"Yes."

"And you will deceive people when it suits your purpose, won't you?"

"There were some things where I felt that my personal privacy as far as my past relationships and things deserved to be able to retain to myself. So whenever I would say something like 'I moved here alone' and then they would interpret . . ."

"I'm not asking you what they interpreted."

". . . ever been married or something like that."

". . . Mr. Earnest, please answer my question. You intentionally misled your friends, didn't you?"

"Yes."

Krantz then returned to the document he'd introduced when Wesley first took the stand. He had the defendant read through one point at a time from the list of things he'd itemized for his divorce attorney. After each one, the prosecutor asked him about the honesty of his statements. Wesley consistently insisted they were true. Krantz introduced two additional handwritten documents of the same nature and took him through the same process until the end of that day in court.

That night, Wes Nance went to bed at 10 P.M., thinking about the trial. He woke up at 3:30 A.M., well aware that Wesley was a better witness this time around than he had been in the first trial. He was more personable and appeared to be doing a better job relating to the jurors. Nance feared that connection could impact the outcome of the trial.

He fretted about what they'd done so far and what they still needed to do before Wesley left the witness box. The prosecution had thus far avoided using Jocelyn's timeline, out of a desire to avoid any inadvertent introduction of hearsay statements written by the victim, but now Nance realized that was a bad strategy. What they needed to do instead was use it but focus in on the statements on that document that were in Wesley's handwriting. Wesley was saying that there was no conflict between him and Jocelyn, that he wasn't in Chesapeake that night, and that he did not have access to Jocelyn's home. His notations on the timeline made his whole story a lie.

On November 19, 2010, the eighth day in Judge Updike's courtroom began with a request from the prosecution to divert from the procedures laid down before the commencement of the trial. The expectation was that anytime one of the attorneys on either team started an examination of a witness, that same lawyer would continue with it through to the end. Wes Nance, however, wanted to finish the cross in order to allow Krantz time to review documents they were considering for submission. Sanzone objected, saying that "it was agreed to have questioning done by only one person on each side for each individual."

The judge responded, "My concern—and I think the concern has always been with allowing questioning by more than one attorney—the concern is repetition. I will allow Mr. Nance to . . . continue with the cross-examination on behalf of the Commonwealth as long as there's not repetition or duplication."

Nance jumped right into his questioning of Wesley. "Jocelyn changed the locks in very early 2006, is that right?"

"Yes."

"Then, Mr. Earnest, can you explain to the jury how you got into her home and wrote on her timeline?"

Wesley turned to the jury, an arrogant smirk on his face; he pantomimed his hands pushing up the pane as he said, "Sure. A window, the second window from the left in the house had to have the sash replaced, but I never did put the locks on that."

A lot of people in the courtroom were stunned. Wesley did not deny that he broke into Jocelyn's home at all. In fact, he sounded as if he was bragging about his cleverness in doing so.

Sanzone didn't like the direction of the questioning or that impromptu revelation from his client and interrupted, "Judge . . . when are they asking about this? What's the date?"

"Excuse me," Nance snapped.

"What date are they asking about?"

"I didn't ask him a date."

"You didn't ask a date?"

"Please proceed, Mr. Earnest," Nance said.

"So the locks had not been put back on that bottom sash of the window," Wesley said.

"And when you wrote on her timeline, you assumed her identity, didn't you?"

"I don't think that's a fair statement at all," Wesley said.

"Your entries were written as if they were written by Jocelyn Earnest, weren't they?"

"I don't think that's . . ."

Sanzone ran to his client's rescue. "Judge, there are no facts in evidence to this."

"I have no further questions, sir," Nance said. "Thank you."

Joey Sanzone took the lead as redirect began. "Mr. Earnest [. . .] he asked a question about the house [. . .] when are we talking about?"

"As best I recall, somewhere middle of 2006 or so."

"That was a year and a half before Jocelyn's death?"

"Yes, sir."

"After the summer of 2006, y'all put the escrow agreement in place [. . .] You got exclusive possession of the house in Moneta [. . .] She got exclusive use of the house in Pine Bluff."

"Yes."

"You were satisfied with that?"

"Yes."

Sanzone asked a few more questions about Wesley's state of mind regarding the divorce and payment of bills, and Wesley answered that the separation had been very cordial, and that he and Jocelyn had had no issues.

Sanzone finished with his client, and the prosecution had no desire to ask additional questions on recross.

Sanzone brought the defense case to an end. "Judge, there's one matter that's just a housekeeping matter to be admitted into evidence, but besides that, we rest."

Now would come the Commonwealth's chance for rebuttal.

FORTY-TWO

The Commonwealth called Investigator Mike Mayhew to the stand as their first rebuttal witness and asked him about the interview with Wesley Earnest on December 21, 2007. Mayhew testified that when he'd asked the defendant about everything he did the week of Jocelyn's murder, he'd never mentioned having David Hall's truck, nor moving any furniture, nor making a trip to Taco Bell, nor having Jesse McCoy clean his car.

On cross-examination, defense attorney Joey Sanzone asked Mayhew if Wesley had ever denied going to Taco Bell. The investigator answered that Wesley didn't deny it because no one asked him about it.

"You asked him questions and he answered every question you asked?" Sanzone said.

"That's correct."

"And you didn't have any follow-up questions that were unanswered at the end of that interview?"

"No, sir. We asked him to go over it three times and he told us every time. And that was what he did those days."

As soon as the Commonwealth recalled Jocelyn Earnest's therapist, Susan Roehrich, Sanzone requested that the jurors be sent out of the courtroom. He argued that Susan's testimony was not proper rebuttal because it was not refuting anything said by Wesley.

Assistant Commonwealth Attorney Wes Nance said that the only purpose of this examination would be references to the comments written by Wesley in a document. The Commonwealth had no intention of mentioning anything written by Jocelyn. The judge decided he wanted to hear voir dire questioning before he ruled on its appropriateness.

Nance handed Roehrich the exhibit of the timeline document that Jocelyn had written for her for identification. Then he asked, "Did she point out certain entries on that timeline?"

"Yes, sir."

"These entries that she pointed out to you, did you recognize the handwriting of those entries?"

"No, sir."

The judge interrupted the questioning, saying that he wanted to know what was in the entries before he could make a decision.

Nance read through the list of alien comments on the timeline, and Sanzone said, "I don't have any problem if they want to say that he wrote that on her timeline, because it's obvious that he wanted her counselor to know those thoughts."

"It almost sounds like now you're saying you don't object to it," Updike said, and overruled Sanzone's objection, saying, "The Court rules that it's proper rebuttal, that it is relevant."

After that, the judge wanted to make sure that the Commonwealth had a witness ready to testify that it was actually Wesley's handwriting on the document. When that was settled, the jury returned and the questioning resumed.

Roehrich identified the document as the timeline Jocelyn wrote at her request and said that the discussion, which took an entire session, occurred at the end of August 2007, eight months after Wesley said he was last in Jocelyn's house. "She was, well, I would say emotionally angry, violated. She was scared."

On cross, Joey Sanzone tried to shake Roehrich's confidence on the date of that meeting with Jocelyn, but he failed.

The Commonwealth's last rebuttal witness was Gordon Menzies Jr., a forensic documents examiner at a forensic science laboratory in Roanoke. He had twenty years of experience in that area, with the last fifteen of them as supervisor. Additionally, he'd been examining forensic documents for thirty-four years and had testified as an expert in that field two to three hundred times. The court qualified him as an expert witness.

He testified that he examined known handwriting samples of Wesley and Jocelyn and he examined the time-line document in question. He said that in his review of the bracketed items, he could confirm with certainty that all, with one possible exception, were in Wesley's handwriting.

Joey Sanzone asked, "Mr. Menzies, you found three categories of writing on here: Jocelyn's, Wesley's, and one you couldn't identify?"

"Correct, sir."

"And you have no idea when these writings were made, do you? I mean, you can't look at the document and tell the age, can you?"

"An absolute time, no, but I would have to say it was after the bulk of the document was produced, whenever that was."

"You don't know when?"

"No, sir, I do not."

Sanzone then pushed the witness to say they were written in 2006 since the latest entry was dated in that year, but he could not get him to commit to any assessment of when they were actually composed since the dates were written in one handwriting and the notes in question were by another hand.

Wes Nance on redirect said, "And, Mr. Menzies, just to explain to the jury a little bit about what Mr. Sanzone was talking about, under each of these dates, were there entries lined up underneath the dates?"

"Yes, sir."

"The ones belonging to Wesley Earnest were at the bottom of each of those letters?"

"They were either at the bottom—particularly the ones that were bracketed in red. However, the ones that I found that were not red bracketed were generally inserted somewhere above that bottom entry and kind of plugged into an available space."

After he stepped down and the Commonwealth announced they had no further witnesses, Sanzone requested to bring Wesley back to the stand for surrebuttal. "I want to call Mr. Earnest to ask him if in 2007, Ms. Earnest ever called him and complained about him writing on a timeline. I want to ask him if [. . .] Ms. Earnest ever took him back to court for being in the house in 2007 [. . .] Those are the questions I want to ask him."

Nance argued that he could have asked those questions during his direct or redirect examination of the defendant and he did not. The judge agreed with the Commonwealth: Sanzone could not recall Wesley Earnest.

Before the jury was brought back into the courtroom, the defense made the traditional motion to strike. "Your Honor, we would renew our motion to strike in this case and state in furtherance of that at this time, the evidence is no longer viewed in the light most favorable to the Commonwealth. And there is no evidence [. . .] that Mr. Earnest was in Forest at the time." He went on to argue that the fingerprint was irrelevant because his client had lived in the home for nine years and could have left it on the paper during that period of time.

He moved then to the question that he was blocked from any presentation regarding possible third-party guilt. "We were prevented from even putting on evidence on stronger circumstances than the Commonwealth has presented to go forward to the jury."

To no one's surprise, Updike said, "Motion is denied. Court finds that there's been sufficient evidence to establish a jury issue as to elements of the offenses charged and that there has been evidence presented by the Commonwealth that is probative. And that is evidence in addition to fingerprint evidence. I do not regard this as a case that relies solely and exclusively or that is based solely and exclusively upon fingerprint evidence."

FORTY-THREE

Wes Nance stood to present the closing argument to the jury. After thanking them for their service, he began his argument. "Wesley Earnest had his testimony planned out yesterday just like he planned out this crime, but, ladies and gentlemen, he made mistakes when he killed Jocelyn Earnest. And those mistakes are the evidence that proves his guilt." Nance took the jury through the things he'd set out to prove in his opening statement.

"I told you that Jocelyn Earnest did not kill herself. And a variety of witnesses have come forward and proven that fact. Dr. Amy Tharp told you that Jocelyn Earnest was killed by a gunshot wound to the back of her head, above and behind her right ear. That gun was held two inches to two feet behind her head [. . .] If you drive from Chesapeake and hold a gun to the back of your wife's head with a fake suicide note already typed up, that is premeditated murder. That is murder in the first degree."

Nance reminded the jury of Marjorie Harris's testimony about the blood stains and patterns. "Mr. Sanzone talked about the secondary head movement maybe happening after the discovery of the body. The blood here doesn't lie. She was moved once, and it was quickly. And it was while she was falling. So it had to be someone who was tall and someone who was strong, perhaps a man who likes sports, perhaps a man who's athletic. Wesley Earnest is that man." Furthermore, he said, "We know this wasn't a suicide because of the note. James Fitzgerald tells you that that note is too short, it's too unemotional, it's too focused on finances. It's not Jocelyn Earnest [. . .] That note doesn't have her fingerprints. That note had no one else's fingerprints but the defendant's."

Nance moved on to motive. "Now, ladies and gentlemen, what is murder? Murder is a problem-solving event. You're eliminating a problem. So who had a problem with Jocelyn Earnest? Now, we know it wasn't the stuff in the house. She died with a little money in her change purse, credit cards. Nothing's taken from the house. So it's not a burglar [. . .] The problem wasn't sexual needs. She wasn't sexually assaulted. She died with all of her clothes on. She was killed because she was Jocelyn Earnest, because of who she was. That's why she was shot in the back of the head. Who had a problem with Jocelyn Earnest? Who was it who said she's hoarding her income? [. . .] Who said she was stalking, verbally abusive, was cleaning out the bank accounts, was running off to Canada? One person was saying that: Wesley Earnest."

Moving on, he said, "The note only points to Wesley Earnest. And part of that is the fingerprint evidence, absolutely. Three different people [. . .] have told you that it's Wesley Earnest's fingerprint on that fake suicide note [. . .] So who are the other two people who know that it's his fingerprints? Patricia Wimmer and Wesley Earnest."

Nance reminded the jurors that both Wesley Earnest and Patricia Wimmer were careful to include copy paper in their listing of the items Jocelyn and Jennifer removed from the lake house. He argued that they did so because they knew Wesley's prints were on the fake suicide note left at the crime scene. He marveled aloud at the improbability of an imaginary killer going to Jennifer Kerns's basement to retrieve a piece of paper to write the note and managing to get one that had Wesley's prints but not a single one from Jocelyn or Jennifer or anyone else. And, on top of that, he managed to transport it to multiple locations without getting his own prints on it. "Is that reasonable? Is that rational? No, ladies and gentlemen, it's not."

He then showed the jurors the note Wesley wrote before his arrest. It had nothing in it about Jocelyn's funeral or burial. It had a long list of financial questions as well as "'if arrested, how?' [. . .] Ladies and gentlemen, that's a confession. That's consciousness of guilt."

Nance turned to the murder weapon that both Jocelyn and Wesley had fired at Roger Earnest's house. "Now there's one thing in the proposals letter . . . written after the December '06 hearing. 'I just wanted to talk with you and you kept refusing. This past fall hunting season was upon us so I wanted to get my guns for the season. I even left you a shotgun in the closet so you could still protect yourself from any intruder.' Talking about her still refusing and then at the end: 'I was getting very bitter.' If Jocelyn Earnest can shoot a three-fifty-seven like nobody's business, why is he leaving her a shotgun?" Nance said, before pointing out, "Guess what went with him to Shameka's house? The gun that killed Jocelyn Earnest.

"And why is that important, ladies and gentlemen? The only evidence you have that Jocelyn Earnest had that handgun in her house was this man's testimony. And this man has admitted that he will deceive or lie to his friends when he's embarrassed. What will he do when he's on trial for murder?

"The third point I mentioned to you was Wesley Earnest's actions in and around and leading up to Jocelyn Earnest's death. You heard about a new one today. During the supposedly noncontested divorce, where she's stalking him, harassing and stealing from him, emptying out his lake house, what did he do? He climbed through the window and wrote on her timeline and he tried to tell you he didn't assume her identity. But you heard what Mr. Menzies said. He wrote on that personal writing of hers as if he were her. He takes on her persona [. . .] just like the person who wrote that fake suicide note. He's learning and he's planning, just like the [visit] . . . that Jennifer Kerns told you about. Now, Wesley argued with the date, but it's either March or November of 2006—a weekday. And what's in session in March or November? School. And where does Wesley Earnest work [. . .]? Chesapeake. And when does he arrive? At night. And he doesn't park in front of the house. He parks past the empty lot at the rental house, if you believe his version. And he's dressed in all black or a dark sweatsuit, the hood pulled over his head. And he comes out of the shadows when Jennifer Kerns gets there. Ladies and gentlemen, he learned from that, too. He learned not to knock. She didn't know he was coming that night. She called Jennifer Kerns with a concerned voice. And when she found out about the timeline, she was upset and scared, and she showed that to Susan Roehrich in August of 2007. This is not an uncontested divorce. This is nasty. And there's a deadline looming. He had to do this before her last name was Branham once again . . ."

Nance addressed Wesley borrowing David Hall's truck and the school sign-in sheet that proved that the vehicle was returned to David on Thursday, the day after Jocelyn was murdered. "Now, ladies and gentlemen, this sign-in sheet is made while David Hall is his buddy, while David Hall didn't realize that Wesley Earnest was going to use his truck to commit murder. So which day does David come in the latest? [. . .] There is no reason to have the joke about running late, if he gets to work at seven thirty-five. It's eight-o-five. It's Thursday. This was made when they were friends. This wasn't planned in the last two and a half years that Wesley Earnest has had to think about his testimony and plan out his testimony."

"[David Hall's wife] tells you that it was Thursday. In fact, remember, she even says it. 'He got it on Monday. Then, he drove it another day. That's Tuesday. He drives it another day, and I'm thinking—that's Wednesday—you still have that thing?' That's what she remembers. And that means it was brought back on Thursday. And that means his wet hair is significant, because he's running late. That means the floorboard stain is significant. When Wesley Earnest pulls the trigger [. . .] he's wearing gloves [. . .] Those gloves get blood spatter on them that didn't get on Jocelyn's hands because she's not holding the gun. And when he gets in that truck to race back to Chesapeake, he just throws them on the floorboard and a little bit of blood transfers. And so he grabs a little bit of bleach and then he just apologizes later.

"[. . .] Now the timing of this case is very key. Jocelyn Earnest last communicates to the world at seven thirty-five when she turns off her security alarm. No, we don't know and nobody knows how soon or later after that she died. We know that her friend, Marcy Shepherd, checked at the house and knocked on the door at about nine forty-five [. . .] and she's not responding by then. There's the window that Jocelyn Earnest died.

"Don't fall into the trap that, well, she falls off the electronic radar right then [. . .] that has to be when she died. Wesley Earnest falls off the electronic radar for sixteen hours when he stops answering his phone, when that phone's sitting in Chesapeake and he's roaring up 460. But we don't know if Jocelyn Earnest had her jacket on because she had just walked in or was walking back out.

The dog is in the kennel, had she already let it out and let him back into his cage so she could go back out that evening? Or did somebody who knew the dog, Mr. Earnest [. . .] get it back in the pen himself? Those are the things we don't know. But we do know that's the window of opportunity for Jocelyn Earnest, and we know it for Wesley Earnest, too."

Nance talked about the feasibility of making the drive from Great Bridge High School to Pine Bluff. "He's there in time to see that door open to know that door is unlocked. He doesn't have to worry about the security alarm. Remember? Jocelyn Earnest only had it on during the day. Once she comes home, it's off.

". . . Jocelyn Earnest is somewhere near that front door. She's got two ways she can go in her house. There's down the hallway to the bedroom—she'll get stuck. Or she can go [. . .] towards the kitchen and the dining room towards the back door [. . .] She doesn't get that far. You don't fight back with someone who's six foot four, athletic, and carrying a gun. Maybe she is running. And Wesley Earnest, towering over five foot [six] Jocelyn Earnest, is able to shoot her in the back of the head and pull her through her own blood, staging the crime scene the way he thinks it needs to be staged.

"Because how do you stage a scene? You stage it to make it look like something it is not. You make it look like a suicide when it's really a homicide. You leave the gun. You leave the fake note. And why do you stage? You stage to distract from the obvious suspect. And who is the obvious suspect? The guy who is totally broke, who's been accusing you of stealing, who's accusing you of stalking, of abasement, of harassment."

Nance then brought up how easily Wesley had manipulated Wayne Stewart at Taco Bell, and his friend David Hall, and how he'd tried to do the same to Rick Keuhne. He urged the jury not to allow Wesley to manipulate them, too. "Ladies and gentlemen, the evidence is there," he said, noting that Wesley's "actions, his ties to that suicide note, his ties to that gun all link together into a web to catch him at his own game. Are you going to believe the evidence in this case or just a whole lot of hot air? Thank you."

FORTY-FOUR

After a brief break, it was time for the defense to offer their closing argument. Joey Sanzone thanked the jurors and explained the importance of their role in the justice system. "When our government made the rules, it was decided that we needed to reflect the fact that it's easy to accuse somebody of something. And you've seen that. It's easy to make people look bad about one thing or another. But proving that an offense took place is another thing altogether. And for that reason we have some real specific rules about what has to take place."

He explained that the most important rule was in jury instruction number two: the defendant is presumed to be innocent. He went on to remind them that the Commonwealth also has the burden to produce evidence to prove the charge. And that, in this case, there is no direct evidence, only circumstantial and opinion. And all of it, he said, must point to opportunity, means, and motive.

"And they just don't exist in this case."

Sanzone disputed Wesley's presumed motive, as well as his opportunity, by pointing to the timing of the drive to Jocelyn's home, the unknown blood and hair in her house, and the argument that David Hall had not even really been late to school on Thursday, December 20, because he'd arrived at 8:05 and wasn't required to be there for the students until 8:15. So the laughter over his tardiness must have happened in an entirely different week, Sanzone speculated, and the Halls "are just mixed up." Despite not having much faith in the Halls' memories, however, Sanzone put more weight in the memory of Wesley's other co-worker, Al Ragas, and his recollection that he and Wesley got coffee together that Thursday at 7:30. Sanzone added that Al had also seen Wesley at the end of the day on December 19 at 4:05 P.M. After that, Wesley went home, then "goes out to get something to eat that night, [where] Wayne Stewart sees him.

"As a jury, the first thing you should make the Commonwealth prove to you is: when did Jocelyn die? That time and distance is the first reasonable doubt. Her time of death is the second reasonable doubt in this case. Four hours and fifteen minutes? Where does it fit in here? Are you going to . . . drive quickly, without even going to the bathroom, stopping for gas or anything, arrive at somebody's front door, knock on the door, kill them, get in your car, and go back home? Is that how it works? Are you able to do it kind of fast like that . . . ? I don't think so. And if you believe Wayne Stewart, just Wayne Stewart, Wesley couldn't have even gotten there until ten fifteen that night.

"And what do you know about Jocelyn and the time of her death? [. . .] And the alarm was disarmed at seven thirty-five at night [. . .] You have to have a code to disarm it. And guess who didn't have the code? Wesley Earnest did not have the code.

"The time of death is clearly established when [Jocelyn] quits answering that phone [. . .] The alarm code is turned off after she stops talking [. . .] So when is the time of death? That is the first question that has to be answered by the Commonwealth. And it's not been answered yet.

". . . I agree with the Commonwealth that the body was moved after she died . . .

"And you do have to make some decision in this case about the truthfulness of the Commonwealth's witnesses. I'm not talking about Investigator Mayhew and Investigator Babb [. . .] They're just working a case [. . .] But some of these other witnesses have told some mighty peculiar stories. And I think the most peculiar and most unusual story comes from Marcy Shepherd [. . .] Because of the fact that she was lying to you about so much of what happened in this case means you can't base any of your decision on what she said."

Sanzone enumerated what he called her lies and said, "And she's not telling the truth about when that body's found and when she finds it."

The defense attorney also disagreed with the Commonwealth's witnesses who had uniformly remembered Jocelyn as happy and looking forward to the holidays. "She was living a troubled life [. . .] She may have been outwardly happy in some ways, but there were a lot of unaccounted portions," Sanzone theorized. Not to mention, "What was that blood doing in the sink just a little ways from where that body is found?"

He suggested that someone overlooked that tiny drop when he was doing cleanup after killing Jocelyn. But that person emptied one trash can because he'd left something in it and he had to dispose of it—of all the receptacles in the house, all were overflowing but one.

Sanzone questioned the kind of people that Jocelyn might have had in her home—"people leaving condoms all over the place [. . .] The people with the hair, the people with the blood, who were they? [. . .] There were a lot of people in that house. We know it. And that's the next reasonable doubt." He cast aspersions on Marcy, Maysa, and Jennifer for not knowing who those people were, and for not knowing anything about the condoms.

"Jocelyn was leading a troubled life [. . .] She was having obvious issues with sexuality. Maybe it really wasn't an issue. Maybe it was fine with her. But she hid it. She and Marcy Shepherd said they hid it. But Marcy Shepherd has told you [. . .] that as far back as 2005, she had been discussing kissing Jocelyn. They discussed kissing one another. They were alone in [the] house after the Christmas party at ten o'clock at night, kissing. And we're all adults. We know what's going on. And we know what's going on since 2005."

Sanzone attacked the financial evidence as inaccurate and misleading, insisting that there were no problems that rose to the level of being a motive for murder. "Go to the direct evidence. Go back to what I said earlier about the evidence that does not require caution." He connected the gun to Jocelyn and pointed to the proof of the gun safe in her basement and the holster found inside of it.

"There are quite a few reasonable doubts here in this case [. . .] I want to get to one that is important [. . .] When they talk about the height of the shot, that is the oldest, oldest trick in the world, because if I'm standing straight up, yeah, you'd probably have to be pretty tall to shoot me in the head, but [. . .] if I'm down here like this," he said as he squatted down, "you don't have to be tall at all.

"Let me just say that the fingerprint evidence in this case is the worst evidence in this case [. . .] This is not a fingerprint ID. This is a partial latent fingerprint ID. The first thing is, we don't know how old the fingerprints are [. . .] Could it have been paper that Wesley touched at some time and somebody took away from Jocelyn's house? Yes. He lived in the house for ten years."

Sanzone talked about the fingerprint expert saying that if there were one discrepancy in the pattern of fingerprints, it was not a match, then reminded the jurors that the prosecution only had partial fingerprints and, therefore, how did anyone know whether or not a discrepancy existed in the unseen part?

He talked about the points of similarity in Wesley's print and the unknown one found on the note. "What did they tell you? Oh, five or six will do. Five or six out of seventy-five or a hundred, that will do, that's fine? What did we have here? We had two guys that disagreed with each other and they disagreed with themselves. They only agreed on . . . that's his fingerprint all right." Sanzone also took exception to one of the experts' lack of notes on the stand. "A good reason for not bringing the notes," he said, "is because he doesn't want me to compare them. And he doesn't want me to see that maybe Mr. Riding had this point and this point and maybe he had this point and that point. About the bottom line is, you'd think if this was an exact science that right off the bat, they'd start out at the same place, but they didn't."

In an attempt to convince the jury that his client was innocent and that the whole case was a patchwork quilt of nonsense, Sanzone referred to the investigation in general and the fingerprint evidence in particular as being "embarrassing." After several warnings that his time was running out, Sanzone finally brought his statement to a close when the judge told him his time was up. "I just ask you to listen to the points I've raised. We have a time limit so we won't go on forever and forever. But you've heard all the evidence, you've heard my argument. I appreciate your time. And I respectfully ask that you find my client not guilty."

Wes Nance now had the floor. "Ladies and gentlemen, what is embarrassing is that Mr. Sanzone would mischar-acterize two experts with over sixty years of experience.

They told you what that exhibit was. They have told that that is his fingerprint and he has, too.

". . . I find it amusing that Mr. Sanzone wants to go into every room of that house except for the room that Jocelyn Earnest is killed in. He wants to go into the bathroom. He wants to go downstairs. He wants to look at the towels on the toilet. Because he knows the stuff that's associated with Jocelyn's death points to his client.

"This house was Jocelyn's home for a decade. She had friends, she had family, she had co-workers over watching a movie. But she was shot in the back of the head in the living room. She had no defensive wounds. There's no reason for the murderer, Mr. Earnest, to be bleeding. She's running away. That blood is an artifact from her life. And I don't know if it was a handyman. I just don't know, but I know it doesn't have anything to do with that. He's talking about forensics in a bathroom when the forensics on the fake suicide note belong to the cheating, in-debt-to-his-eyeballs husband.

"We talk about a lot of minor points, and we object and y'all go in and out, but let's just think about that for a moment. The fake suicide note has the fingerprints of the husband who says she's stealing from him, harassing him, stalking him, emptying out [. . .] his lake house. This is contentious.

"Does Wesley Earnest need to know the alarm code? He climbs through windows, ladies and gentlemen. He assumes her identity when he takes that personal writing, that timeline, and puts the same song and dance that you heard yesterday. They're almost exact quotes. That's the manipulation that she got sick of. That's the manipulation she refused to have contact with anymore. She stood up to him.

"No, that same manipulation, all the folksy stories that he told with a smile yesterday when he's on trial for murder, that's what pulled [Taco Bell employee] Mr. Stewart in. He thought Wesley was going to lose his job. That's what he told you. He thought he was doing somebody a favor. That's the manipulation you saw at work yesterday. And that's the manipulation that was at this crime scene.

"Now, let's talk a little bit about Jocelyn's friends and Marcy Shepherd [. . .] He wants you to let a murderer go because of missing text messages? And why do we have that report? Because Marcy Shepherd told the police [. . .] And one of the missing emails is: I'm going to my counselor. And you know the other thing that's missing: a motive to kill. In a text message?

"[. . .] And where is Jocelyn after those missing text messages? She's at her counselor's and she's happy, because she doesn't know what's chugging like a freight train up 460 waiting for her. He doesn't need the alarm code. And, of course, everything's fine and dandy, except for in August of 2007 when Jocelyn shows that timeline. What did Susan Roehrich see? She saw anger. [Jocelyn] looked violated. She was scared. That proves identity right there.

"Ladies and gentlemen, you heard from a tire store manager, a preacher, forensic scientists. You heard from Wes's friends that he's lied to. You've heard from a variety of people who have told you he committed this crime, but there's another person, a silent person who told you he committed this crime. And that's Jocelyn Earnest. That woman was scared of him. And the position of her body says that she was killed by somebody strong and somebody tall. And I know what Mr. Sanzone's trying to do, but let's talk about that old trick. That shot was straight."

Wesley, Nance argued, had already confessed to the crime by his actions. "When he's wondering how he's going to get arrested, he's telling you he did it. When he says, 'It's my three-fifty-seven,' he's telling you he did it. When he says, 'It looks like a suicide over a failed relationship,' he's telling you, ladies and gentlemen, that he did it. And finally [. . .] he's reading from a script. It's the same script he scribbled on the timeline. It's the same script that he fed y'all yesterday. But it's the script also that he left at the scene, the staging of the crime scene. What's he trying to tell you? The murderer is trying to tell you: 'I killed myself over debt because there's my suicide [. . .] that's my gun.' The people who loved Jocelyn, what did they tell you? She was happy, and she didn't have a gun.

"He is reading from the script he planned," Wes Nance said, pointing at Wesley Earnest. "Ladies and gentlemen, don't let him get away with it."

The judge's instructions to the jury were typical fare, pointing to the need for unanimity in any determination of guilt. He explained the law necessitating secrecy of the identity of the alternates prior to the commencement of deliberations. He pulled two jurors then sent the remaining twelve back to the deliberation room at 2:28 P.M. on November 19, 2010.

The jury returned with a verdict four hours later, at 6:57 P.M. Jocelyn's family and friends all clutched one another's hands—sharing their fear, their anxiety, their hope.

The signed verdict document passed from the foreperson to the clerk. Then the words of the verdict filled the courtroom: "We, the jury, find the defendant guilty of first degree murder as charged in the indictment. We, the jury, find the defendant guilty of use of a firearm in the commission of first degree murder as charged in the indictment."

Wesley Earnest showed no reaction when the verdict was read.

FORTY-FIVE

Jocelyn Earnest's mother, Joyce Young, took the stand first during the penalty phase of the trial, which started just minutes after the verdict was announced. Inconceivable pain was etched across every inch of her face.

Wes Nance asked, "Could you tell the jury about Jocelyn?"

"She was a genuine person. She was somebody that you would want as a friend, somebody that you could trust. She would help people. She was loving. There's just so many adjectives that I could use for her. She was part of me, a very deep part that I'll never have."

"Ms. Young, how has your daughter's murder affected you?"

"It's something you never expect to bear. The loss is like no loss that you ever have [. . .] There are no words to describe the loss. It's so deep. And it's not one that will ever go away. It changes you forever. I'm not the person that I used to be. I'm not the mother that I used to be. And I'm not the wife that I used to be. I'll never get that person back. It just feels that something so precious has just been ripped from me. I just feel like—at times, like some wild animal just wants to get out. I just need to scream. And I just know that I'll never get her back. I'll never be able to celebrate anything with her. Holidays—like Thanksgiving—is coming up. She'd always come home for Thanksgiving. And we—my other daughter—we'd always go shopping Black Friday. And we'd get up really early and shop all day and into the night. And it was something we did every year. And Christmas—Christmas is so special. And we'll just never have that. It just changes [. . .] everything. You just—like I said—there are no words to describe the loss. There just aren't any words. It goes way beyond her. She was just a single, intelligent, beautiful, caring person. And I loved her dearly."

After that passionate response of grief, the defense wisely had no questions for the witness.

Another layer of pain was excavated when Bill Branham stepped into the box. When asked to introduce himself to the jury, he went straight to the memory of his daughter. "My name is Bill Branham. And I'm Jocelyn's father. And I live in Little Rock, Arkansas. So I didn't have as much time to spend with Jocelyn as I would have liked. But the times we had together were wonderful . . . I was planning on retiring in early 2008, and I was looking forward to being able to spend more time with Jocelyn.

"Jocelyn had developed a hobby of photography, which I'd been doing for, oh, twenty years or so, serious photography. And Jocelyn had become a good photographer. She was really learning a lot of stuff. And, you know, when I'd buy new equipment, I'd pass my old stuff down to Jocelyn just to learn on. And that Christmas 2007, I had gotten her a really nice macro lens that enables you to take real close-ups of flowers and insects and things like that, because she really enjoyed that and I enjoyed it. And I was looking forward to teaching her how to use that . . . I won't have those outings. I really liked this part of the country and thought we'd have a great time exploring.

"And I can still hear in my mind when we'd talk on the phone, she had this little . . . giggle, this kind of catchy laugh. And I hope I never get to the point where I can't hear that or I forget what her laugh sounds like because I'll never hear it again in real life. And I have all those wonderful memories that we shared . . . They're still good memories, but they have this touch of sadness, because Jocelyn's not here anymore. She was taken away. And I miss her. My life is not going to be the same. It hasn't been the same since December 2007."

Again, the defense refrained from any cross-examination.

A third branch of agony sprouted from the testimony of the next witness, Jocelyn's younger sister, Laura Rogers. Wes Nance asked, "What did Jocelyn mean to you?"

"Jocelyn was just everything. My parents divorced when I was two. And she was like a mom and a best friend, my big sister when I needed her to be. She was my confidant and my yard sale buddy. She would teach me things, but she was also learning from others. She was just the best person that I've ever known. She was not judgmental. She would help anyone who needed it [. . .] She's beyond words really [. . .] I miss her terribly."

"Laura, how has the loss of your sister impacted you and your family?"

"I'll never, ever be able to forget having to tell my parents that my sister was killed. I'll never be able to take the memory away of my dad being interrupted at dinnertime to hear the news. He had driven up to Pennsylvania to come home for Christmas and never got to see her. I remember my sister was with me the first time when I found out I was pregnant. And she had been with me through all my miscarriages. See, the reason I didn't get to see my sister when she was home that weekend was because I had had a miscarriage. And we had talked on the phone and she said, 'That's all right, I'll see you again in, like, a week.' And I'll never get that week. And I carry that forever. But through the grace of God, I now have a one-year-old son, and I know she's watching over him. And he will definitely know about his Aunt Jocelyn."

When she finished, the defense again passed up the opportunity to ask any questions.

Another type of immeasurable sorrow was carried by Wesley's mother, Patricia Wimmer. Joey Sanzone asked, "What type of person was Wesley growing up?"

"He was always my pride and joy. He was obedient. He was always there wanting to help me."

"What do you mean by that?"

"Well, anything in the house or round outside, whatever, he'd be there . . . We were kind of companions an awful lot, especially after his dad and I got divorced when he was about twelve [. . .] And he would be the little man around the house, change locks on doors or whatever for me [. . .] One of our fondest memories was when he graduated from high school and he and I took a trip out to California to visit my family, my mother and sisters."

"Wesley and Jocelyn, did you spend time with the two of them?"

"Yes, I did."

"Did you see any disagreements between the two of them?"

"No [. . .] They were like two peas in a pod [. . .] My first memories of them is laying on the floor watching sports games together on TV [. . .] He always respected her."

"It's been said that [. . .] anything a man could do, Jocelyn could do just as well. Did you find that to be true?"

"She was a trooper. She was [. . .] competitive [. . .] She was always good [. . .] And they would do things together and, yeah, they got along great."

"Since all this has taken place, you've spent a lot of time visiting Wesley?"

"Yes."

"Have you seen him angry?"

"No, no."

With courtesy to the injured loved ones equal to that demonstrated by Joey Sanzone, Wes Nance had no questions for Patricia Wimmer.

Before the jurors who found Wesley guilty considered the sentences, the attorneys gave their final arguments.

Wes Nance thanked the jurors again and said, "When Wesley Earnest took Jocelyn Earnest's life, he didn't just kill one person. He destroyed a whole family. And I ask you as you consider his fate to consider that this was a crime that took planning, that took a cold-hearted approach of a gentleman who could drive for three and a half hours to get to his wife's home, to shoot her in the back of the head. That gives you an indication of the type of individual that you will be presenting your fate to. Thank you."

Joey Sanzone mentioned Wesley's lack of a criminal record, noting, "He's forty years old essentially and has lived his life as a law-abiding citizen for all these years." He highlighted the range of punishments available to the jurors, even in first degree murder cases, "because some are worse than others. Some defendants are worse than others. So I would simply ask you not to let emotions rule, but to consider what the law means when it does create a range such as that [. . .] You made your finding. But as you complete it, I would just ask that you add a modicum of mercy in your decision of a sentence of Mr. Earnest. Thank you so much."

Judge Updike reminded the jurors that their decisions on punishment must be unanimous. The jury returned to the deliberation room at 7:26 P.M. They had a question about parole, and were told that no, Virginia law says that no person sentenced to incarceration for a felony was eligible for parole. "The defendant will not be eligible for parole upon any sentence imposed. Does that answer your question?" the judge said.

"Yes, sir. Thank you."

At 8:30 that night, the jury returned with their decision. "We, the jury, having found the defendant guilty of first degree murder, fix his punishment at imprisonment for life. We, the jury, having found the defendant guilty of use of a firearm in commission of murder, fix his punishment at imprisonment of three years." All the color drained from Wesley's face as he turned and whispered to his mother before being led from the courtroom.

More often than not, incarceration was a place where inmates put on weight, but not Wesley Earnest. Dressed in a dark suit, he was rail thin with sunken cheeks for his sentence hearing on Tuesday, January 25, 2011.

Judge Updike asked, "Do you have a final statement?"

"No, sir," Wesley replied.

The judge passed down the sentence recommended by

the jury: life in prison without parole and an additional three years for use of a firearm in the commission of a felony.

Joey Sanzone told reporters that the defense strategy was constrained by the rulings of the judge. "A lot of the things we wanted to tell the jury could not be told."

He announced his intentions to appeal and indicated that his effort on behalf of his client could possibly challenge existing case law in Virginia.

On November 29, 2010, Joey Sanzone had filed documents concerning the planned testimony of Jennifer Mnookin, the UCLA law professor engaged in a study about the reliability of partial fingerprints. It was the first step toward an appeal on the grounds that when the judge did not allow her to testify as an expert witness and did not let her offer an opinion contradicting the Commonwealth's expert, Wesley Earnest did not get a fair trial.

Oral arguments were heard before a three-judge panel in the Court of Appeals of Virginia on September 12, 2012. Wes Nance was present, as were members of Jocelyn's family. Nearly three months later, the decision reached its ruling that the court had not abused its discretion, and the verdict issued was affirmed.

On August 2, 2013, the Virginia Supreme Court turned down the defense's appeal of that decision. Joey Sanzone was disappointed. "We believe that there are fundamental errors in the reliability of fingerprint evidence and jurors should be informed of that." Because of his faith in his argument, he still hoped that, in time, new developments in forensic science would prove him right. Sanzone sent a letter to the forensic science department requesting that they preserve the blood and DNA evidence in this case.

Now incarcerated at the Sussex I State Prison in Waverly, Virginia, Dr. Wesley Brian Earnest is simply inmate number 1426979.

The end of appeals helped the family and friends of Jocelyn Earnest to move on with their lives. Still, every holiday, every birthday, every memory continued to be tinged with sorrow.

Jocelyn's sister, Laura, contributed often and at length on an online memorial page but never with more poignancy than when she wrote: "This morning, when I was outside, I heard a bird crowing so loudly I felt like it was right beside me. As hard as I looked to find it, I did not see it anywhere. I began to cry and then I smiled. This warm feeling came over me. I knew the bird was there, but I didn't see it. Just like you are still with me, I just can't see you."

AFTERWORD

Writing *Under Cover of the Night* brought back memories of another woman I wrote a book about: Susan Mc-Farland in *Gone Forever*. Jocelyn, like Susan, was professionally successful and cherished by co-workers, friends, and family. Both seemed to have lifestyles that did not put them at risk of dying violent deaths. But these women were caught up in disintegrating marriages with narcissistic spouses who hid a secret side of their lives. Both of their husbands were convicted of their murders.

According to the United States Bureau of Justice, 3.8 percent of all homicides in this country involve women dying at the hands of their husbands. Although three-quarters of these killers had prior criminal records, it was not the case with Wesley Earnest or Richard McFarland. Depending on the study reviewed, 67 to 80 percent of men who murder their wives have physically battered them beforehand—for many it was escalating violence that finally turned fatal. Yet neither of these women were injured by their husbands until the ultimate, fatal act of domestic violence that ended their lives.

What can we do to prevent this loss of life? Awareness of the reality that this possibility exists is the first step; recognizing narcissism and the dangers it presents is another.

A review of the symptoms in the *DSM-IV-TR* reads like a description of Wesley Earnest. Narcissists possess a "grandiose sense of self-importance," "exaggerate their achievements and talents," and are "preoccupied with fantasies of unlimited success." They believe that they are "special or unique," display "arrogant, haughty behaviors or attitudes," believe "others are envious," and "require excessive admiration." Many people who encountered Wesley Earnest felt just that way about him. How many times had Wesley told his co-workers and friends that he was independently wealthy? What about his frequent insistence on being addressed as Dr. Earnest?

Narcissists are also "interpersonally exploitive" within relationships and "take advantage of others to achieve their own ends." Wesley forced Jocelyn to forsake her dream of a simple cottage on the lake in exchange for the monument to achievement that he built. He used Dave Hall to borrow the truck that helped him commit murder. He manipulated Wayne Stewart at Taco Bell into providing an alibi.

Finally, a narcissist has a sense of entitlement and unreasonable expectations of favorable treatment. Wesley expected his attorney to believe his lies. He expected the same of law enforcement, and of both juries. He really thought he was smart enough and charming enough to convince others that the story he'd told was reality.

In his book *People of the Lie*, M. Scott Peck took it a step further, writing: "In addition to the fact that the evil need victims to sacrifice to their narcissism, their narcissism permits them to ignore the humanity of their victims as well. As it gives them the motive for murder, so it also renders them insensitive to the act of killing. The blindness of the narcissist to others can extend even beyond a lack of empathy; narcissists may not 'see' others at all."

In *The Gift of Fear*, Gavin de Becker wrote about a dangerous myth in spousal murders, that they happen in the heat of the moment, when "in fact, the majority of husbands who kill their wives stalk them first, and far from the 'crime of passion' that it's so often called, killing a wife is usually a decision, not a loss of control." And the evidence of Wesley stalking Jocelyn is overwhelming and undeniable.

What can we do? We can learn all we can about the warnings that foreshadow spousal homicide. We can explore the psychology of intimacy turned fatal. We can teach ourselves to cultivate our intuition and never fear acting on it or speaking out about genuine concerns to others. We all need to see others and be effective in our evaluations of them. We all need to discern between ungrounded fears and intuitive responses to the often subtle signals of danger. Jocelyn Branham ignored her intuition on her wedding day, allowing warning signs to pass unheeded because she did not want to look foolish, or to inconvenience or disappoint her family and friends. How often have we all done exactly the same thing?

However, would leaving him at that altar have protected her against the ultimate act of violence? Maybe, or maybe he simply would have acted sooner. If she had kept her home security system armed 24/7, would she still be alive? It would have made Wesley's mission more difficult to achieve, but he could have ambushed her on her way from her home to her car or in a secluded spot of Canadian woods. Killers are very determined people.

To my knowledge, Wesley has never been professionally diagnosed with any level of narcissism or personality disorder. My judgment on his psychology is merely my opinion, based on evidence of his behavior shown in two trials and backed by many who have crossed his path and by two juries in a court of law.

There are others with a different viewpoint, including his mother, Patricia Wimmer. Another person who still proclaims Wesley's innocence is his attorney, Joey Sanzone.

He said, "I don't know anyone who would put together such a complex plan and I don't see that person in Wesley. You'd have to have so many different talents and that is not how Wesley lived . . . Wesley is very pleasant and engaged. He's not brooding or mad at life."

Sanzone also retains serious doubts about the evidence in the case. The blood found in Jocelyn's home, although far removed from the actual scene of her death, bothers him. "Familial DNA may still be an issue on the blood in the bathroom. We may get a cold hit someday. I think the killer is the person whose blood was found, or someone who was there with that person."

But the biggest issue of all for the defense attorney remains the fingerprint evidence. "This will be like the Sam Sheppard case but on a different issue. It will be alive, years from now." He bases that faith on the evolving nature of all forensic science. He believes that, like many other techniques that have been turned on their heads in the past, the science of latent prints will undergo a similar sea change. He feels that the sins of expectation bias, the assumption of the number of points needed to absolutely identify a specific individual, and the current inability to correlate friction ridge measurements to the pressure applied will be altered by more research and we'll end up throwing out much of what is now accepted as gospel as junk.

The massive changes in forensic science never cease to amaze, so I have to conclude that it is possible that he and Dr. Jennifer Mnookin may be right. But to me, the case was hardly even reliant on the print evidence anyway. Latent prints aside, I felt that the circumstantial evidence in this case pointed unwaveringly to one person: Wesley Earnest.

Whether I am right or wrong, one thing will always remain true. The violent death of Jocelyn Denise Branham Earnest inflicted a heavy loss on many people who will feel the grief for decades. And so I add another woman to the roll call of those I wish I'd had a chance to know in life. I do so with the fervent hope that this book will lead someone, somewhere, to act to save their own or another woman's life and keep one more name from being added to my list.